# INDIANS OF THE
# SOUTHEASTERN
# UNITED STATES
# IN THE LATE
# 20TH CENTURY

# INDIANS OF THE
# SOUTHEASTERN
# UNITED STATES
# IN THE LATE
# 20TH CENTURY

Edited by J. Anthony Paredes

THE UNIVERSITY OF ALABAMA PRESS

Tuscaloosa and London

Library of Congress Cataloging-in-Publication Data

Indians of the southeastern United States in the late 20th century / edited by J. Anthony Paredes.
    p.    cm.
    Includes bibliographical references and index.
    ISBN 0-8173-0534-3
    1. Indians of North America—Southern States—Social conditions. 2. Indians of North America—Government relations. 3. Indians of North America—Southern States. I. Paredes, J. Anthony (James Anthony), 1939–
E78.S65I53   1992                          91-15048
975'.00497—dc20

British Library Cataloguing-in-Publication Data available

*For tribes that do not slumber*

# CONTENTS

# ILLUSTRATIONS AND TABLES

## Photographs

## Maps

## Tables

# ACKNOWLEDGMENTS

We are all deeply indebted to the southeastern Indian peoples and communities who are the subjects of our essays and without whose cooperation and assistance our work would not have been possible; individual authors have acknowledged and thanked the people of various groups as they thought best. I hope that those who read what we have to say about them here will be pleased even if they might not agree with everything we say.

As editor, I thank my friend and colleague James C. Sabella (University of North Carolina, Wilmington) for having invited me to put together the Southern Anthropological Society symposium that was the basis for this collection in the first place; I thank my wife and colleague Elizabeth D. Purdum for all her help (including some last-minute editing of papers for oral presentation) in putting the SAS symposium together and seeing me through the subsequent years of turning the symposium papers into this book; I thank my "New Mexico traveling companion" (inside joke, dear reader) and colleague Jack Campisi (State University of New York College, Oneonta) for his commentary on the symposium papers even though he is not represented in the pages of this book; I thank two anonymous readers for The University of Alabama Press whose criticisms and suggestions markedly improved our final essays; and I thank Erika Esan, Precious Martin, and—especially—Bridget Beers and Janet DuPuy for their faithful typing (I refuse to use the high-tech barbarism, "word processing"). Special thanks to DuPuy, Adriana Demaio, and Elizabeth Stanton for assistance in preparing the index. To Beverly Denbow we all owe much gratitude for her superb copy-editing. Finally, I indulge my prerogative as editor to thank my parents, Antonio and Mildred, and, in this instance, pay special tribute to my mother, who grew up hard on a poor farm at Barbee Creek in northern Tuscaloosa County and who passed along to me her own familial tradition of being "part Indian." I hope she takes particular pride in this book on southern Indians being published by The University of Alabama Press.

# INDIANS OF THE
# SOUTHEASTERN
# UNITED STATES
# IN THE LATE
# 20TH CENTURY

# INTRODUCTION

## J. Anthony Paredes

The first native people encountered by Europeans in what is now the United States were within the boundaries of the present-day southeastern states. In the sixteenth century *conquistadores* from Spain trekked across peninsular Florida northward into what was to become the Deep South, searching for gold, fame, power, and eternal youth. They left in their wake disarray, destruction, and the terror of strange new diseases. Massive depopulation followed. By the seventeenth century Europeans were settling the coastal areas of the South from Virginia to Texas. Further depopulation, dislocation, and annihilation of whole tribes proceeded apace.

In the interior, eventually the descendants of the survivors of those first deadly encounters with Europeans rebounded and regrouped, albeit into less complex, less populous polities. Actually, by the latter half of the eighteenth century the populations of the major "Indian nations" were steadily increasing (Paredes and Plante 1982). In the eighteenth century the Cherokees, Choctaws, Chickasaws, Creeks, and, later, the Seminoles had become forces to be reckoned with, courted, appeased, and manipulated, as Englishmen from the Atlantic seaboard, Spaniards from Florida, and Frenchmen from the Mississippi competed for economic advantage in the slave and hide trade, military supremacy in the control of ports and pathways, and, ultimately, political control of the vast, rich new world of North America.

Following the Anglo-Americans' successful revolt against their king in England, the American Southeast became the scene of new struggles. The native peoples, whether resisting or accommodating the ever-growing for-eign presence, were nonetheless ever-tightly entangled in a trap (self-made or otherwise) of technological dependency and economic indebtedness. Soon their land became more valuable than their services as hunters, slave catchers, warriors, and concubines. The Indians had to be moved. Neither statesmanship nor military resistance could deflect the expanding tide of people descended from Europeans and Africans that moved inward, leav-ing only here and there tiny islands of Native Americans in remote areas of the coastal plains. The interior tribes were to be removed—by economic inducement if possible, by chicanery if need be, or by force if all else failed. And, thus, the infamous "Trail of Tears" of the Great Removal. By the midnineteenth century, the bulk of the native population, numbering in the tens of thousands, had been removed to what is now Oklahoma. Their descendants live there still. This book is not about them.

Despite what was one of the most massive relocations of human popula-tions in history until the twentieth century, the Great Removal did not take all the native peoples of the Southeast. Some small tribes, as in Virginia, remained under the protection of local state governments; others retreated to remote areas not immediately desired by whites and eventually received in the later nineteenth and early twentieth centuries official federal sanc-tion to remain. Yet others languished for decades in a kind of social and political limbo in their homeland. Some eventually were removed to Oklahoma as late as the early twentieth century, as in the case of some of the Choctaw of Louisiana (Bushnell 1909:3) and Mississippi (Debo 1934:246, 273–76). Others, such as the Poarch Creeks, in the latter half of the twentieth century finally won official federal government sanction as Indians. Many others, especially those groups with greatly mixed tribal and racial backgrounds (the most well known of these being the Lumbee Indians of North Carolina), remained in the Southeast as distinctive ethnic communities but occupied an anomalous place in the ever-more complex and changing racial and ethnic composition of the American South; some of these groups are currently pressing for official recognition from the federal government as Indians. This book is about all of these Native American groups that have remained in the Southeast, from the tidewaters of Virginia to the Louisiana bayous, from the mountains of western North Carolina to the Everglades of Florida. It is about these groups as they were in the late twentieth century, on the eve of the 500th anniversary of Co-lumbus's historic voyage that changed everything. The southeasterners were among the first to feel the sweeping impact of the arrival of other human beings from across the Atlantic, but they, the southeastern Indians, remain there still as an ever-more visible Native American presence.

The aboriginal cultures of the Southeast were the most complex that the early European explorers encountered north of the Rio Grande. These native peoples practiced intensive cultivation; built massive earthen temple mounds; produced elaborate art tied to the glorification of a religious and political elite; formed dense, populous towns approaching classification as urban centers; and were on the brink of creating true states. Despite the disruption caused by the early explorers, the descendants of these incipient states were still impressive to the settlers and traders a hundred and more years later. Thus, the native peoples of the Southeast have had a special fascination for foreign observers and thinkers since almost the beginning of European settlement.

Already by the late eighteenth century major scholarly works were being published on the southeastern Indians (e.g., Adair 1775), some of which remain to this day as important ethnological and historical sources. Through the early nineteenth century the tradition of proto-anthropology continued in the writings of such as Benjamin Hawkins (1848). By the later nineteenth century various southeastern Indian groups had become subjects for study by the first generation of professional anthropologists (e.g., Mooney 1890) as well as historians reflecting on an earlier period of American expansion as the frontier era was drawing to a close in the West (e.g., Halbert and Ball 1895).

Using these earlier sources and documents as well as salvage ethnography in Oklahoma and in the East, twentieth-century anthropologists continued work on the early cultures of the Southeast. Their contributions ranged from Swanton's monumental synthesis (1946) to such specific, technical works as Eggan's classic study of changes in Choctaw kinship (1937).

In the latter half of the twentieth century there has been a growing body of ethnological work on specific groups who remained in the South, including works by Sturtevant (1954), Fogelson (1961), and Kupferer (1966), to mention a very few of the earlier studies of this type. Not to be overlooked in this regard, either, is Berry's survey (1963) of racially anomalous groups that are not neatly categorized as black, white, or Indian, even though the book is regarded by some as controversial and even racist. The older tradition of areal syntheses of traditional culture and history has also continued, among both anthropologists and historians, notably Hudson (1976) in the case of the former and Cotterill (1954) and Wright (1981) in the case of the latter. While there appears to be now some slackening of general ethnological interest in the area (archaeology is, of course, flourishing as it seems to be everywhere these days), there seems at the same time to be a flowering of interest in the "Indian history" of the region among professional historians, such as Green (1982), Merrell (1989), and Perdue (1983).

Among historians Williams (1979) has done the most to bring together the often neglected stories of those remnants of the once populous nations, and others, who remained in the Southeast. The early history and later experiences of the main bodies of the tribes removed to Oklahoma had been to some extent a subject of enduring interest to some historians, such as Young (1961) but most especially the widely respected "grand lady" of Indian history, the late Angie Debo (e.g., 1934, 1941). Those who remained in the East, however, did not generally attract the attention of modern historians as they had anthropologists. It is not surprising, then, that when Williams assembled the contributors to his book most of them were anthropologists. Several of these, plus a lone historian, also contributed to the present work.

Given Williams's fairly recent compilation, one might ask: "Why another book on southeastern Indians?" There are two principal reasons. First, often for lack of knowledgeable scholars, the earlier work did not include a number of groups, especially the smaller, more obscure, and problematic groups laying claim to Indian identity in the modern South. In this book the coverage is much more complete. Through state survey articles for Virginia, North Carolina, South Carolina, and Louisiana, a variety of lesser-known tribal remnants and "composite" groups are represented in addition to the better-documented groups such as Catawba, Lumbee, and Tunica, to say nothing of tribes that had been subjects of early anthropological study, such as the Cherokee and the Pamunkey. A separate chapter had been planned for this collection on the Mowa Choctaws of Alabama—one of the largest, most well-established but controversial groups seeking official recognition as an Indian tribe. Mowa leaders raised certain objections to inclusion of the chapter, so the author, Susan Greenbaum, withdrew her manuscript. Hence, despite their current efforts to gain official recognition as Indians, the Mowa Choctaws are omitted from this work as they were from the Williams book. (In earlier literature [e.g., Stopp 1974] the Mowas are identified by the locally pejorative term, "Cajan" ["Cajun"]; the term "Mowa" was derived from the names of their home counties, Mobile and Washington, in the same way that the name "Haliwa" of the North Carolina Haliwa-Saponi was coined from Halifax and Warren counties.)

The Walter L. Williams book is essentially a series of historical overviews covering the period from the Great Removal to the present, as we should expect from a work edited by a historian. In this respect the work stands as a basic reference and guide to the histories of the groups represented. Williams and French (1979) further expand the usefulness of the work as a sourcebook with their thorough and well-organized bibliographic essay. Nonetheless, in the interest of presenting comparable historical narratives, the contributions to the earlier volume were limited in their descriptions of current states of affairs and the very recent past among the groups included. Thus, the second purpose of this present volume is to provide a fuller accounting and assessment of social, political, and economic circumstances of southeastern Indians near the end of the twentieth century.

The American Indian peoples remaining in the Southeast are exceptionally diverse. Some, such as the Miccosukees and Seminoles, are among the least acculturated in the entire United States, clinging firmly to native language, religion, world view, and even some elements of material culture, and they maintain a relatively "pure" gene pool. Others, such as the Poarch Creeks, have retained very little of native language and culture but have maintained a solid identity as Indian throughout history even though they have mixed considerably with non-Indians, especially in recent decades. Yet others are of uncertain tribal origins and their claim to an Indian identity is a matter of continuing debate.

Southeastern Indian groups have been especially noteworthy generally in American Indian developments of the latter half of the twentieth century. Beginning in the late 1960s, if not earlier, millions of U.S. citizens began to lay claim to some degree of Indian ancestry, more often than not from some southeastern tribe. Claims of being "part Cherokee" by Americans of European and African descent have become a standing joke in "Indian country" (cf. Carter 1988). At risk of appearing to be unfair to the much-maligned Cherokees, it must be noted, too, that the Eastern Cherokees have acquired a reputation of being the quintessential "tourist Indians," in part because some of their people seized the economic opportunities of being located next to one of the most frequently visited national parks in the United States, Great Smoky.

In the 1980s the Southeast became a major testing ground for just what does constitute an Indian tribe and what its powers are under United States law. In the first instance there is the perennial, still unsolved problem of who and what type of sociopolitical group, exactly, are the Lumbees (cf. Blu 1980, Campisi et al. 1987). There can be no question about their separate identity as an ethnic group to be reckoned with (as the Ku Klux Klan found out in the 1950s),[1] but their legal status as an Indian tribe is still not fully resolved. The legal and historical questions surrounding Lumbee tribal identity and status notwithstanding, they are, at least loosely speaking, one of the largest Indian tribes in the United States, with a total population in excess of 40,000 members. Moreover, following the issuance in 1978 of federal guidelines whereby previously unrecognized groups may petition for acknowledgment as an Indian tribe under United States law (Greenbaum 1985), the Southeast has been one of the prime areas from which such petitions have been forthcoming. As of 1987 (Quinn 1987) one-third (34) of the total of such petitions (104) had come from groups in the Southeast; 2 of those had been approved (Tunica-Biloxi and Poarch Creek), bringing those petitioners into the fold of federally protected Indian tribes; 7 other petitions had been denied, and the remainder were still pending. In addition, there is a miscellany of other tactics being used by various groups to secure their status as Indians, ranging from the efforts of the once federally recognized Catawba of South Carolina to regain that status to a number of groups in various states, such as the Nansemond of Virginia, seeking official state recognition but, at least for the moment, not actively pursuing federal recognition. Yet a number of others are in the very early stages of trying to prepare petitions for federal recognition (e.g., some Cherokee descendants of north Georgia).

One hundred and fifty years earlier, it was in a Georgia case, *Worchester v. Georgia* (1832), that the U.S. Supreme Court laid the foundation for the legal principle of federal Indian tribal sovereignty (cf. Cohen 1982:232–35). Again, it has been from the Southeast that have come some of the most dramatic modern tests of the limits of tribal sovereignty. Specifically, the Seminoles of Florida paved the way for the Indian bingo phenomenon that swept the country in the 1970s and 1980s, Indian-owned high-stakes bingo parlors unrestrained by regulations of the surrounding state by virtue of tribal sovereignty. Similarly, the Seminoles and, less dramatically, the Choctaws of Mississippi have been at the forefront of testing the limits of tribal governments' exemption from state jurisdiction in other ways on reservation lands, thereby realizing important avenues for economic development. Finally, from the Seminoles in the 1980s came a case, involving the killing of a Florida panther, wherein the principles of tribal sovereignty and Indian religious freedom were reaffirmed even when the killing of an animal belonging to a federally designated endangered species was at issue.

While Indians remaining in the South after the Great Removal might have been conveniently forgotten and ignored by chroniclers of the Old South, the descendants of those native peoples are very much a visible and palpable part of the eastern Sun Belt renaissance that is the New South. Little wonder that southern Indians (and, frankly, some fake Indians) are enjoying a greatly renewed and often sympathetic attention from the press and the electronic media. For instance, the self-proclaimed "progressive" intellectual magazine, *Southern Exposure*, devoted a whole issue to "Indians of the South" in 1985. *Southern Exposure* might be a little strident and a bit out of the popular mainstream, but even that bellwether of New South tastefulness, *Southern Living* magazine, from time to time publishes items with an Indian theme (e.g., Engle 1989).

In this volume are assembled essays by the most prominent anthropologists, and two historians, Kersey and Taukchiray, currently studying contemporary Indians of the Southeast. With the exception of the chapter by Rountree, shorter versions of these chapters (along with one by Greenbaum) were first presented at the 1986 annual meeting of the Southern Anthropological Society in Wrightsville Beach, North Carolina. The papers were presented as part of an invited session, organized by Paredes, on modern Indians of the South. All the contributors were instructed to develop their essays around a loosely constructed outline of topics, including population, political organization, economic conditions and development, government relationships, retention of elements of traditional culture, and other current conditions in general. George Roth, one of the discussants for the original SAS session, provides here a concluding, overview chapter; Roth brings very special insights to the question of Indian tribal status and character in the modern South by virtue of his position as senior anthropologist with the branch of the Bureau of Indian Affairs that reviews petitions for federal recognition.

We have produced here what we believe to be an important panoramic, ethnographic snapshot of Indians of the American Southeast near the end of the twentieth century, still surviving nearly 500 years after the *conquistadores* first splashed ashore on the Florida coast.

It almost goes without saying, given the rapid changes under way in southern "Indian country," that despite our best last-minute updating efforts, what is presented here will already be out of date in some respects by the time the book appears in print. But that is of necessity true of all ethnographic accounts. It is equally true, however, that the greatest value of any ethnography lies in its presentation of the unfolding of human possibilities in a particular place at a particular time without regard for the relentless flow of cultural change that engulfs us all. It is, of course, from the comparative study of such ethnographies that ethnologists, along with archaeologists, ethnohistorians, and others, attempt to contribute to a general theoretical understanding of cultural phenomena. Although we all aimed for the "ethnography of the present," we will be gratified if our work is judged only to make a contribution in the tradition of that wonderful, liberating scientific fiction from anthropologists of yore: the ethnographic present.

# 1

# INDIAN VIRGINIANS
# ON THE MOVE

*Helen C. Rountree*

The Indian groups to be found in Virginia today[1] are descended from the Algonquian-speaking Powhatan groups of the coastal plain, with the exception of the Amherst County people whose ancestry apparently derives from various Siouan and Iroquoian groups of the piedmont and mountains (see map). All the Virginia groups have non-Indian ancestry as well, as their English, Welsh, and Irish surnames demonstrate. Because they are thus "mixed-blood" people, as well as up-to-date (i.e., anglicized) people in their ways of life, Anglo-Virginians have long questioned their "Indianness." Indians were formerly subject to Virginia's "race" laws, which were highly discriminatory to anyone not "purely" white (Rountree 1990). The reservation groups were particularly visible and came under more public pressure, which made them de facto the leading upholders of "Indianness" in the state. In consequence, the political and economic status of all the groups was severely depressed until the civil rights era (Bastow 1975; Berry 1963, 1972, 1978; Blume 1950; Feest 1978; Pfaus 1947, 1949; Rountree 1972a, 1979, 1986, 1990; Seaman and Wailes n.d.; Speck 1925, 1928; Stern 1952; Wailes 1928).

The period of the 1960s through the 1980s saw tremendous improvements on all fronts in Indian lives. Indian people have fully used the opportunities presented to them by a more liberal era. Significantly, instead of assimilation there has been an increase in Indian pride and Indian tribal and intertribal activities during that period. Thus Virginia in the late 1980s had eight Indian groups, all in stages of organization and state recognition.

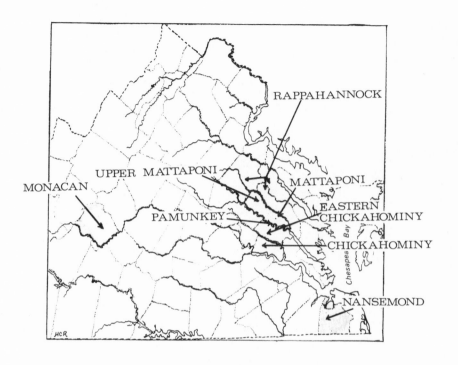

Locations of Modern Virginia Indian Tribes


Two of the eight Virginia tribes have reservations dating from colonial times. The Pamunkey have about 1,200 acres and about fifty people, and the Mattaponi have about 125 acres and a population of sixty. Both reservations are in King William County, about thirty miles east of Richmond. The number of people in residence for both groups is only a fraction of the people genealogically entitled to live on the reservations.

Five incorporated groups lack reservations but possess state recognition as Indian tribes. These are the Upper Mattaponi Tribal Association (about 60 adults enrolled plus about 35 children; King William County and Richmond metropolitan area), the Chickahominy Tribe (about 550 enrolled; Charles City County), the Chickahominy Tribe, Eastern Division (42 adults enrolled plus 29 children in 1985; New Kent County), the United Rappahannock Tribe (about 150 enrolled; Essex, Caroline, and King and Queen counties), and the Nansemond Indian Tribal Association (94 adults enrolled in 1986; city of Chesapeake and adjacent cities). All of these groups have additional, eligible relatives who have not formally enrolled.

Late in 1989 the sixth nonreservation incorporated Indian group in Virginia received state recognition. This was the Monacan Indian Tribal Association in Amherst County (about 300 living in the county, with more living away), formerly known in literature by the extremely derogatory—and inaccurate—name of "Issues." This group has a long if somewhat inexact tradition of Indian ancestry, perhaps largely from the historic Siouan-speaking Monacan Indians (Houck 1984).

None of these groups has federal recognition as Indians, although several of the organized nonreservation groups have seriously considered applying for it. Their success would be long in coming, due to the extensive burning of county records in Virginia during the Civil War as well as at other periods. For Virginia Indians who lost their reservations, documentation for the crucial "middle centuries" of continuous group existence lay in the county records, which in all but four counties are gone now. Ironically, federal recognition would come relatively easily to the reservation groups, because the colonial- and state-level records made about them have survived better. Yet the reservation people have so far declined to seek recognition on the grounds that they are doing well as they are and have enough bureaucrats to deal with already.[2]

The major impetus to activism among the Virginia groups in the civil rights era was the Coalition of Eastern Native Americans, an information-spreading organization founded in 1971 by a steering committee that included the then-chief of the Mattaponi Reservation, Curtis L. Custalow, Sr. CENA did not survive the 1970s, but it served two invaluable purposes while it lasted. First, it showed Native Americans throughout the eastern United States that their local experiences with prejudiced non-Indians were normal, not isolated instances peculiar to only a few places. Second, it showed group leaders how they could improve the lot of their people through federal grant moneys outside the funds allocated to the Bureau of Indian Affairs. Most Virginia groups joined CENA and benefited accordingly.

After 1971, Virginia Indian groups began applying for and getting moneys directed at two areas of their lives: education and economic development. These were the areas, they felt, that needed the most improvement the soonest.

Education has always been a crucial issue between Indians and non-Indians in Virginia. In colonial times the English wanted to "educate" and anglicize Indian children, while Indian parents demurred. In postcolonial times the Indians began to realize that literacy was a necessary defense for a beleaguered minority and, now much anglicized themselves, they sought an education for their children while the white-dominated state and county governments demurred. When publicly funded segregated schools became the rule after the Civil War, Indian children were expected to attend the "colored" schools, which would have made them legally "colored" forever afterward. Therefore, fighting for and winning a publicly funded "Indian" school became a badge of Indianness in Virginia, even if the school offered few years of coursework. The Pamunkey got a state-supported school by 1890, the Mattaponi a separate one in about 1919. The Chickahominy managed a school before 1910 but the county did not support it until 1922 (when the Eastern Chickahominy fissioned off, they set up a school of their own); the Upper Mattaponi Indians managed to get a county-supported school in the late 1800s and again in 1917, the Nansemond in 1890 for a few years and again in 1922. The Amherst Indians attended a church-provided school staffed by a teacher paid by the county, while the Rappahannocks could get no one of their three counties to provide them with a school until the 1950s, when they had to donate the building themselves. However, high school offerings came much later: to the then-combined Pamunkey and Mattaponi school in 1958, to the newly combined Chickahominies' school in 1950 (eleventh grade in 1954), and to the Nansemond through dispersal to various white city schools from the 1930s onward. The Amherst people and the Rappahannock did without until integration came. Any youngsters wanting more education than was offered locally had to leave Virginia, usually for church-supported schools such as Bacone College in Oklahoma. In the late 1940s the high school on the Cherokee Reservation also admitted Virginia Indian students; the commonwealth of Virginia paid the tuition of Pamunkey and Mattaponi students because of their treaty status.

Integration in 1965–68 therefore ended an important public symbol of Indian identity and group achievement, and many Indian parents were deeply dismayed. However, parents on the two reservations succeeded in negotiating special concessions for their children in the county schools, again because of their treaty status. The children were to have free tuition to county schools, free books, and free school dental checkups. (This is the one and only kind of health care rendered specifically to Indians anywhere in Virginia.) Parents in other groups spent several uncomfortable years while their children went to schools with black children and white children went to local "segregation academies." It was federal grant moneys in the 1970s—allocated to Indian communities because they were unique ethnic components in their counties—that allowed parents on and off the reservation to make themselves felt as Indians who were active in the school systems once more.

In 1973 the Mattaponi got a grant of $3,200 to supplement county expenditures on their children's schooling, and in 1975 the Chickahominy Tribe got money for a remedial summer program in reading and mathematics, both grants coming from the Department of Health, Education, and Welfare. The real impetus for education, however, came with moneys for adult education aimed at job training.

Indian groups in Virginia began getting federal moneys for economic and community development simultaneously with education funds. In 1973 the Pamunkey Indians received Comprehensive Employment and Training Act (CETA) money for environmental protection measures through the Coalition of Eastern Native Americans. In 1975 the Mattaponi got a grant of more than $100,000 to improve their housing, and in the process of getting it they had to draw up a housing code for the reservation. The Pamunkey got federal grant moneys totaling $310,000 after 1977 from the Economic Development Administration and the Department of Housing and Urban Development to build their museum/craft shop/meeting hall (dedicated in 1980). After 1980 they got further moneys from HUD to refurbish existing houses or replace them with trailers and to install septic and well systems for houses still lacking them. The Pamunkey also received funds from CETA and the Governor's Employment Training Council to encourage the making of more pottery and to help Indian personnel to qualify for running the museum. The Mattaponi have used CETA funds to refurbish their old schoolhouse as a tribal-cum-craft center, which is open to the public by appointment; they also have a museum and an educational trading post that are in private ownership.

In 1975 several Virginia Indian communities (Pamunkey, Mattaponi, and both Chickahominies) received part of a $124,522 CETA grant for job placement among southeastern Indians, administered that year through the United Southeastern Tribes (USET), an organization based in Nashville (later changing its name to United South and Eastern Tribes). The jobs in question were mainly blue-collar jobs. In succeeding years more CETA funds were acquired and administered through community action agencies in various counties. From 1977 through 1981, CETA funds were directed in part toward the organization of classes in Indian crafts, $126,500 being used for crafts alone in 1979. By 1981 all the administration of these CETA funds was in Indian hands (a Pamunkey, Warren Cook, and a Chickahominy, Michael Holmes).

When CETA funding ended in 1981, the administrative organization already in place renamed itself the Mattaponi-Pamunkey-Monacan Job Training Partnership Act Consortium and began applying for and getting federal moneys specifically for adult education and job training. The name "Monacan" was included because Warren Cook, the head of the consortium, contacted and drew in the Amherst County Indians. Under the aegis of the consortium, many Virginia Indians have gone back to school to get vocational training or to earn their GED (Graduate Equivalent Diplomas). Meanwhile, several Chickahominy, Mattaponi, and Rappahannock people have earned advanced degrees on their own, several of them in education.[3]

An increased number of Indians today hold white-collar jobs. There are store and restaurant owners (Chickahominy and United Rappahannock), store managers (in several groups), teachers in all grades (Chickahominy and United Rappahannock), engineers (Mattaponi and Chickahominy), officers in the military (United Rappahannock), a medical doctor (a Mattaponi–Upper Mattaponi), a nuclear engineer/consultant (United Rappahannock), accountants (Mattaponi and United Rappahannock), a veterinarian (Chickahominy), a self-employed printer (Upper Mattaponi), a postal inspector (United Rappahannock), and a lawyer (Chickahominy). There are also shop foremen and labor union officers (in several groups) and owners and operators of trucking firms (Chickahominy), logging contractors (United Rappahannock), and a construction company (Eastern Chickahominy). These jobs are more readily available in cities like Washington, Richmond, Newport News, Portsmouth, and Lynchburg. Thus many younger Indian people have moved to urban areas, until most of the Upper Mattaponi Indians live today in the Richmond area and most of the Nansemond Indians live in Portsmouth, Norfolk, or Virginia Beach. Those who want to live in their rural home counties must often commute, a problem that is particularly acute on the Pamunkey Reservation, located some fifty miles by road from the nearest large city (Richmond). The Chickahominy Tribe is the only one to make a concerted effort thus far to keep its young people in the community. The problem in Charles City County is that building sites are very limited, so in 1984 the tribe succeeded in buying a large plantation to subdivide for its members.

The Indians of Virginia are well able to enter fully into the economic life of the commonwealth as individual citizens. They have been monolingual English speakers for nearly two centuries. Their preferred housing and transportation are identical to that of their non-Indian neighbors, although reservation people tend to purchase mobile homes rather than build houses, which they could sell later only to other Indians. Clothing is ordinarily that of non-Indian Americans except for an occasional ornament of beadwork; for special "Indian" occasions many people have regalia. Their tribal religious centers are Christian churches, all of them Southern Baptist except for the Nansemond, whose church is United Methodist, and the Monacan, whose mission is Episcopalian. Their use of time is the same as that of white Virginians, at least during working hours. They keep up with many relatives, but those relatives do not have the same economic hold upon them that kinsfolk do in some western tribes (i.e., Virginia Indians can accumulate the money for a middle-class life-style almost with impunity). They have few enough culturally based conflicts in dealing with non-Indians that escape through alcohol and drug use is minimal among them. Their Indianness derives mainly from very strong traditions of Indian ancestry and beliefs about the nature of Indian history, and these do not hinder them from participating successfully as individuals in Virginia's economy.

Not surprisingly, then, tribal enterprises so far are all of the small-scale variety in Virginia. Ideas like bingo parlors do not find favor with these conservative Protestants, and no group has yet tried to start a factory of any kind. Several dozen people, however, are participating in tribal craft guilds, partially to make money and primarily to continue their heritage and reinforce their identity as Indians. The crafts include beadwork in geometrical Plains Indian and floral eastern Indian styles, both traditional coiled and modern molded pottery, some leatherwork, and some basketry. Those who can afford the time (usually retired people) are going to an increasing number of powwows, county fairs, and non-Indian community gatherings of all kinds—usually by invitation—wearing their regalia, selling their wares, and answering questions the public puts to them. The public relations value of these appearances is incalculable.

Indians who are more prosperous and more active as an ethnic group in their communities could easily be felt as a threat by their non-Indian neighbors if their interactions with these neighbors were not so carefully managed. In fact, relations between the Virginia Indian groups and their neighbors are generally very good, though not entirely free of some tension.

Nonreservation Indians in Virginia are full citizens in their counties, their state, and their country, and they have been so ever since they lost their reservations (in the case of the Algonquian groups) or left their original Indian communities (in the case of the Monacan). The nonreservation groups that are formally organized are organized only as corporations, and the corporations have no special jurisdiction that conflicts in any way with local civil authority. "Citizen" Indian people pay taxes, go to court, vote, and occasionally put up a political candidate. Marvin Bradby, the Eastern Chickahominy chief, has been a member of the New Kent County Planning Commission since 1974 and chairman of it since 1982; Stephen Adkins, a Chickahominy member of the Council on Indians, has been on Charles City County's school board since 1974. Indians' relations with local school boards, however, are sometimes touchy, particularly over the always volatile issue of library and classroom books. Presentation of history, of course, is the delicate issue, and many of the history books that Virginia schoolchildren read are still heavily biased against Indians. At this writing, Indians appear only in the early chapters, being shown in illustrations with Mohawk (not Powhatan) haircuts and discussed in the text only as tomahawk-wielding enemies.

The two reservations are legally not a part of King William County. They therefore pay no county taxes, have special reservation licenses for their cars, and so on. Yet many reservation people, especially on the tiny Mattaponi Reservation, own off-reservation land, which they formerly used as hunting territories and now sometimes divide up for building sites for their children. They pay county property taxes on these lands like other people.

Reservation people come under the jurisdiction of the county sheriff whenever they leave their reservations, but the sheriff has no direct power over them while they are at home. Miscreants (committing either misdemeanors or felonies), who are extremely rare on either reservation, would have to be fetched away by a state trooper. Because both reservations have allowed the commonwealth of Virginia to pave their roads (Mattaponi in 1956 and Pamunkey in 1982), state troopers and anyone else can enter the reservations and remain there as long as they stay on the roads. There being no tribal police, the Indians would call the troopers if trouble with outsiders arose. Prosecutions between Indians and outsiders would start in the county court, where they would follow the ordinary course of non-Indian court cases. If a dispute occurs between two reservation Indians that cannot be settled by the tribal government, that dispute is also referred to the King William County Court, with the normal appeal procedures available beyond that.

The two reservations have also had problems with fishing rights and claims upon their boundaries throughout the twentieth century. The fishing rights are those of fishing without licenses being required, an interpretation of the still-current Treaty of Middle Plantation (1677) that was formally upheld in the Code of Virginia of 1950. The boundary disputes have been both with neighboring individuals and with the Chesapeake Corporation, a large paper company in the county, and they continue to arise because neither reservation has ever been officially surveyed. When such a dispute materializes, the Pamunkey and Mattaponi Indians can telephone the governor and/or the state's attorney general for legal advice. Most of the boundary disputes have been successfully settled out of court.

The foregoing account shows that the reservations' relationship with the commonwealth of Virginia is somewhat informal. Virginia has never had any sort of Indian bureau. It is simply understood, sometimes after a hurried consultation with the governor or attorney general in person, that reservation tribes in distress can call directly upon state agencies for certain local civic services. The reservation people carefully keep up their personal contacts with the governor by paying him a "tribute" (actually quitrent) of game or fish every Thanksgiving, according to the terms of their treaty. They do so in regalia, with the media attending, and that often misleads the public into seeing the event as a less serious matter than it is.

Pamunkey Indians paying their tribute to the governor, 1970s style (ca. 1975). Tribute in game or fish is stipulated by the Treaty of 1677, which is still in force for the two surviving reservations. (Courtesy *Richmond News Leader*)

Virginia has had one major land case based upon the reinterpretation of the 1790 Indian Non-Intercourse Act, and that land case concerned the Pamunkey. The Nansemond considered but then shelved a similar land case because the old Nansemond reservation in Southampton County was sold to a non-Indian in 1792. The Pamunkey case derived from the condemnation in 1855 of a twenty-two-acre strip of land across the northern part of their reservation for the building of a railroad to West Point, Virginia. The Indians were not adequately compensated either then or later, and the railroad is still there and in daily operation. The tribe began to take legal action in 1971 with local advice. In 1975, when the Native American Rights Fund was called in, the case began in earnest. The railroad finally agreed to settle out of court in 1979, with the agreement that some unused land was returned to the Pamunkey and the rest of the land was to be returned as well if the tracks were ever abandoned. Reparations of $100,000 were to be paid, including rent on the land for the next decade, after which a regular rent was to be negotiated and paid in succeeding decades. The Pamunkey and Mattaponi tribes have both begun looking into other losses of their land since 1790 (and these have actually occurred), so there may be other land cases in the future.

Formal political organization is a long-established fact among most of the Virginia groups; the only recent changes have been in the number of Indian groups that are organized according to a basic model that first appeared on the reservations.

The Pamunkey and Mattaponi reservations have a form of government that evolved by the midnineteenth century, by which time the people there were much anglicized (Rountree 1990:chaps. 7–8). The old matrilineal, monarchical system, in which women often inherited ruling positions, was defunct by 1750 and was replaced by an assembly of all the adult males. By the 1830s one to three "headmen" appeared as leaders of the assembly, though all the men still signed tribal documents. Then sometime after the Civil War, a single headman came to be called a "chief," and he and several councilmen began to be elected every four years. Since then, chiefs have usually been reelected for as long as they wished to serve, and there has been a slight tendency for sons of chiefs to become chiefs as well, though not necessarily their fathers' immediate successors. The duties of the chief are to preside at meetings, act as official spokesman for the tribe, and, occasionally, to mediate disputes within the tribe.

When the Mattaponi Reservation separated administratively from the Pamunkey Reservation in 1893, the Pamunkey pattern then in use was copied. Male suffrage was assumed on both reservations, in imitation of Anglo-Virginian society of the time. That customary rule has been retained ever since, though it has never been formally inserted in the tribes' written bylaws (which are not open to the public). The Pamunkey and occasionally the Mattaponi have taken the custom of female exclusion further, ruling that women of their tribes who marry nonreservation men (even Indian ones) may not live on the reservation for the duration of the marriage. Thus it is daughters who have built houses on privately owned lands adjacent to the Mattaponi Reservation. Most of the reservation women have long been resentful about the discrimination, but they have not been able as yet to muster the male votes needed to effect a change.

Both reservations have chiefs, assistant chiefs, and several councilmen (the Pamunkey have seven, the Mattaponi a minimum of three). Elections are normally held every four years, unless there is a retirement or death or, in the case of the Mattaponi, the chief exercises his right to accept only a two-year term. In order to vote, a person must be genealogically Pamunkey or Mattaponi, male, aged eighteen or older, and in residence on the reservation for at least six months per year. Tribal meetings are held quarterly in the renovated schoolhouse/tribal center at Mattaponi and in the new museum/auditorium at Pamunkey. Any Mattaponi voter can attend the quarterly council meetings, which thus double as "tribal" meetings. The Pamunkey have quarterly tribal meetings with required attendance and more frequent council meetings that are closed to voters unless they have specific business to transact. On both reservations, the nonvoting women and outsiders (including non-Mattaponi husbands living at Mattaponi) can attend any of these meetings only by invitation when they have business to present. Meetings are conducted formally, using Robert's Rules of Order. The issues discussed in a meeting are not supposed to be broadcast, although somehow the whole tribe usually knows about them soon afterward.

Each reservation also has trustees (seven for the Pamunkey and four for the Mattaponi). These people are merely advisers drawn from the more prosperous white citizenry of the area. Once a major bulwark between non-Indians and Indians who could not vote or even testify in court, the trustees are seldom needed today. Reservation leaders are more likely to consult state officials or pan-Indian organizations by telephone.

The nonreservation groups that are formally organized are technically corporations, formed according to the standards of the state corporation commission. This arrangement is strictly a twentieth-century phenomenon. The groups existed in earlier times, but they did not feel a pressing need to organize in self-defense until the Jim Crow era and later. When they did organize, they followed the reservations' pattern of officers and government, although they updated their suffrage rules and allowed women to vote and hold office. The Chickahominy were the first to organize, in 1901, and were followed by the Rappahannocks in 1921 (and again in 1974), the Upper Mattaponi in 1923 (and again in 1976), the Eastern Division of the Chickahominy (due to a fissioning) in 1925, the Nansemond in 1984, and the Monacan in 1989.

All of the organized groups have an elected chief, one or more assistant chiefs, councilmen (five for the Eastern Chickahominy and Nansemond, seven for the Upper Mattaponi, nine for the Chickahominy, eight to ten for the United Rappahannock, and four or five informally appointed elders for the Monacan), and, for the Upper Mattaponi, Nansemond, and Monacan, a secretary and a treasurer. These are the official titles of the officers in all groups except the Chickahominy Tribe, where the above titles are unofficial and the official designation of the officers is board of directors. The secretaries, and treasurers, and several of the directors/council members are women.

In the late twentieth century, when sophisticated, energetic leaders are a necessity, several of the chiefs (Eastern Chickahominy, Upper Mattaponi, and Monacan) have been men in their forties and early fifties. In the other groups, the chiefs are much older men who are held in high respect and who have younger assistant chiefs doing much of the administrative work. Among the "citizen" groups is a tendency, paralleling that on the reservations, for sons of chiefs to become chiefs; Oliver Adkins (now deceased; Chickahominy), Captain Nelson (United Rappahannock), and Earl Bass (Nansemond) have been recent cases in point.

The officers in all these groups are elected by men and women aged eighteen and over (sixteen and over among the Eastern Chickahominy). The frequency of elections varies. The Eastern Chickahominy hold elections annually, the United Rappahannock every three years, the Upper Mattaponi and Nansemond every four years, and the Chickahominy every year for staggered three-year terms. The Monacan hold an election when an office becomes vacant. Each group has a written set of bylaws, technically open to the public but private in fact, covering membership requirements, elections, committees, and so forth. Tribal meetings are run according to Robert's Rules of Order. Considerable variation occurs in the frequency and openness of these meetings. The Nansemond and the Upper Mattaponi have general tribal meetings every month with refreshments before and afterward; attendance is closed to the public except by invitation. Their council meetings are held separately once a month and can be attended by nonofficers only by invitation. The United Rappahannock have only quarterly council meetings, which are not open to tribal members or outsiders unless they have pertinent business to present. The Eastern Chickahominy have two general tribal meetings annually plus quarterly tribal council meetings, both of which are open to tribal members but not to outsiders unless invited. The Chickahominy have one general annual meeting, with six council meetings per year that are open to tribal members but closed to others except by invitation. The Monacan have called meetings, closed to the public except by invitation, that are held on an average of once a month. Their meetings of tribal officers, also held about once a month, are closed to nonofficers unless invited.

All of the organized groups are more or less the product of one or two energetic people.[4] The main obstacle today, now that segregation is over and racial tensions have ameliorated, is finding resourceful, sophisticated leaders who have the time to contact and coordinate meetings of their kinsmen. Nowadays, with a greater dispersal of kinsmen to nearby cities and with much more complicated bureaucracies to contact, the pressure on leaders is even greater. The Nansemond achieved their formal organization within only two years (1983–84) because their prime mover, Assistant Chief Oliver Perry, Sr., is a retired civil servant with grown children and plenty of time.

All the Indian groups in Virginia have requirements for membership and, in the case of the reservations, residence thereon. Because residence is

the prime goal of applicants for the reservations, and because present allotments of the communally owned land must be subdivided to accommodate
new arrivals, there is a ceiling on membership, which the tiny Mattaponi
Reservation has all but reached (they have a waiting list there). All the
Virginia groups also have people who are eligible for membership but who
have chosen not to join, because of either geographical distance or lack of
interest. Thus the population figures cited at the beginning of this chapter
are enrollment figures; real populations are nearly impossible to calculate.

Only one Virginia group specifically allows dual tribal membership.
That is the Upper Mattaponi, who have intermarried for years with the
Mattaponi Reservation people. The Upper Mattaponi chief in 1984–88
was Linwood Custalow, M.D., the son of an Upper Mattaponi mother and
a Mattaponi father (who is coincidentally the current Mattaponi chief).
Dr. Custalow lives and has his practice in Newport News, which precludes
his meeting the residence requirement on the reservation where he grew
up. He and his sister, Shirley McGowan, an officer in the consortium who
lives adjacent to the Mattaponi Reservation, are members of both their
parents' tribes, but they are allowed to vote only among the Upper Mattaponi, he because he lives away and she because she is female.

The requirements for membership in the Virginia tribes are primarily
genealogical. Kinship in all the groups is bilateral, so it does not matter
which parent supplies the Indian ancestry (though the United Rappahannock group prefers that ancestry be on the father's side). Applicants must
show family connections that the group in question recognizes. For most
of the groups, this recognition is achieved informally through the memo-
ries of the elders. An exception is Gertrude Custalow, the church secretary
on the Mattaponi Reservation, who is now keeping a genealogy of her
people so that legitimate but distant relatives can be treated fairly. Literacy
came late to most of the Virginia Indian groups and most of the crucial
courthouses were burned, making documentation of family lines nearly
impossible beyond a century and a half ago. The Nansemond, in contrast,
require very formal proofs of Nansemond ancestry because they can afford
to. Their ancestors became literate early and kept some very old religious
books with family records in them; thus this group has compiled (with my
help) a genealogy based on documents going back to the Nansemond Indians of the early seventeenth century. In all the groups, applicants for membership are also screened for character, because public image means a
great deal to such a small ethnic minority.

One specifically "Indian" gathering of long standing in Virginia is aimed
at both celebrating a group's "Indianness" to the general public and
providing Indians of various tribes with a chance to socialize. This is the
Chickahominy Fall Festival. Usually held on a Saturday afternoon in late

September or early October, the festival is publicized in the local media and through invitations sent to friends. For many years after its inception in 1951, this affair was organized by Chief Oliver Adkins and held at the tribal school, next door to the tribal church; after the school was lost to the county during integration, the Jamestown Festival Park played host until a new Chickahominy tribal center was finished in 1978. The festival has always featured speeches by invited guests (one principal speaker has been the United States commissioner of Indian affairs) and noncompetitive exhibition dancing by the Chickahominy Redmen Dancers and any other guests who wished to participate (since 1985 two United Rappahannock dance teams have appeared). The guest dancers nearly always demonstrate pan-Indian, Plains-inspired drumming, singing, and dancing; the Chickahominy dancers have their own style, which features programmatic numbers such as the Welcome Dance and the Courtship Dance. Craft concessions have multiplied in recent years, with more tribes from Virginia and other states represented each year. Chickahominy-run game and food booths have been a fixture since the early 1980s. Today the preparations for the festival are so complicated that a large committee has to do the work.

The Nansemond began following suit in January 1985, when they celebrated their state recognition with a "pig-pickin'." In 1986 they also held a spring festival and since 1988 they have held a September "homecoming," open to the public, which they hope will become an annual event parallel to the Chickahominy Fall Festival. These events are primarily for Indians of other tribes and then for invited guests, although a local television station usually covers them. Nansemond gatherings feature speeches, dancing by the Chickahominy and Rappahannock dance teams, and crafts displays. At the first two outings, in 1985–86, meals featuring barbecued pork were served, but there were no concessions, at the Nansemond's request; the aim of both affairs was purely social.

Many of the host people and most of the Indian guests wear some sort of regalia to these gatherings. The minimum outfit is "civvies" with a beadwork or turquoise-and-silver ornament of some sort; even some tribal officers dress this way on occasion.[5] The next step up, for men and women among the Nansemond at least, is ribbon shirts over slacks; some add headbands, beadwork ornaments, or knee-high leather moccasins. Full regalia for Virginia women is long, fringed, beaded dresses of leather or leather-like fabric. Those who favor a more traditional Virginia Algonquian style wear their dresses over one shoulder only. Full regalia for men varies, depending upon status as a dancer, nondancer, or tribal chief. Male dancers wear a loincloth over slacks (leather preferred) or shorts or bathing trunks, fringed and beaded leather vests, Plains-inspired feather headdresses, moccasins, and, occasionally, Plains-style feather bustles. Nondancers who are not chiefs wear fringed and beaded leather shirts and trousers and often moccasins. Chiefs wear the same regalia, usually in leather, but they add headdresses (the Eastern Chickahominy chief's clothing is black velvet without fringes). The headdresses of chiefs longer in office are standard Plains-style war bonnets. However, since the early 1980s the old Algonquian-style upright wild turkey feather headdress has come into fashion. These garments are being custom-made for sale by women on the Mattaponi Reservation, and Gertrude Custalow is currently (in 1990) making a feather cape as well.

Other Indian gatherings in Virginia are more private, so regalia is generally not worn to them. The tribal Baptist churches have homecomings during the summer that are staggered to allow people from other groups to attend. The full day includes Sunday school, morning worship service, a picnic, and then either a gospel concert or the first service in a week-long revival. Marriages and funerals also draw many friends from other tribes and become major social occasions. The funerals of chiefs and assistant chiefs are especially important events, often covered by the media; however, only at Mattaponi does there seem to be a custom of wearing regalia at such times.

Virginia Indian gatherings center around buildings, which become symbols of the groups using them. All religious occasions, of course, take place in the churches, which are kept scrupulously clean and frequently renovated. The Eastern Chickahominy recently built a completely new church with a $45,000 grant from the Virginia Baptist General Board's State Mission Offering. All of the groups except the Nansemond have a church of their own that is either a Baptist church with the tribal name in its title or, in the case of the Monacan, an Episcopal mission church established especially for them. The Nansemond received a Methodist mission in 1850. Some Nansemond have gone there ever since, although with the dispersal to nearby cities, that congregation, now a United Methodist one, is mostly white. When the Nansemond began holding formal meetings again, that congregation invited them to have the meetings in the church.

Schoolhouses are still important buildings to the Indians in Virginia. The Pamunkey, whose few children were sent to the Mattaponi school in 1951, used their building for many years as a trading post for the selling of pottery; today it is used for storage. The Mattaponi have renovated their schoolhouse and made it into a tribal center. The two Chickahominies lost their Samaria School, but its proximity to the Chickahominy Tribe's church keeps it fresh in their minds. The Nansemond got a schoolhouse on their church grounds at two different periods, but no building remains. Instead the group has cooperated with the city of Chesapeake to erect a

Table 1. Virginia Indian Groups in the Mid-1980s

| | Reservation | Enrolled Adults | Universal Suffrage | Annual Festival | Dance Team | Tribal Center | Museum |
|---|---|---|---|---|---|---|---|
| Pamunkey | X | ca. 50 | | | | X | X |
| Mattaponi | X | ca. 60 | | | | X | X |
| Upper Mattaponi | | ca. 60 | X | | | X | |
| Chickahominy | | ca. 550 | X | X | X | X | |
| Eastern Chickahominy | | 42 | X | | | X | |
| United Rappahannock | | ca. 150 | X | | X | | |
| Nansemond | | 94 | X | X | | | |
| Monacan | | ca. 550 | X | | | | |

historical marker on the spot. The Upper Mattaponi lost their Sharon School to the county when integration came, although the Indians had contributed so much to the purchase of land and building materials that the county's title to the building was questionable. In 1985 the tribe carried out a campaign to get the school back, culminating in a meeting with the King William County Board of Supervisors in which their testimony was bolstered by the chiefs of the Pamunkey, Mattaponi, and Chickahominy (dressed in regalia), by an ethnohistorian (myself), and by several of the most influential white citizens of the county. They got their building back and have renovated it for a tribal center. The Monacan use a room in their mission church's parish hall as a tribal center.

Tribal centers may soon outweigh churches as the most important symbol of group identity and cohesiveness. Those tribes that lack convertible buildings seek to build one in order to house tribal meetings, craft guilds, adult education, and public events. The basic requirements of such a building are a meeting hall, a kitchen, workrooms, and lavatories. Ideally that means a large building. The Chickahominy, the largest tribe in the state, built such a building with their own money in 1976–78. The Pamunkey used federal funding to build a combination museum and meeting hall-cum-kitchen. The Eastern Chickahominy have made do with a trailer bought for the purpose. The Mattaponi have redone their schoolhouse. The Upper Mattaponi are doing the same, and meanwhile they rent the cafeteria of King William High School or, more rarely, use their church. The United Rappahannock have bought land and are now raising funds for a building. The Nansemond have scarcely begun work on a tribal center; they have their meetings in the church, smaller meetings in private homes, and public gatherings at a dance hall near the church.

Virginia Indian people have been members of other Indian organizations for a long time. Oliver Adkins, the Chickahominy chief, was a member of the National Congress of American Indians for several decades and was a member of the board of the now defunct Coalition of Eastern Native Americans. Linwood Custalow, the Upper Mattaponis' physician/former chief, is a founding member and past president of the Association of American Indian Physicians and was formerly another Virginia member of the NCAI. He has also served on the board of trustees of Bacone College, where he did his high school work. Other Upper Mattaponi living in New Jersey are active members of the Powhatan-Renape Nation there. Some Rappahannocks joined the American Indian Movement in the 1970s. Curtis Custalow, the former chief at Mattaponi, was a prime mover in organizing the Coalition of Eastern Native Americans; he was also a member of the board of directors of the Native American Rights Fund for several years and has now been replaced there by his nephew, Kenneth Custalow, the Mattaponi accountant.

Virginia had no bureaucracy of any kind for Indians until recently. The commonwealth was concerned only with reservation Indians, whose treaty rights had to be protected and who could call the governor or the attorney general directly for help. In 1972 the governor made a move toward including Indians in policymaking when he appointed the Mattaponi and Chickahominy chiefs to be members of the Governor's Minority Economic Development Advisory Commission. In 1977 Warren Cook, a college-educated Pamunkey, was appointed governor's adviser on Indian affairs on the assumption that the "Indians" concerned were only reservation people.

In 1982 the nonreservation organized tribes (Chickahominy, Eastern Chickahominy, Upper Mattaponi, and United Rappahannock) began to campaign for state recognition, something the Chickahominy had attempted unsuccessfully in the early 1920s. With the help of a Chickahominy-hired lobbyist and of Hardaway Marks, an influential delegate who had known the Chickahominy for many years, the four tribes got the General Assembly to appoint a Joint Subcommittee to Study the Historical Dealings and Relationships Between the Commonwealth of Virginia and Virginia Indian Tribes. They also began working with the Indian Information Project of United Indians of America, an organization whose members are mainly Lumbees, to collect documents and organize testimony in cooperation with the subcommittee. They did not consult the reservation groups, who for some time feared a threat to their own legal status and remained aloof. The crucial hearing, with leaders of all the tribes (including the reservations) and an ethnohistorian (myself) testifying, was successful. House Joint Resolution 54 was passed in January 1983, giving official recognition to the two Chickahominies, the Upper Mattaponi, and the United Rappahannocks (part of whom had fissioned off immediately before and taken another name).[6] Publicity surrounding this event incited Oliver Perry, Sr., of the Nansemond to begin organizing his people;[7] they achieved state recognition through another resolution exactly two years later. The Monacans followed suit, eventually receiving recognition in 1989.

State recognition under the law of 1983 means that an Indian group, already formally organized with a tribal roll, is formally recognized as such; the commonwealth makes no comment thereby on the people's status before 1776, when the colonial government existed. Recognition carries no services at all with it. The only thing it does is to bolster the credibility of Indian groups seeking federal moneys for community development and the like. Given the sophistication of the Virginia Indians today in dealing with local, state, and federal governments, that is plenty.

The resolution also established the Virginia Commission (now renamed Council) on Indians that is the successor of the joint subcommittee in that it has five Indian and five non-Indian members. Most of the Indian members are chiefs or assistant chiefs in their tribes; originally there was only one female member, a United Rappahannock, but now there are several.[8] Because the law setting up the council is the same one dealing with recognition of nonreservation groups, the Indian tribes represented on the council are all nonreservation tribes. The council cannot speak for the reservations; only the adviser to the governor on Indian affairs can do that, and belatedly but very sensibly he has been made an ex officio member of the council. Even then, the council has no authority over anyone; its function is strictly advisory. For instance, Indian groups seeking state recognition are now expected to get the advice of the council, which is in turn expected to set definite guidelines on the matter. In 1988 the nonreservation and reservation groups jointly established United Indians of Virginia, an informational and advisory body that parallels the council in many ways. But it, too, serves only as a forum and lacks authority over anyone. Those wanting the *official* cooperation of any Virginia tribe, as the Jamestown Festival Park recently has in renovating and Indianizing its museum, must in the end deal with the chief of each tribe. Although intertribal cooperation is reaching new heights in Virginia, the tribes are still separate and entirely autonomous entities, as they have always wanted to be.

The civil rights era destroyed a major symbol of identity among Virginia Indians through the closing of the tribal schools. Yet the era's positive effects on Indian lives have been greater than any of the Indians dared to hope for at the time. With much expanded opportunities for education and employment, Indian people all across Virginia have moved into higher economic brackets, with consequent improvements in their health, their morale, and their general standard of living. The next generation now has a firm foothold in gaining further improvements.

Tribal organizations have become more active, partly because of a milder "racial" climate and partly because of a greater awareness of other eastern Indians' organizations and goals. Groups without formal organizations have taken steps to remedy that weakness, for in the late twentieth century being formally organized is a vital part of successfully being Indian in Virginia. Schools as identity symbols have been replaced by tribal centers, in which members maintain their kin ties, practice the arts connected with their heritage, and plan new community projects, often with federal funding behind them. Litigation over lost reservation land has been fought and finally won. And most of the groups without reservations have achieved state recognition as Indians, a goal they scarcely dared to dream of in the 1960s.

Non-Indian Virginians used to predict that, whenever they had the chance, the people claiming so consistently to be Indians would melt away into the white population. That prediction has not come true. Integration and civil rights laws did not bring assimilation. Instead they brought greater economic and political power to a people who still feel they are Indians and have never really wanted to be anything else.

# 2

# ADAPTATION AND THE CONTEMPORARY NORTH CAROLINA CHEROKEE INDIANS

*Sharlotte Neely*

The Eastern Band of Cherokee Indians has constituted the largest federal reservation in the Southeast since the reservation's founding on traditional tribal lands in 1889.[1] Land holdings number 56,574 acres scattered across the counties of Swain, Jackson, Graham, and Cherokee in the mountains of southwestern North Carolina. While the U.S. census for 1980 shows 5,482 Indians living on or near the reservation, the Eastern Band itself counts more than 9,000 enrolled members. Although North Carolina has a larger Indian population than any other southern state, the Cherokees are the only group within the state's borders to have federal reservation holdings.

Because the Cherokees, unlike many other southeastern groups, have reservation land, an Indian language still spoken by a few Cherokees, unique crafts, an undisputed relationship to prehistoric and historic Indians, and other characteristics that non-Indians associate with "real" Indians, the Cherokees have not had to "prove" their Indian identity despite intense intermarriage with whites and the loss of many traditional traits. The most notable Cherokee traits still in existence are in the areas of family life, values, healing, art, and language, although the number of Cherokee language speakers is rapidly declining (Neely 1979).

After the Great Removal, about 1,000 Cherokees in North Carolina remained behind in the mountains to form the nucleus of the Eastern Band (cf. Finger 1984). Price (1953) suggests that there was a pattern to the selective survival of the Cherokees and other Indians in the Southeast. In-

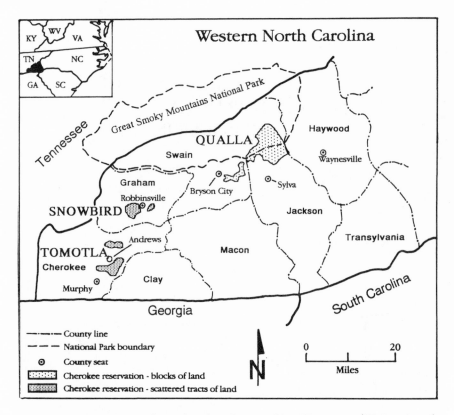

Locations of North Carolina Cherokee Communities (Courtesy of University of Georgia Press)

dian groups on lands classified by whites as ecologically marginal, like swamps or mountains, have survived best. From the Cherokee Removal of 1838 until the 1880s and 1890s the Eastern Cherokees were largely a homogeneous group, both culturally and racially. By the end of the nineteenth century, however, there was less state land available that whites really valued, and many whites, lured by the hope of obtaining ownership of "free" Indian land under the federal government's policy of allotment, moved onto parts of the North Carolina reservation (Kupferer 1966:232). Even as late as 1928, Cherokee writer Henry Owl could remark: "The enrollment took a sudden spurt in 1928 because of the plans for allotment, and many names on the list will not stand too close scrutiny for eligibility" (Owl 1929:142).

As Gulick (1960) has noted, the Cherokee reservation lands are among the most rugged in their region of the mountains, and within the reservation "white Indians" are more likely to reside on what flat bottomlands are

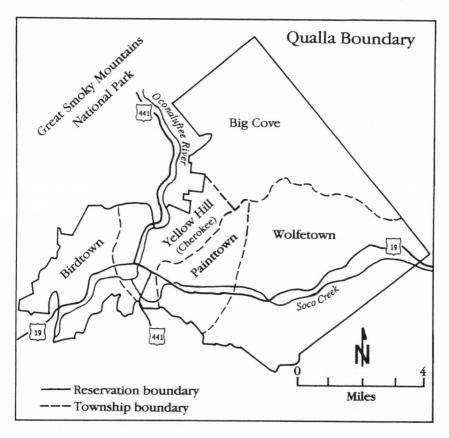

Detail of Qualla Boundary Reservation (Courtesy of University of Georgia Press)

available. Fullbloods are left with extremely rugged holdings. The "white Indians" whom fullbloods resent are Cherokees of minimal Indian ancestry and whose behavior conforms to white America's Protestant Ethic.

The Cherokees have survived in the southern Appalachian Mountains for at least the last four thousand years and have always exemplified a generalized adaptation. Originally, Cherokee subsistence was achieved through a combined approach of gardening, gathering, fishing, and hunting. Even today, most wage laborers supplement the support of their families through those endeavors although the reservation is too overpopulated to rely heavily on exploiting natural resources or on farming.

During the twentieth century, Eastern Cherokee history has been characterized by depressing economic trends, which have contributed to acculturation. In the midnineteenth century, before population increases placed excessive demands on the limited land base, most Cherokees adequately provided for their needs by farming. Yet by 1908 most Cherokees were reported as living in poverty, because, as a government official stated, "there are few opportunities in that part of North Carolina where they live for them to earn money, and they are obliged to depend upon their sterile little farms" (Litton 1940:225).

As the population steadily increased, with no corresponding increases in the size of the reservation, the Eastern Cherokees were less and less able to depend on farming as a means of livelihood. By the 1950s only about 10 percent of the people supported themselves by farming, and by the 1970s not one Cherokee family received its livelihood from that source (Gulick 1960:39). Despite the fact that the Cherokee population has increased ninefold in the last century and a half, the land base has not increased at all.

This decline in farming has meant that more Cherokees have turned to other occupations, which have often taken them off the reservation into wage labor. World War II and subsequent wars have taken numerous Cherokee men away from North Carolina and exposed them to the larger world. Many of these veterans later left the reservation for jobs or commuted to neighboring areas by automobile to find work.

By the 1950s, tourism provided more income to the reservation than any other form of regular employment, but it was not adequate. Tourism provided many jobs, so that unemployment during the summer dropped to 1 percent, but most of these jobs were low paying and limited to the summer months. During the winter, unemployment soared to 20 percent, and the average yearly income for most Cherokees was only one-fifth of the national average (Gulick 1960:39). In 1958 the local Bureau of Indian Affairs superintendent wrote that because of the "dire need" among the Cherokees, there was "much actual hunger" (Williams 1971:48).

Unemployment and underemployment have always been problems for the North Carolina Cherokees because of the lack of large-scale industries nearby and the distance from urban areas. The tourist industry has been enhanced by the reservation's close proximity to the nation's most visited park in the Great Smoky Mountains. Despite that advantage, however, Cherokee tourism has always had major problems. Foremost is the fact that Cherokee tourism has been a summer event. Highways that are jammed with cars from Memorial Day to Labor Day are deserted for the rest of the year. Summers are thus busy for most Cherokees because they can find jobs but still must spend time tending their gardens as well. Besides its seasonal nature, other drawbacks to tourism include low wages, the fact that the largest tourism enterprises are white owned, and the fact that many shops stock cheap imitation Indian crafts from Haiti or Taiwan. By the 1970s, however, some economic progress had been made, and Cherokee incomes had increased from 20 to 60 percent of the national average; but most families still needed more than one employed family member just to make ends meet (Eastern Band of Cherokee Indians 1972:33–35).

The tribal council has made some major strides in the last ten years to exert more control over the tourist industry. The council has considered setting standards for craft items sold on the reservation. In 1976, the Eastern Band opened the doors to the magnificent new Cherokee Museum. Through this museum—along with the older living village exhibit, Oconaluftee, and the outdoor drama, "Unto These Hills"—it is possible for tourists to gain a reasonably accurate view of Cherokee prehistory and history. A tourist visiting the expanded Qualla Arts and Crafts Co-op can find high-quality genuine Cherokee crafts instead of the rubber tomahawks sold amid the full-scale aluminum tipis and plastic bison in the shops along the main strip.

Nothing, however, has had the effect on Cherokee tourism or the Cherokee economy generally as a phenomenon of the last decade. In 1982, the Cherokees followed the lead of the Florida Seminoles and other Indians on federal reservations and began offering opportunities for tourists to play high-stakes bingo. In less than two years, the Cherokees "cleared $500,000 from 65,000 players" (Anderson 1984). Profits now range from $600,000 to $1,000,000 annually. In addition, bingo provides an annual payroll, most of it to Indians, of about $500,000. Since 1987 the tribe has taken over direct operation of bingo with a three-person board of directors. The tribal council has contracted with either Cherokees or a mixed group of Cherokees and whites to run the operation. Seventy percent of bingo profits goes to the tribe and 30 percent goes to the operators. The tribe's profits are used on projects that focus on what tribal attorney Ben Bridgers calls "health, education, and welfare issues."

A ripple effect from bingo occurs both on and off the reservation. Motels that used to make money only in the summer and lose money in other seasons now at least break even or better no matter what the season. Swain County, which has the largest Cherokee population in the state, estimates that since the advent of Cherokee bingo, welfare payments have decreased by nearly a third.

Bingo is a good example of an adaptive survival strategy on the part of Cherokees and other federal Indians. The ability of the Cherokees to tap into diverse federal, state, county, and tribal resources has always been impressive. Even ten years ago, while some Cherokees in the Snowbird community were employed through the tribe's Mainstream Program, others were employed by Graham County's Mainstream Program. At the same time, two Graham County deputy sheriffs who were Snowbird Cherokees were paid by the tribe but technically employed by the county.

Now that Mainstream, CETA, and other federal programs are drying up under Republican administrations, Indians have had to be inventive in tapping into new resources. One new source exists at the state level. In 1970 the Cherokees joined with the Lumbees and other North Carolina Indians in an organizational effort that resulted in a state commission on Indian affairs. Once the commission was functioning, however, the Cherokees declined to participate. One reason may have been the Cherokees' perception at the time that the commission would not benefit the Cherokees as much as other Indians. For other Indians the creation of the commission was an important step in establishing their Indian identity. The Cherokees felt more secure in their own Indian identity and may have even felt that, in allying with nonreservation Indians, Cherokee identity could be harmed. Also, while the commission was originally set up to promote Indian crafts and culture, it was not lucratively bankrolled by the state. Besides, at the time the Cherokees were already involved in a regional group, United Southeastern Tribes (USET).

In 1986, however, the Cherokees changed their position and joined the North Carolina Commisison of Indian Affairs. Like every other Indian group in the state, except the Lumbees, the Cherokees have two seats; the Lumbees have three because of their large population. The benefits to the Cherokees were immediately forthcoming: 1986 was the Year of the Native American in North Carolina; as a result the legislature awarded the commisison $65,000, and the Cherokees received $7,500 of that sum. While normally the commission does not have large sums of money to disburse, it can function to lobby the legislature for funds to benefit Indians. In 1986 the commission was instrumental in securing $30,000 for the Cherokees' program to prevent unwanted pregnancies.

High-stakes bingo exists because of Indians' ability to juxtapose their federal and state status. While the Cherokees are now working more closely with state government, the success of their bingo enterprise requires that they maintain some legal distance from the state. A string of court cases involving the Seminoles seems to indicate that if a state allows bingo at all, that state has no power to regulate bingo on a federal Indian reservation (Fragin 1985:35). Forty-two of the fifty states allow bingo, which makes their bingo laws regulatory and therefore not applicable on federal reservations within their state boundaries. Only if bingo is illegal in a state and therefore criminal as gambling can a state disallow bingo on a federal reservation. The Seminoles got high-stakes bingo rolling in 1979, the Cherokees joined in 1982, by 1984 at least fifty tribes were in the bingo business, and by 1985 at least eighty were (Fragin 1985:35).

Cautious of the problems the Seminoles experienced with county and state officials in Florida, the Cherokees carefully consulted with the attorney general's office in North Carolina before opening their bingo hall.

State law sets an upper limit of $500 a game on bingo. Cherokee bingo is higher stakes, and twice a year there are $1,000,000 games that cost a player $500 to participate. So far, however, North Carolina has made no attempt to close down Cherokee bingo, and the Cherokees have been involved in no litigation.

The profits the Cherokees are making at bingo, however, are not as high as the Hollywood, Florida, Seminoles who can run games every day of the week with nearby Miami and Fort Lauderdale to draw on for players. The Cherokees are in a more remote area and run games only two weekends per month. The bingo operators spend a considerable amount of money busing in players from places as far away as Cincinnati, Ohio. Despite travel problems, however, bingo has partially solved one of the major problems with Cherokee tourism: how to attract tourists to the reservation in the fall, winter, and spring. At one time, the tribe considered attempting to solve the winter tourism problem by opening a ski resort. Ultimately, it was decided that the winters were not cold or snowy enough for a ski resort to be a good investment. High-stakes bingo surely brings in more tourists.

While bingo has, at least in part, solved many financial problems, it has created some ethical ones. As on other reservations, concern exists that organized crime may become involved. Because private investments, not government or bank loans, are largely used to finance high-stakes bingo, this may be a legitimate concern on some reservations. The Cherokees converted an old textile mill into their bingo hall and lease it to private contractors who assume financial responsibilities and run the bingo games for 30 percent of the profits. Organized crime concerns aside, some Cherokees and local whites, who as groups are both largely fundamentalist Christians, have wondered about the morality of making money off any form of gambling, including bingo. Other concerns have revolved around questions of whether the tribe is making its fair share of profits after the payroll, expenses, and the contractor's profit are taken care of.

For a while there were concerns that legislation might pass through Congress outlawing Indian bingo. Various bills were proposed that would either protect or eliminate high-stakes bingo. There was fear that if legislation passed allowing the states to control Indian bingo, then high-stakes games would end as state bingo laws were applied to reservations. Some nonprofit groups who use bingo to raise funds and have felt the competition from reservations advocated state control. What did pass in 1988 was legislation that preserved high-stakes Indian bingo while restricting the expansion of Indian gambling into the casinos and dog tracks proposed by some tribes. While the Reagan administration opposed gambling on moral grounds, bingo represented the kind of entrepreneurial enterprise that former Secretary of the Interior James Watt complained was lacking on reservations. The profits from high-stakes bingo also benefited the Reagan administration by masking the budget cuts to federal reservations.

Bingo is not the only financial boost the Cherokees have experienced in the last two decades. In 1972, $1,855,254.50 was awarded to the Eastern Band by the Indian Claims Commission for all Cherokee lands lost to non-Indian control. Despite the protests of traditionalists on the tribal council who wanted the money invested and the profits used for some common good, such as retirement benefits and college scholarships, the money was eventually divided on a per capita basis (amounting to less than $250.00 per person) and has been dissipated. By contrast, a bingo commission decides on an annual basis how bingo profits are to be spent for group projects. Per capita distribution of the bingo profits is prohibited by law.

Thus, as some resources disappear, others emerge. Starting in 1962 the Qualla Housing Authority functioned to improve dramatically housing on the Cherokee reservation by either building new homes or significantly improving old ones. During the first fifteen years, more than 600 houses were built or improved, reducing the fraction of substandard housing from nearly 90 to less than 60 percent (Eastern Band of Cherokee Indians 1972:47; *Cherokee One Feather* 1975). The housing authority has had a major impact on the quality of reservation housing, and today the total number of houses built exceeds 1,100.

Ironically, the same reservation status that has paved the way for the lucrative Cherokee bingo had blocked efforts to upgrade housing. Because reservation land cannot be used as collateral in securing a bank mortgage, Cherokees, like other federal reservation Indians, had previously been unable to finance adequate housing. After all, one of the ideas behind the concept of a reservation is that such land cannot be lost to Indian control, not even to bankers. By creating the Qualla Housing Authority and tapping into government money to provide home loans, Cherokees were able to finance new houses of superior construction. Costs were kept low because the houses were semiprefabricated and most of the labor was done by the families themselves on land to which they held possessory rights.

In the late 1970s the Cherokees founded a children's home to have someplace on the reservation to house Cherokee children not in their parents' care. Many Indian groups have been concerned about the loss of Indian children to whites through either foster homes or adoption. In 1978, the Indian Child Welfare Act was passed into law. This legislation makes it difficult for non-Indians to adopt Indian children because priority is given to tribal governments to place Indian children in Indian adoptive or foster homes. Before the law many Indian children were annually adopted by white parents and were, from the Indians' point of view, lost to their own people and culture. In addition, Indian children removed from their parents' care by the courts were often placed in white foster homes. The primary reason for placing Indian children in white foster homes was not that Indian foster parents were lacking but that it was easier to find white homes that met the statistical criteria of having indoor plumbing, enough bedrooms, central heating, and the like. Often those types of criteria mattered more to the courts than whether Indian relatives were willing to take in the children. Now in such cases Cherokee children can at least be kept on the reservation near their families and enrolled in reservation schools by placing them in the Cherokee Children's Home. The children's home meets all the criteria of the courts and is a good example of how adaptive the Cherokees can be in dealing with outside forces. In 1990 the Cherokee Children's Home and Cherokee Boys' Club took over direct control of all schools on the Qualla Boundary, ending almost a century of Bureau of Indian Affairs control. Funding still comes from federal taxes.

Other changes have occurred. In the mid-1970s, the Bureau of Indian Affairs, which was then responsible for education on the main reservation, the Qualla Boundary, constructed a new high school. The old high school had become so structurally unsound that the second floor could not safely be used. The new Cherokee High School by contrast even has such luxuries as a swimming pool and gymnasium. Programs were begun to teach the dying Cherokee language, crafts, and other cultural traits. The tribe has plans to expand such programs.

Also in the 1970s, the Indian Health Service finally expanded the small Cherokee Hospital and worked with the tribal council to construct a clinic in the Snowbird community fifty miles from the main reservation. The problem of adequately staffing either facility still exists with the Cherokees and all other federal reservations because the salaries of Indian Health Service physicians are not competitive with salaries elsewhere and because reservations are largely located in remote, rural areas not attractive to those in the medical profession. The Cherokees try to compensate for the lack of professional staffs by training themselves in emergency first aid methods, running their own rescue squads, and entering into contracts with private physicians and county hospitals.

Today band membership is based on a minimum of one-sixteenth Cherokee blood degree, although in the past the degree has been as low as one-thirty-second. It is a system that attempts to define Indians genetically rather than socially. Although it is unlikely that Cherokees with near minimal blood degree would ever be classified as cultural traditionalists, the number of Cherokees living like their white neighbors has continued to include more and more people with near maximal blood degree.

The Snowbird Cherokee community is a noteworthy exception. While

*Above:* A Cherokee woman puts the finishing touches on a basket at the Oconaluftee Living Village, where tourists may view traditional Cherokee life. (Photo: Thomas C. Donnelly, 1990). *Below:* A new Qualla Housing Authority home stands next to the old house in which a Snowbird family previously lived; the old house was later razed. (Photo: Sharlotte Neely, 1975, Courtesy The University of Georgia Press)

*Above:* Shirley Jackson Oswalt runs the Snowbird Community Store, which dispenses school supplies and other necessities to those in the Snowbird Cherokee community. *Below:* The Cherokee Tribal Council House where decisions are made on topics as diverse as land disputes and education. (Photos: Thomas C. Donnelly, 1990)

the percentage of what Cherokees term "white Indians" has increased on the main reservation and the only Cherokee language speakers there tend to be elderly, Snowbird has a high percentage (over 75 percent) of full-bloods and Cherokee speakers. Living on scattered tracts of reservation land in Graham County, fifty miles southwest of the main reservation, the Snowbird Cherokees consciously work at preserving their traditions, like language, while having intense relations with local whites among whom the Cherokees' land is scattered.

The Snowbird Cherokees represent the best example of a generalized adaption among the modern Cherokees. They garden, gather, fish, and hunt to supplement their wage-labor jobs. Snowbird women make some baskets to be sold in the tourist shops on the main reservation but otherwise are not so dependent on the tourism business, which in addition to paying low wages and being seasonal is often dominated by whites and "white Indians."

The people of the Snowbird community have become adept at adapting to the modern world without sacrificing their traditionalism. The community led the way in seeking nontribal economic resources, such as those of county government, in order not to be totally dependent on tribal resources. When the federal government paid the Eastern Band of Cherokees nearly two million dollars for Cherokee lands permanently lost to whites, only the Snowbird Cherokee council members suggested the money be used for some group good, demonstrating the traditionalist Snowbird community's adherence to the old Harmony Ethic value system of the Cherokees that focuses on putting the needs of the group above the individual's, being generous with the poor, and sharing resources. The method suggested for using the money for group good was quite modern, however; Snowbird suggested the money be invested and the interest alone used (to supplement the pensions of the elderly and the college tuition of the young), leaving the principle to continue earning interest. "White Indians'" wants won out, however, and there was a per capita distribution of the money, which is now spent.

No matter what the cultural outlook of an individual Cherokee is, however, there are advantages to identifying ethnically as a Cherokee Indian. Many of the advantages are economic. Band membership's most basic economic advantage is access to reservation land and thus new houses. With lands held in trust by the federal government and legally a corporation under North Carolina laws, the band's assets consist of its land with the band's members functioning as stockholders. Although reservation lands cannot be "owned," individual band members can have "possessory rights" to tracts of land that can be sold to, bought from, willed to, or inherited from any other band member. Access to land provides definite economic opportunities, even though the reservation is too crowded and the land too poor and mountainous for large-scale farming.

The cheap price of reservation land, sometimes acquired for free if inherited, compares favorably with more expensive off-reservation land and high rents in nearby towns. Many Cherokees survive more inexpensively by living in homes on the reservation and commuting long distances to find work than by moving closer to their off-reservation jobs. For the few who hold lands adjacent to major highways on the main reservation, there is a profitable business in either leasing land for tourist enterprises or in operating those enterprises themselves. Access to land has also meant access to the band's housing program.

The current attraction of band membership can be illustrated by the recent efforts of a peripheral Cherokee community to reassert its Cherokee identity. Located more than sixty miles southwest of the main reservation and largely comprising people phenotypically white, the Tomotla community of Cherokee County has not always been so eager to assert its Indian identity, and in the recent past people there may even have intentionally misrepresented their ethnic status. Their lands, however, do have reservation status. Even as early as the Swetland Roll of 1860, most Indians in that area were of minimal blood degree and probably should be grouped with pre-Removal hill-country Cherokees who lived to the south. In 1950 the U.S. Census Bureau numbered only 24 Indians in the community, and not for the previous seventy years had the community numbered more than 40 people. But in 1970 the Tomotla community officially numbered 71 Indians, and in 1973 it was able to muster enough people to the polls to defeat the neighboring Snowbird community of 320 fullblood Cherokees, thereby seizing two seats in the tribal council. In other words, it seems probable that until the last twenty years many people in the Tomotla community were identifying as white, even to census takers. By 1980 the Tomotla population had officially grown by 166.2 percent to 189.

When the two new representatives from Tomotla were seated at tribal council in 1973, a council member from the main reservation admitted he had not previously known of the existence of the Tomotla community—they had kept such a low profile as Indians. At a meeting a few weeks later, people from the previously unrecognized Tomotla community voiced their demands for a share in the band's low-cost housing program, which had previously overlooked them. By more actively asserting their Cherokee ethnic identity and grasping a share of the power in band affairs, the community had acted in its own best interests and benefited itself economically. In 1975 plans for building new houses included this community. The community continues to have some representation in council and to make itself heard on important issues. "White Indian" communities have been supportive of Tomotla's efforts, while fullblood communities have expressed resentment. While a shaky compromise exists between Tomotla and Snowbird (each controls one of their township's two tribal council seats), the Tomotla/Snowbird controversy is just one example of the factionalism between minimal and maximal blood degree Cherokees that is ongoing.

In its 1973 dispute with the neighboring fullblood Snowbird community over the council election, the new Tomotla council members and their constituents had to defend their lack of Indianness. Unlike their Snowbird neighbors, they do not largely look Indian, do not speak the Cherokee language, and do not manifest other Cherokee traits.

Though rarely does an entire Cherokee community choose between emphasizing or deemphasizing its Indian identity, depending on whether it is adaptive to do so or not, some Cherokee individuals are continually confronted with the choice. Most of these individuals are the so-called white Indians, people with minimal Cherokee blood degree. Because they look white, speak English fluently (and rarely speak any Cherokee), and conform to Euroamerican cultural standards, these individuals can usually be accepted as white simply by ignoring their Cherokee background. Cherokees with maximal blood degree, such as the Snowbird Cherokees, do not have this choice. Phenotypically they appear Indian, often speak Cherokee or speak English with a Cherokee accent, and frequently conform to Indian behavior patterns. These fullbloods often resent white Indians who can alternate between two ethnic identities as the occasion demands. Again, it is possible to look to census records for proof of some white Indians' shifting identity. U.S. Census Bureau records for 1970 show 3,245 Indians residing in the four North Carolina counties in which reservation lands are located. The band's enrollment office for the same time period, however, "reported over 7,000 enrolled members [of the Eastern Band of Cherokee Indians], with an estimated 5,000 living on or immediately adjacent to the Cherokee Indian lands" (Eastern Band of Cherokee Indians 1972:11). That is a difference in estimated local population of over 1,700. Although fullbloods are not burdened with the personality conflict inherent in an unstable ethnic identity, they are not afforded the social and economic advantages of a shifting identity.

Tribal laws and practices used to be full of provisions that limit the participation of minimal-degree Cherokees in situations where a "real Indian" is needed. Although blood degree alone does not determine one's cultural real Indianness (and there are a few fullbloods who are not thought of as "real Indians"), blood degree and ability to speak the Cherokee language are the two most important attributes of "real" Indians. Physically looking and sounding like an Indian is important in convincing outsiders that the Cherokees have not totally blended into mainstream America. To be principal chief or vice-chief, for example, one had to be at least one-half Cherokee. In a tribal referendum of 1987 the white Indian majority voted to eliminate blood degree requirements for holding tribal office that were more restrictive than those for band membership. That year the Eastern Band of Cherokees elected their first chief of less than one-half blood degree, Jonathan Ed Taylor. The Bureau of Indian Affairs provides scholarship money only to Cherokees of at least one-fourth blood degree. Maximal-degree Cherokees thus have attempted to take care to exclude minimal-degree Cherokees from participation in some aspects of Cherokee life. Perhaps it is this exclusion that serves to justify minimal-degree Cherokees' sometime participation in white American society.

Especially in the last twenty years a growing awareness of Indian identity has occurred among the Eastern Cherokees. For many it is an effort to maintain a simultaneous identity as "real Americans" and "real Indians." Each autumn, after the tourist season, the Eastern Cherokees hold their Fall Festival. Other Indians from as far away as New Mexico, Florida, Oklahoma, and New York attend, further reducing the Eastern Cherokees' isolation not only from the world of white Americans but other Native Americans as well. After the 1972 Fall Festival, when the first resurgence of Indian identity was at a peak on the Cherokee reservation, the *Cherokee One Feather* (1972:3) ran an article that said: "The old fair has become a festival, and festival means sharing, celebration, and ceremony. . . . The major attractions at the Fall Festival were ethnic: Indian customs, culture and self image. Perhaps one bumper sticker summed it up: 'Brothers rejoice! It's in to be Indian!'"

Traditional stickball games and booger dances, thought to have been acculturated out of existence, are performed each fall alongside Ferris wheels and cotton candy concessions, but they are performed. Also, each year the tiny Snowbird community in Graham County hosts a "Trail of Tears Singing" at which Western Cherokees from Oklahoma are the special guests. The Cherokee language is spoken, and traditional foods like bean bread are consumed.

Far from culturally or physically disappearing, the North Carolina Cherokees are increasing in numbers and striving to preserve a core of uniquely Indian traits. The stereotype of the "vanishing Indian" does not apply to the Cherokees. They are surviving both physically and culturally.

# 3

# STATE-RECOGNIZED INDIANS OF NORTH CAROLINA, INCLUDING A HISTORY OF THE WACCAMAW SIOUX

*Patricia Barker Lerch*

This chapter is on the Indians of North Carolina. In the first section, I describe the geographic distribution and size, the surname pattern, the religious structure, and the political organization of four contemporary Indian groups known as the Lumbee, the Coharie, the Waccamaw Sioux, and the Haliwa-Saponi. This necessarily brief section can only introduce the subject of Indians in North Carolina today. For a historical account of the Indians of North Carolina, one should consult Theda Perdue's useful publication *Native Carolinians* (1985). In the second section, I present a case study of the Waccamaw Sioux Indian group. Certain issues that have been important in achieving recognition provide themes around which to describe events in the history of the Waccamaw people. I have chosen the annual Indian powwow, a contemporary Indian event, to demonstrate the saliency of Indian identity and heritage in community life. In order to make sense of the Waccamaw struggles to gain recognition, I suggest that the concept of articulation (Lurie 1971) may assist us in understanding how this Indian people managed to persist until the present.

One of the most important themes in the history of Indian-white relations in North Carolina is that of recognition. I am using recognition in this chapter in the sense that it refers to the state of affairs in which a governing body grants certain rights and privileges to an Indian group. I would like to suggest a typology of Indian people in North Carolina even though I am aware that this makes a complex situation overly simple. But some readers may be unfamiliar with Indian people in North Carolina, and this typology may help them see how the Indians are defined in part by whether or not they have recognition.

Recognition is the yardstick with which Indians are measured in North Carolina, ranging from those who have full or partial federal recognition to those who have state recognition to those who have no recognition by any level of government. First, there are Indians who live on a federal reservation and who have legal rights to the services and programs of the Bureau of Indian Affairs. The Eastern Cherokee are the only representatives in the state of this type. They can be said to have full federal recognition. Second, there are Indians whose existence has been officially noted by the federal government but who do not receive any of the services or assistance offered by the programs of the bureau. The Lumbees are in this category; the federal act (70 Stat 254) designating them "Lumbee Indians" does not extend a federal trust relationship to them nor does it provide the basis for the services reserved for recognized tribes. Third, there are Indians who live in named communities and groups or who affiliate with urban Indian associations who have legal recognition from the state of North Carolina. These groups and associations are assisted economically, socially, and politically by the North Carolina Commission of Indian Affairs. The Waccamaw Sioux, the Coharie, the Haliwa-Saponi, and the Lumbee are in this category (this list is not meant to be exhaustive). Finally, in the fourth category there are Indians who live either in communities or groups or are dispersed throughout the general population but who have neither federal nor state recognition. Seeking the rights associated with recognition by either the state or the federal government is a major theme in the history of the Indians of North Carolina.

## Indians of North Carolina

It is difficult to write in general terms about the Indians of North Carolina because each group has its own special history and a good deal of this history remains to be written. While many Indians are dispersed throughout the general population, most inhabit identifiable communities that are named and known as "Indian" to the residents and their neighbors. These little communities are further organized into named groups like Lumbee, Coharie, Waccamaw Sioux, and Haliwa-Saponi. Family and kinship, common schools, churches, and political organization define the group boundaries. Yet, some of these same institutions cut across community and group lines, linking individuals to Indian people across the state through intermarriage, religious denomination, and Indian politics. A

## North Carolina Indian Tribes

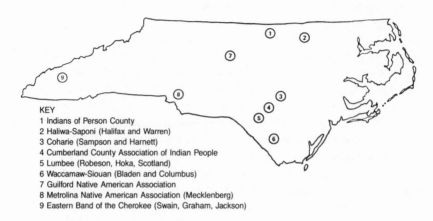

KEY
1 Indians of Person County
2 Haliwa-Saponi (Halifax and Warren)
3 Coharie (Sampson and Harnett)
4 Cumberland County Association of Indian People
5 Lumbee (Robeson, Hoka, Scotland)
6 Waccamaw-Siouan (Bladen and Columbus)
7 Guilford Native American Association
8 Metrolina Native American Association (Mecklenberg)
9 Eastern Band of the Cherokee (Swain, Graham, Jackson)

Locations of Modern Indian Groups in North Carolina (Courtesy of North Carolina Commission of Indian Affairs)

good place to begin, then, is with a description of the location and the geographic distribution of the Indian population.

## Geographic Distribution

According to the 1980 federal census, 64,536 people of American Indian descent live in North Carolina, including 4,844 on the Eastern Cherokee reservation (U.S. Bureau of the Census 1984:15). Most North Carolina Indians live in rural areas (50,275), but many (14,261) live in metropolitan regions (U.S. Bureau of the Census 1982:14). Twenty-five counties appear listed in the census with 200 or more people of Indian descent within their borders: Bladen (321), Buncombe (295), Columbus (1,175), Cumberland (3,644), Davidson (205), Forsyth (451), Gaston (257), Graham (379), Guilford (1,348), Halifax (1,217), Harnett (487), Hoke (2,578), Jackson (2,411), Mecklenberg (1,404), Moore (316), New Hanover (258), Onslow (589), Randolph (252), Richmond (443), Robeson (35,528), Sampson (884), Scotland (2,062), Swain (2,502), Wake (505), and Warren (640) (1982–83:18–19). The urban Indian population is concentrated in Fayetteville (3,644), the Greensboro–Winston-Salem–High Point area (2,303), Charlotte-Gastonia (1,837), and Jacksonville (589) (1982:18–19). The Indian people of Graham, Jackson, and

Swain counties are primarily Cherokee (U.S. Bureau of the Census 1984:24).

Most of the North Carolina Indians live within two major geographical areas: a southeastern ten-county cluster and a north-central four-county cluster just south of the Virginia state line. Within these two areas are identifiable and distinct communities for each of the state-recognized Indian groups. The largest, with forty thousand people, is the Lumbee group, which lives primarily in thirty-three separate communities in Robeson County. The four major Lumbee communities are Prospect, Pembroke, Fairgrove, and Magnolia. In addition, Lumbee people have migrated to the surrounding counties of Hoke, Cumberland, and Scotland. The Coharie group, which numbers between three and four thousand, lives in several small clusters in Sampson County including Holly Grove, New Bethel, Shiloh, Harrells, and Averybourough, and, in Harnett County, they live in the community of Dunn. The fifteen hundred Waccamaw Sioux have settled into three major communities: Ricefield, in Bladen County; Buckhead, which straddles Bladen and Columbus counties; and St. James, in Columbus County. The Haliwa-Saponi group's Halifax-Warren community has about three thousand members.

The state's urban Indians are served by the Cumberland County Association of Indian people in Fayetteville, the Metrolina Native American Association in Charlotte, and the Guilford Native American Association in Greensboro. The Cumberland County Association of Indian People reaches approximately fifteen hundred people in the Fayetteville urban area and throughout Cumberland County. The Metrolina Native American Association in Charlotte works with forty-six hundred people in a ten-county area, a majority of whom are Lumbee Indians (Lerch, Berde, and Levy 1986:3–7). In Greensboro, the Guilford Native American Association offers programs to about three thousand people originally drawn to the region in the 1970s by jobs in the furniture markets and textile mills (Revels 1981:65). These three urban associations are recognized by the North Carolina Commission of Indian Affairs as official Indian organizations.

North Carolina Indian people live outside the state, too. Over the years, Lumbee, Waccamaw, Coharie, and Haliwa-Saponi Indians have left their home communities for such cities as Baltimore, Detroit, Los Angeles, Richmond, Newport News, Hampton (Virginia), and Virginia Beach. According to Makofsky (1982:76), perhaps as many as four thousand Lumbees are in Baltimore alone. Many were attracted by the prospects of employment, many have gained skills in business, and many have returned to their home communities to establish local Indian-run enterprises (Richardson 1976:31).

While the majority of the state's Indian people are affiliated with one of the above groups or associations, there are other communities of Indian people in North Carolina. Among these are the Person County Indians, who were recognized by the state in 1913, and many others that do not have state recognition. The latter include the Meherrin Indians of Hertford County, the Eno-Occaneechi of Alamance and Orange counties, the Tuscarora of Robeson County, and the Hoke County Cherokees. Less is known about these people, and the discussion that follows does not include information on any of the currently unrecognized state groups. Thus, a need exists to extend research interests into this area.

## Common Surnames

The Lumbee, Coharie, and Waccamaw are located in a southeastern ten-county cluster (Bladen, Columbus, Cumberland, Harnett, Hoke, Moore, Richmond, Robeson, Sampson, and Scotland). Their proximity to each other has increased intermarriage and facilitated exchanges of ideas and strategies of adaptation throughout their history. Some hint at the linkages can be observed in the surnames common to each group. A brief survey of the surnames found in each group reveals a pattern of overlap. A degree of overlap also occurs among the three groups and the urban associations, although no single Indian group shares its surname list completely with any of the others. However, we do not know the frequency of intermarriage in the present or the past. Based upon a sample of households from the Waccamaw group, the frequency of intermarriage is extremely low today: Waccamaw-Lumbee 3 percent and Waccamaw-Coharie 1 percent. The Haliwa-Saponi do not share their surnames with any of the other three Indian groups or with the urban associations perhaps because of their relative isolation from the others in the north-central area just south of the Virginia state line (see Table 2). It is typical to find that within the Indian groups three or four surnames dominate the group because of endogamy, or the practice of marrying someone from one's own family or community. Endogamy, group name, and geographic location promote group solidarity. Intermarriage, even at a low rate, and church membership connect members of one local group to another.

## Religious Expression

The Christian religion is the dominant religious expression of the Lumbee, Coharie, Waccamaw Sioux, and Haliwa-Saponi. The major de-

## Table 2. Geographical Distribution of North Carolina "Indian" Surnames by Regional Associations

| Surnames | | | Indian Associations | | |
|---|---|---|---|---|---|
| | 1 | 2 | 3 | 4 | 5 |
| Brooks | | X | | | X |
| Bell | | X | | | |
| Blanks | X | X | | | |
| Brewington | | X | X | | |
| Carter | | X | X | | |
| Freeman | X | X | | | |
| Graham | X | X | | | |
| Hammonds | X | X | | X | |
| Hunt | X | X | | X | X |
| Jacobs | X | X | X | X | X |
| Locklear | X | X | | X | X |
| Lowry | | X | | | X |
| Maynor | | X | | X | |
| Moore | X | X | | | |
| Oxendine | | X | | | X |
| Strickland | X | X | | | X |

*CODE  1 = Waccamaw Siouan Development Association
      2 = Lumbee Regional Development Association
      3 = Coharie Indian Tribe
      4 = Cumberland County Association of Indian People
      5 = Metrolina Native American Association

Note: This table shows the overlapping pattern in Indian surnames occurring in the five associations; it does not reveal either the frequency of surnames within regions or the entire complement of surnames characteristic of individual Indian groups.

nominations include Baptist, Methodist, Church of God, Holiness, and Freewill Baptist. Lesser known are the Lumber River Holiness Methodist, Mormons, Seventh Day Adventists, Freewill Holiness, Bible Freewill, Primitive Baptist, Assembly of God, and Church of Christ. In one listing of Indian churches ($N = 141$), most had Indian ($N = 115$) pastors (Brewington 1976:19).

Religion offers a structure that both strengthens and circumvents community and group ties and loyalties. Indian pastors connect congregations of people in distinct communities and in different Indian groups. Pastors are rarely hired full-time by one congregation but travel between two or more churches. Thus, pastors link one community to another and sometimes link one named Indian group to another, too. For example, one pastor may travel between a Lumbee community church and a Waccamaw community church and through him, his sermons, and his activities, the members of these two different churches may become acquainted. Indian church associations also connect congregations of people in distinct communities and in different Indian groups. Indian churches can be connected to each other because they belong to a denominational association of Indian churches. Such associations have played an important role in the history of North Carolina Indians. The Burnt Swamp Baptist Association is a good example of how religion cuts across group loyalties and defines the boundaries of that part of the population that is of Indian descent.

The Burnt Swamp Baptist Association, surveyed in the 1970s, is predominately a Lumbee association. Of the forty-eight churches affiliated with this association, forty-four are Lumbee, two are Waccamaw, one is Coharie, and one is Haliwa-Saponi (Brewington 1976:21). The association was organized in 1875 specifically for Indian churches; and, as the second article of its 1910 constitution read, "this association shall be comprised of members chosen by the different churches in our union, who shall be known, designated and styled as Indians or lineal descendants of Indians."[1]

It may seem unusual for a church association to be in the business of giving formal recognition to Indian churches. But as the history of the Waccamaw Indians, covered later in this chapter, shows, recognition as Indian has always been an important feature of Indian history in North Carolina. Designating a church as "Indian" is seen as problematic today when the membership of most Indian church congregations is multi-ethnic. Despite a preference for "marrying in," interracial marriages remain a characteristic of many Indian congregations (Brewington 1976:19).

The Burnt Swamp Baptist Association gave the Indian churches a voice in religious affairs within the state. In addition to organizational ties that united these Indian congregations in the various denominations, the Indian communities lying in close geographical proximity to each other long enjoyed traveling to each other's church revivals in late summer and fall. This intermixing has promoted common ties and political alliances among the state's Indians.

**Published Sources.** Some readers may wish to learn more about specific Indian groups. The Lumbees receive more attention from scholars and writers than any of the other three groups (see Blu 1980; Dial and Eliades 1975; Evans 1971; Makofsky 1980, 1982; McPherson 1915; Perdue 1985; Ross 1987; Swanton 1934; Tamarin 1974). Throughout their modern history, they have been known variously as the Croatan (1885–1911), Indians of Robeson County (1911–13), Cherokee Indians of Robeson County (1913–53), and Lumbee Indians (1953–present) (Perdue 1985:61–68). Karen L. Blu (1980) details the social history of Lumbee ethnicity in her book *The Lumbee Problem: The Making of an American Indian People.* A more recent in-depth historical account of Lumbee origins is presented in the Lumbee petition for federal acknowledgment prepared by the Lumber River Legal Services (LRLS). The petition clarifies Lumbee tribal origins and traces their ancestry in large part to the Cheraw and other Siouan-speaking tribes of the Carolinas (LRLS 1987:2). Other than general references in historical accounts of North Carolina Indians (Lee 1965; Milling 1969), only the Haliwa-Saponi (Dane and Griessman 1972) and the Waccamaw (Alexander 1950; Lerch 1988) are covered in separate studies.

Because the Indians of North Carolina have Indian, white, and, sometimes, black ancestors, they have been described in general sociological and geographical surveys, along with many other peoples, by terms such as "mixed bloods," "American isolates," "tri-racial isolates," "folk societies," "racial islands," and "marginal peoples." These labels obscure differences among such groups by grouping those in which the Indian ancestry is the most vigorously maintained along with those who do not maintain a strong Indian identity. The survival of these so-called marginal groups is attributed to a number of factors, including their physical isolation from whites, their structural isolation from whites and blacks based on practices of endogamy, and their close-knit community life (Gilbert 1946; Price 1953; Berry 1963, 1978; Pollitzer 1972; Thompson 1972; Frazier 1966; Dane and Griessman 1972; Griessman 1972).

Earlier studies took an important first step by tracing the geographical distribution of people with mixed heritage and by identifying some of the features of their environment that contributed to their persistence through time. But now, because we know more about those who maintain their Indian ancestry and identity above all else, we must take the next step by researching the social dynamics within specific Indian communities and groups. Developing a taxonomy of human societies is a function of social science. Looking for differences within larger categories is also an important goal of social science. In other words, I am arguing in favor of more specific social and historical studies on groups such as these.

## Political and Economic Goals

Let's return now to our overview of the Indian groups and organizations of North Carolina by looking at their political structure. We will begin with the largest, the Lumbee. The Lumbee Regional Development Association (LRDA), chartered in 1968, is granted authority by the state to act as an interim governing body until the Lumbees succeed in their petition to obtain full federal status. The LRDA is controlled by an elected seventeen-member board of men and women. This board oversees state and federal programs and administers economic development projects for the Lumbees. The Lumbees have never had a tribal chief. LRDA is headquartered in Pembroke, Robeson County. Similarly the Coharie Intra-Tribal Council, organized in 1975, is the present governing body of the Coharie people of Harnett and Sampson counties. Seven members, three from each county and one rotating chairman, are chosen in a popular election held during the annual Coharie festival. As early as 1944, the Coharie organized and operated the state-funded East Carolina Indian School where Indian children from surrounding counties, who were eligible to attend this school, boarded in the homes of Coharie people. The Waccamaw Siouan Development Association (WSDA), established in 1970 to represent the Waccamaw Sioux of Columbus and Bladen counties, is governed by a seven-member board elected to serve for terms of three years. In addition, WSDA has a hired staff. The Waccamaws have had a chief since the early part of this century who offers leadership in community affairs and advises the board. The Haliwa-Saponi Indians organized a governing council in 1954 to help meet the educational needs of the Indian children, and the first tribal school opened in 1956. After its closing in 1968, the school building became the site of community functions. The Haliwa-Saponi Indians are governed by a chief and an eleven-member council elected by the group members.

**North Carolina Commission of Indian Affairs.** Responding to pressing social problems of poverty and illiteracy, in 1970 members of the North Carolina Indian groups persuaded the political leaders of the state to establish a commission of Indian affairs. A planning committee, with members from the Lumbee, Coharie, Waccamaw, Haliwa-Saponi groups, and from the urban associations, met to discuss the organization and goals of the soon-to-be formed North Carolina Commission of Indian Affairs (Maynor 1976). The commission's purpose, as outlined in legislation passed in 1971, is to act as a liaison between federal and state programs and the state-recognized Indian tribes and associations, to provide aid and protection to all Indians, to assist Indian communities in social and economic development, and to promote recognition of, and the right of, Indians to pursue cultural and religious traditions considered by them to be sacred and meaningful. The commission includes representatives from the governor's office and the state-recognized groups and associations.

The North Carolina Commission of Indian Affairs is empowered by the state to extend official state recognition to Indian groups. Thus, after its formation, the commission granted recognition in 1971 to the Coharie, the Waccamaw, the Metrolina Native American Association, the Guilford Native American Association, and the Cumberland County Association of Indian People. Prior to this date, the state extended a similar recognition to the Lumbee in 1953 and the Haliwa-Saponi in 1965. (The Eastern Band of Cherokee Indians may participate in the commission if they so choose.) Until the formation of the commission in 1971, the state had reacted slowly to the needs of the Indians of North Carolina (Perdue 1985:56–57).

In 1979 the commission reported the administration of several federal programs supporting the social and economic development of the state-recognized Indian tribes and organizations. These programs covered job training, social services, literacy, and housing (Jones 1979). For example, in 1978–79, one-half of the commission's budget came from the popular CETA (Comprehensive Employment and Training Act) program that provides funds for public service jobs, short-term work experiences, classroom training, job counseling, and a variety of support services. Through federal funding, the Coharie, Waccamaw, and Haliwa-Saponi Indians began to provide day care, meals for the elderly, and other services to their communities. Literacy levels were raised through the help of VISTA community workers. The Housing Assistance program (Section 8) of HUD assisted low-income families in acquiring standard rental housing on the open market. The economic, educational, and health problems of the 1970s plagued many Indian groups on into the 1980s (Presti 1981:1–3). While some programs have continued until 1990, many people believe that solving these problems is tied to achieving federal recognition as Indian tribes.

**Recognition.** The issue of recognition excites the North Carolina Indian tribes and groups as no other in recent history because through recognition, they believe, their economic and social development goals will be realized. When the North Carolina Commission of Indian Affairs was established in 1971, the commissioners set guidelines for the future recognition of state Indian groups. These guidelines call for rather stiff requirements, including providing documentation in support of the petitioning group's Indian status from other Indian groups within the state with whom the petitioning group may be related, from county, state, and federal authorities, and from anthropologists and other scholars. Documented evidence of traditions and evidence of participation in grants from sources or programs designated as "for Indians only" are also acceptable. In addition, unrecognized Indian groups petitioning for state Indian status must demonstrate descent from an Indian tribe indigenous to North Carolina within the last 200 years and show that their members are one-quarter Indian blood. These rather rigorous regulations underscore the significance recognition receives within the state.

Some sentiment exists among those yet to be recognized that these regulations are unreasonably tough. At the same time, federal recognition imposes equally rigid requirements on the tribes and groups seeking it. According to the guidelines set forth by the Branch of Acknowledgment and Research of the Bureau of Indian Affairs, recognition means acknowledgment of the Indian tribe by the secretary of interior that results in a special "government-to-government" relationship under which the acknowledged tribe may seek government services and funding reserved only for such federal tribes. At both state and federal levels, recognition provides access to special funds and programs reserved for Indian tribes and organizations to aid in their social and economic development.

## Articulation Vs. Assimilation in Waccamaw History _____

Indian–non-Indian interactions in the state of North Carolina are best understood as an example of what Nancy Lurie calls "articulation" in interethnic relations. Lurie (1971:419) defines the meaning of articulation as it refers to Native American communities. A minority community articulates its cultural identity each time it uses that identity in its interaction with the dominant society. It gives expression to its cultural identity as a minority. This expression prevents the minority from being totally assimilated into the dominant society.

Articulatory relations must be consciously maintained. Community members cannot allow others to define them but must assert themselves before the representatives of the dominant society. Some individuals choose the easier path of assimilation. Articulation becomes one means to identity maintenance. Peterson (1972) discusses a similar pattern in the Mississippi Choctaw communities where assimilation, separation, and out-migration offer choices in minority-majority relations. Peterson's separation concept is closest to the concept of articulation as it is used here. The Waccamaw Siouan Indian community illustrates the complexities inherent in managing articulatory relationships with the dominant society. We begin with a brief overview of the early history of the Waccamaw.

## Probable Ancestry of the Waccamaw

The first person to make a serious study of the history of the Waccamaw Sioux people of Columbus and Bladen counties was a young man named James E. Alexander. Alexander became acquainted with members of the Freeman Indian family when in 1949 he moved to Whiteville, North Carolina. In exchange for his room and board, he agreed to research the origins of the Indian people of the tiny communities of Buckhead and Ricefield whose governing body called itself the Council of the Wide Awake Indians. He worked closely with the Reverend R. T. Freeman, chief spokesman for the community. (Their efforts to win federal recognition through legislative action are discussed below.)

Alexander's research (1950) led him to the conclusion that the Indians were descendants of the historic Waccamaw and Cape Fear Indians, two tribes classified with others speaking a Siouan language who once inhabited the same land.[2] Three kinds of evidence support this conclusion. First, there is similar territory and location. Second, there is evidence that household heads representing the prominent Indian families deeded land in this area as early as 1800.[3] Third, there is support for Indian ancestry in the special census category in which the household heads and their families were being placed.

The movements of the historic Cape Fear and Waccamaw Indians can be traced before the beginning of the nineteenth century when the named ancestral families of the modern Waccamaw began to register deeds to land in the area. The territory and hunting grounds of the historic Waccamaw and Cape Fear Indians extended from the coast as far inland as the Great Green Swap, the Waccamaw River, and Lake Waccamaw, bordering the communities of the modern Waccamaw. Today the land is drained, but in the past the Indians inhabited small islands of high ground where they farmed, fished, and hunted. A Spanish explorer, Gordillo, visited the Cape Fear coast in 1521 and described the first encounter with the historic Waccamaw. According to John R. Swanton (1946:203), "Guacaya" (pronounced "Waycaya" in English), a word that sounds like Waccamaw, appeared on a list of tribal provinces furnished by the captive Francisco of Chicora who was rescued by Gordillo during his visit to "St. John the Baptist" River (identified later as the Waccamaw River at Winya Bay).[4] Verazzano, an Italian explorer of the Cape Fear River region, sighted Indians there in 1524 (Wroth 1970:78–79). A century later, in the 1660s, William Hilton of Barbados made two voyages to the Cape Fear River where he reported favorably on both the Cape Fear Indians and the conditions for European settlement (Lee 1965:70).[5]

The Cape Fear, Waccamaw, and other "Eastern Siouans" essentially comprised small autonomous tribal groups that never presented a serious political threat to European settlement (Mooney 1894:6). They lived along the vanguard of European colonization where their aid, friendship, trade, and alliance held the attention of the Europeans. Feeling the pressure of colonization, they were altered permanently by European settlement patterns, diseases, wars, and hostility.

The Tuscarora War of 1711 and 1712 and the Yamasee War of 1715 entangled both the Waccamaw and the Cape Fear Indians in their battles (Lee 1965:67, 76). A Colonel Barnwell who hoped to recruit "Wachamaw" and Cape Fear Indians as allies against the Tuscarora may have been the first to actually use the name Waccamaw (Barnwell 1909:43; Lee 1965:77; South 1972:32–33).[6] On Barnwell's return trip from New Bern, North Carolina, to Charles Town, South Carolina, he traveled south across Lake Waccamaw and down the Waccamaw River, presumably through the territory of these two tribes.

According to an Indian census of 1715, some 610 Waccamaw men, women, and children were located in a village about one hundred miles northeast of Charles Town (Swanton 1946:203). This village was apparently the southern boundary of a territorial range that stretched from just south of the Neuse River to within one hundred miles of the Charles Town (South Carolina) settlements.[7] During the Yamasee War (1715) the Waccamaw (along with the Cape Fear Indians) were of sufficient size to threaten the company of Colonel Maurice Moore who traveled south through Cape Fear country to aid Charles Town. It is reported that his vessel that would transport his army and eighty captives waited for him somewhere along the Cape Fear River (Lee 1965:80–81). These Tuscarora and Yamasee wars altered permanently Indian-white relations in the region. The Cape Fear Indians, greatly weakened by the wars, became less important to the European settlers thereafter (Lee 1965:80–81; Milling 1969:226). After peace, the Commissioners of the Indian Trade, located in Charles Town, considered moving a trading factor closer to the Waccamaw at Uauenee (McDowell 1955:111). By 16 December, a Mr. Waties, the Waccamaw trading factor, was told by the Commissioners of the Indian Trade to slow down the sale of guns and ammunition to the Waccamaw because they were using their guns to raid the Wineau for cattle. The Waccamaw supplied slaves to Charles Town in this trade partnership (McDowell 1955:137).

A short war, the "Vocamas War," broke out in 1720 and culminated in the successful pacification of the Indian territory along the northeast border of the Charles Town colony (Swanton 1952:101; Milling 1969:226–27). After 1720, frontier turmoil made it more difficult for the authorities to locate the Waccamaw and the Cape Fear Indians. We learn that some Waccamaw reportedly were settled near the Catawba of South Carolina in 1717 (Swanton 1946:203), others were raided and captured by the Seneca Indians in 1725 (Mereness 1961:138), and some Cape Fears are believed to have settled in the parishes of St. Stephen and St. John near the Pee Dee Indians under a chief called "King Johnny" (Swanton 1946:103). And still others placed the Cape Fear Indians and the Waccamaw back in their old territory near Lake Waccamaw perhaps as late as 1734 (Sprunt 1916:40), leaving open the possibility that one or both of these groups remained in the vicinity of Lake Waccamaw beyond that date.[8] The whereabouts of the Waccamaw were still of concern to the British as late as 1755, as a letter to King Haigler of the Catawba from Governor James Glenn of South Carolina indicates. The governor tried to pressure Haigler into persuading the Waccamaw to settle near the Catawba.[9] It is unclear from this correspondence, however, whether the governor was successful. The remnants of the Waccamaw and the Cape Fear Indians probably removed themselves further into their old territory eventually to reside in the vicinity of the modern Waccamaw community.

From this brief history of the probable origins of the modern Waccamaw community we can observe some of the long-term effects of acculturation. First, the Waccamaw and Cape Fear Indians were skilled traders both with other tribes and with Europeans. They learned to use guns and ammunition in their wars against each other and the English. They raided more sedentary and acculturated Indians for cattle. The Indian trade supplied them with many goods of European manufacture. They were well equipped materially and psychologically to hide in their old territory and reconstitute themselves as an acculturating Indian community, adapting modified Euroamerican farming techniques to their old swampy homeland.

## Nineteenth Century

The modern Waccamaw ancestors appear in the first federal census of the population in 1790 listed in the category "All Other Free Persons." Census enumerators of that time went into the countryside to enumerate the households. They reported their own opinion of the racial status of the people in their census blocks. Census enumerators who could not directly talk with household members listed the people in the household based upon their own knowledge of the community or on what neighbors reported about the inhabitants of a particular household. The choices were limited: white, slave, and all other free persons. The special status of the Jacobs family, one of the major families of the modern Waccamaw community, is evident as early as 1800, when the federal census of Bladen County listed most as "All Other Free Persons" (U.S. Census Office 1976). All Waccamaw family surnames are consistently referred to in this fashion in this early census. Their special status is evident in that there were very few people listed in this manner in all of Bladen County, where only 152 of a total county population of 7,028 (including 4,577 white and 2,299 slave) were listed in this fashion.

The category "All Other Free Persons" is open to interpretation. It could refer to any of four kinds of people. First, it could refer to freed Negro slaves. Second, it could refer to free Indian people (Swanton 1934:5). Third, it could refer to people of mixed Negro and white heritage. Fourth, it could refer to people of mixed Negro and Indian heritage. The fourth possibility seems among the most remote because of the "divide and rule" policy of whites who deliberately and systematically encouraged the separation of Indians and Africans in the southeastern United States during the eighteenth century (Willis 1963:157–76). Whites feared for their very survival as a minority surrounded by two large "colored populations," and Willis shows how they created hostility between blacks and Indians in order to prevent an alliance that would drive whites out of the region forever. Whites tried to prevent slaves from escaping to Indian territory and Indians from remaining too long in the vicinity of enslaved blacks (Willis 1963:161–63). Fear, suspicion, and hatred were encouraged on the part of Indians for blacks and vice versa. Willis argues convincingly that "Whites created much of the hostility between Indians and Negroes in the eighteenth century" (1963:176). The possibility that "All Other Free Persons" refers to freed Negro slaves also seems unlikely because if the ancestors of the Waccamaw were freed Negro slaves without Indian ancestry, as some communities in the region were, why did they not maintain a similar pride in their status as free Negroes that characterizes such communities? If the Waccamaw ancestors fall into the category of people with mixed Negro and white heritage, it seems more likely they would have tried to assimilate into the dominant society eventually as whites rather than creating a fiction that they were Indians. In the early 1800s there was little incentive to be Indian, and as time passed, and with the passage of the Indian Removal Act of 1830, Indian heritage would have offered far fewer advantages than white heritage would have. The second possibility thus seems the more likely, that the Waccamaw ancestors were primarily of Indian ancestry and that they transmitted this knowledge generation after generation within their families, instilling a pride in their children and recounting stories of their traditional ways.

The events of the end of the nineteenth century brought the Waccamaws out of isolation into a position where they negotiated with their white neighbors primarily to provide public funds to support Indian education. The leaders at the end of this century are the children and grandchildren of those categorized as "All Other Free Persons" at the beginning of the century. The Waccamaw actions were influenced by those of the Lumbee, the largest population of Indian people in the state at the turn of the century.

## Twentieth Century

**Council of the Wide Awake Indians (1910–1950).** The earliest remembered governing body of the Waccamaw people is the Council of the Wide Awake Indians. The council's actions reflect a concern over the funding of Indian education that was widespread in the state among Indian people at the time. Following the Civil War, the North Carolina legislature added thirty-three amendments to the state constitution providing for, among other things, separate schools for whites and blacks, forbidding miscegenation between whites and nonwhites, and ending local control over county government (Lefler and Newsom 1973). This system provided schools for whites and blacks. Throughout the state, Indian people refused to send their children to black schools, which were the only option open to them as they were denied admittance to the white schools. The establishment of Indian schools for the Croatan (Lumbee) in 1885 by the state of North Carolina opened the way for other Indian communities (N.C. Laws, chap. 51:92–94, 1885). Recognizing the potential voting power of the Croatan, the Democrats supported the movement to fund Indian education (LRLS 1987:31). The smaller Indian communities followed the lead of the Croatan and petitioned to have themselves designated Croatan in order to secure funding for Indian education. For example, by 1910 the Coharie of Sampson County organized their first Indian school.

The year 1910 was a crucial one for the Waccamaw, too. The Council of the Wide Awake Indians, perhaps in place earlier than that year, included representatives from the major families. These "men of age" deliberated in homes, in churches, and later in the settlement schools. They traveled and communicated community concerns to county and state government bodies. The school board minutes of Columbus County in 1898 note that "the school committee . . . [is to] be notified to organize the mixed race of said township into an Independent district of their own."[10] By placing representatives on the local school committees, the council sought to safeguard direct participation of Indian parents in the education of their children.[11] However, these early schools were not officially recognized by the state as Indian schools,[12] but de facto control over the student body fell to the Indian committee members. An example from the 1920 board minutes shows that the school committees successfully petitioned the school board to remove non-Indian children from their school.[13] Oral history of these years describes them as ones during which the council learned how to influence the local white school administrators. A record of their requests before the Columbus and Bladen school boards leads to the conclusion that the Waccamaw leaders were cognizant of the fact that as early as 1885 the state of North Carolina opened schools for the "Croatan" Indians of Robeson and adjoining counties (Blu 1980:78–79), and they sought repeatedly to have themselves designated "Croatan" Indians in order to have the right to state-funded Indian schools within their communities.

**Recognition and Schools.** The Waccamaws lacked the strength in population size to politically influence local county and state representatives. Thus, the decision to be included in the Indian population as "Croatan" was the only option. As Lurie (1971:419) points out, Indian leaders frequently borrow successful strategies of articulation from one another as they test various ways to accomplish their objectives. General dissatisfaction with the name Croatan resulted in its disuse, and by 1913 the former Croatan were known as the Cherokee.[14] From 1913 until 1953, Cherokee was synonymous with Indian within the state, protected by state law, and provided with state tax dollars to support education (Blu 1980:80–87).

However, the Waccamaw did not abandon until 1927 the tactic of being designated as Croatan. An early reference to this effort appears in 1914 in some correspondence between the state school superintendent, F. T. Wooten, and a federal Indian agent, O. M. McPherson, who was in charge of an investigation into the conditions of the Croatan Indians of southeastern North Carolina (McPherson 1915:237–38). Later, in 1920, an entry in Columbus County school board minutes shows that through their attorney, Donald McRackan of Whiteville, North Carolina, the council argued that inasmuch as the Croatan of other counties had already won separate Indian schools, their rights as Croatan Indians were being denied.[15] McRackan described the Indian community:

> We have residing in our county a class of people known as the croatan-indians who inhabit one school district exclusively with the exception of one colored child who is within school age.

> Of course there are white people living within the same district, but I mean there are no negroes living therein except the one mentioned.[16]

McRackan was perplexed as to why the county board refused to provide the funds, for it was clear to him and, in his opinion, to anyone else who saw them that they were of Indian descent:

> I do not know what evidence that can be furnished the board stronger than for the people to appear before the Board and show from their personal appearance, which it seems is sufficient to satisfy any Board that they are not negroes.
> They have good features, straight hair and red cheeks and do not bear any negro resemblance.[17]

But McRackan was informed by E. C. Brooks, the state superintendent of public instruction, that "the law does not compel the County board of education to provide separate schools for the Indians of its county."[18] The decision to fund or not fund the Indian school was left to the local school board. The Waccamaws, angered by the decision of the local board, took matters into their own hands and were reprimanded by the local board, which threatened to take them to court unless they opened their schools to all "colored" children.[19] Frustrated, some Indian parents withdrew their children from the county schoolhouse in 1923 and moved them to their church, where they could go to school without interference.[20] Other Indian parents responded to the situation by beginning construction of their own schoolhouse.[21] This situation was evidently acceptable to the Columbus school board, because the Council of Wide Awake Indians, led by W. J. Freeman, convinced the school board to reimburse the tribe for expenses incurred during the use of "a church for school purposes two years."[22] That year (1924), an Indian family deeded land to the board for a school in the Indian settlement at St. James.[23] Evidence that the school authorities went along with this solution appears in the board minutes for 1927 when the two Indian-controlled schools in the settlements and their respective supervisory committees appeared on the county school list.[24] In the 1920s, tribal effort concentrated on controlling entry to the Indian community schools and on pressing the local board to fund them as Indian schools. Tribal leaders worked simultaneously on both local and state levels.

In 1927 the Waccamaw leaders hired Thomas Johnson, an attorney from Lumberton, North Carolina, to assist them in winning funding for Indian schools in their community.[25] Once again a successful strategy for articulation was adopted from the Lumbees of Robeson County. "Croatan," no longer in use, was replaced by "Cherokee" in reference to people of Indian descent.[26] Chapter 213, Public School Law, passed in

1927, granted the Cherokee of Columbus County public funds to support Indian schools. No action was taken to implement the law. By 1928 the school board's inaction caused the tribal council to press mandamus proceedings through their attorney. Then in 1929 the Columbus County Board of Education and the Columbus County commissioners lobbied successfully for the repeal of Chapter 213.[27] This action stopped the flow of state and county funds to the support of Indian schools.

With characteristic persistence, the name of the Waccamaw leader W. J. Freeman continued to appear in the board minutes presenting the needs of the Indian community, including that of well-trained Indian teachers.[28] St. James committeeman, George Mitchel, asserted his Indian status when he refused to accept a position on the school committee until the board granted him recognition as an Indian.[29] Then, in 1933, the tribe experienced a victory when the Bladen County Board of Education, accepting the fact that the Waccamaw deserved separate Indian schools, granted them permission to open the first such school within their community on the Bladen side of the county line.[30] This first county-funded Indian school was known as the Wide Awake Indian School. Stimulated by this success, tribal members living in Columbus County once again renewed their efforts and petitioned the board to officially designate the St. Mark's School (held in the community church by the same name) an Indian school.[31] Their petition failed, but they maintained their efforts until 1945 when the Columbus County Board of Education finally agreed to support separate county schools for Indians.[32] Throughout this struggle, the Council of the Wide Awake Indians played an important role by providing leadership that presented the Indian position to the local and state education officials. The county and the state provided schools for "colored" children throughout this period, so the option to assimilate was always present. The Indian leaders chose to articulate with the dominant society based on their cultural and ethnic identity as an Indian community.

**Federal Recognition 1940–1950.** The euphoria over securing public funding for Indian schools gave way eventually to the stark reality of the poor social and economic conditions under which the Indians struggled to educate their children. One observer of the Wide Awake Indian School in the Buckhead community reported the following conditions:

> the windows are poorly spaced and furnished only about one-half of the light needed, dark, dirty walls aggravate this condition. The blackboards are poor and insufficient. The seats are old, and not the proper size. Especially in the classroom used by the seventh and eighth grades the desks are so crowded together that there is hardly leg room for the pupils, and desks

designed for one person are occupied by two. There are no instructional supplies.[33]

If these deplorable conditions alone were insufficient to stir the council leaders' desire to seek federal aid, the barriers placed on Indian youth who wanted to continue their education beyond the primary level were probably motivation enough to push them toward federal recognition. According to a survey of the educational needs of the Indian children in 1950, access to higher education was denied primarily because of the financial burden of boarding high school children in Sampson County, where they would attend the Eastern Carolina Indian School.[34]

The Council of the Wide Awake Indians appointed W. J. Freeman to the position of council chairman in 1940.[35] Under his leadership, the council members embarked upon a course they hoped would end in the federal recognition of all or some portion of the Indian community. Freeman acted as chief spokesman for the council, a position that had evolved during the previous twenty years when he had repeatedly appeared at school board meetings to argue the Indian case. Just before the Waccamaw were to present their case to Congress, this position passed in 1949 to W. J. Freeman's younger brother, the Reverend R. T. Freeman.[36] The Reverend Mr. Freeman and the council hired James E. Alexander, a white man, to help research their community history and to represent them in Washington as they pursued federal recognition. This was consistent with their earlier pattern of working through white brokers or lawyers who would represent Indian interests. When the council submitted supporting documents to the U.S. Congress and the Bureau of Indian Affairs in 1949, they referred to themselves as the "Council of Wide Awake Indians, Waccamaw Tribe of the Siouan Nation."[37] This was the first time that the terms "Waccamaw" and "Siouan" appeared in print in an official way referring to the Indian communities.[38]

In November 1949, members of the Council of the Wide Awake Indians traveled to Washington, D.C., with James E. Alexander. They visited the BIA offices to get advice on how to pursue their objective of federal recognition.[39] Through Alexander the tribe also made contact with the Association on American Indian Affairs of New York City. The president of the association, Oliver LaFarge, and the association's executive director, Alexander Lesser, both anthropologists, strongly supported the Waccamaw effort.[40] LaFarge described Alexander as a "strong friend" of the Waccamaw.[41] The Washington attorney and counsel to the association, Felix Cohen, reviewed the Waccamaw case and drafted a bill to the U.S. Congress that became known as the Waccamaw Bill (H.R. 7153, H.R. 7299).[42] In consultation with Cohen, the Waccamaw voted to place their lands in trust in order to establish a land base for the Indian families living in the Buckhead area. This was done to prevent any further loss of land-holdings. At a meeting in the Buckhead area, 157 Waccamaw adults signed a resolution stating their support of the terms of the Waccamaw Bill.[43] The legislation proposed two steps: (1) to give the Waccamaw Indians protection regarding their lands, and (2) to give them rights and privileges as a tribe under the Indian Reorganization Act of 1934.

The bill was submitted to Congress in the spring of 1950 and was directed to the House Committee on Public Lands, which in April of that year referred the matter to the Bureau of Indian Affairs. LaFarge wrote in support of the bill:

> The facts in this case speak for themselves. These people are descendants of a small Indian tribe which was by-passed by the course of discovery, exploration, and settlement. The documents show that the present Waccamaw group resides on lands which are part of the area inhabited by Waccamaw people for hundreds of years.
>
> Today, these Indian families are in need of help in many ways. Perhaps most of all, they need what they refer to as "recognition" as Indians to give them back their self-respect.[44]

In August 1950, the Bureau of Indian Affairs returned a negative response to the House committee, recommending that the Waccamaw Bill be defeated. While sympathetic with the Waccamaw case, Dale E. Doty, assistant secretary of the interior, expressed fear that recognition of the Waccamaw would encourage many other state-recognized Indian groups in North Carolina as well as other eastern states to seek federal recognition.[45] Thus, despite considerable effort on the part of the association, this recognition effort was defeated by the late summer of 1950. LaFarge remained convinced that the Waccamaw Bill should have been passed, as the following remark written twelve years later indicates: "About 1950, we tried to get recognition for the Waccamaws of [North] Carolina, a group that is lower than a snake's belly in relation to its neighbors, but we did not get to first base. I think that a group such as this probably has a stronger claim than many of those in the East."[46]

**Economic Development.** In the years following, the Waccamaw leaders turned inward and focused on addressing local issues of economic development. They continued their practice of articulating with the dominant society as Indians, seeking to overcome poverty, discrimination, and prejudice. The Council of the Wide Awake Indians, Waccamaw Tribe of the Siouan Nation pressed local authorities for improvements in roads, drainage, electrical services, and schools. Between 1950 and 1955, the council and the school committees lobbied for allocation of funds for construction of a new Indian school building large enough to accommodate grades one through eight. Just ten years prior to the passage of the Civil Rights Act of 1964, Waccamaw students attended secondary school in their own community at the Waccamaw Indian High School.

In the 1960s the lobbying activities of the council shifted to the school committees and the Waccamaw Indian Improvement Club, a group of Indian men from the major families. This shift was accompanied by a change in leadership as the old "chief," R. T. Freeman, stepped aside for his nephew, Clifton Freeman. The younger Freeman worked closely with his own hand-picked council and with the Waccamaw Indian Improvement Club. The old council had sought Indian recognition in order to fund Indian schools, and it had succeeded on the county and state levels by 1945. But their efforts failed to win federal recognition in 1950. With new leadership, other issues related to economic development dominated the next decade.

The 1960s ushered in a new era of development for the Waccamaws and their leaders. The failure to secure federal recognition in 1950 encouraged the Indian leaders to devise a plan that would make them increasingly self-sufficient and less dependent on the need to be federally recognized in order to economically develop their communities. Thus, when the Waccamaw Indian Improvement Club was formed, it adopted the strategy of attracting outside investment and industry into the Indian community. Working closely with the new chief and his council, the club was instrumental in attracting a small audiodevice company into the community on the site of the former Waccamaw Indian High School, abandoned after school desegregation (ca. 1967). The club also pursued employment for Waccamaw people and sent representatives to the county seats to lobby for the hiring of Indians. In addition, the 1960s witnessed the expansion of a major paper company and a major utility company, both of which provided jobs for Indian people. The new "chief" and his council successfully secured five acres of land from one of the paper companies. This acquisition had significance as a symbol of the Indians' progress. This land, tribal land, would become the focus of future community events and would publicize the physical presence of the Indian community to its neighbors. Thus, during the post-1950 period, the Indian community leaders strengthened their ties to local government and industry in order to promote economic development for their people. Throughout this decade, the Waccamaw never stopped presenting themselves to outsiders as Indians nor did they abandon their crusade for recognition as Indians.

The Waccamaw leaders gained an understanding of grantsmanship as they applied for funding from county and state agencies. The 1960s and 1970s also witnessed a major shift in federal policy affecting Indian people. This new era—the era of self-determination—spanned the administrations of Kennedy, Johnson, Nixon, and Carter. New social and economic programs of the "War on Poverty," the "Great Society," and the "New Frontier" offered aid to poor people of all ethnic groups, including Indian organizations and communities lacking federal Indian status. For example, the Office of Economic Opportunity allowed unrecognized American Indian organizations to apply for assistance from such programs as Job Corps, Neighborhood Youth Corps, Operation Headstart, VISTA, Legal Services, and Community Action programs. Thus, federal recognition per se was no longer a special barrier to receiving federal aid as it had been in earlier eras. In 1973, the Office of Economic Opportunity functions for American Indians were transferred to the Office of Native American Programs in the Department of Health, Education, and Welfare—later changed to Administration for Native Americans in the Department of Health and Human Services. These programs became critical for the Waccamaw in the 1970s and 1980s. During the 1970s, the Waccamaw obtained county and state support for a day care program and building. The teachers and staff continue to be funded under Title XX program funds administered through the North Carolina Commission of Indian Affairs. In 1972 Chief Clifton Freeman and others formed a nonprofit development association in order to promote the tribe. This association became the present Waccamaw Sioux Development Association, and, with its creation, an evolution in tribal political organization took place. According to the bylaws of the association, the tribe must elect a nine-member board of directors to run its affairs. The position of chief became essentially symbolic, stripped of its former administrative functions. The new tribal board members are elected by secret ballot with voting open to all tribal members over eighteen years old. This system led to the "retirement" of Chief Freeman and his council. Since 1978 an elected tribal council, chair, and the paid staff of the association have continued to pursue the tribe's development. After the death of Chief Freeman in 1985, his daughter, Priscilla Freeman Jacobs, assumed some of his former duties and, in May 1988, was installed as the chief of the Waccamaw Siouan Tribe.

The formation of the Waccamaw Siouan Development Association (WSDA) has been extremely important to the Waccamaw. Since its formation, it has pursued self-sufficiency as a long-term goal. This pragmatic policy has been even more important because of the current reduction in federal funding to programs that offered the most help to the Waccamaw in recent years. To achieve self-sufficiency in the future, the association plans to work closely with county and state agencies. The North Carolina

Commission of Indian Affairs has provided assistance to the Waccamaw by offering workshops, seminars, and advice on how to attract industry into the Indian area. Most recently, the commission's economic developer has advised the Waccamaw on the process of establishing a tribal industry capable of generating revenue to support the future staffing of the association and other tribal projects. The association has helped several Indian farmers develop aquaculture projects, raising catfish to sell to the supermarket and restaurant chains in the southeastern area of North Carolina.

**Community Festivals: Powwow.** Throughout the Waccamaws' recent history their Indian identity was guarded and maintained consciously through their efforts to articulate with the dominant society. The former council focused on ensuring that non-Indians gave the group the rights due them as Indians, such as publicly funded Indian schools. By the mid-1960s, the country was moving uniformly toward desegregated public education, and consequently the Waccamaw were forced to give up their community Indian schools. The old symbol of their Indian status was to give way to a new institution, the powwow festival, which had much broader meaning than the community school. The first few years after desegregation involved the Waccamaw leaders in several statewide Indian activities, beginning with the incorporation of their development association and followed by their participation in the formation of the North Carolina Commission of Indian Affairs. These activities culminated in the initiation of the first annual powwow within the Waccamaw community.[47]

The word "powwow" refers to a festival held and sponsored by one or more tribes or communities.[48] It can occur at any time of the year and for any occasion. Most powwows include secular dancing, last a few days to a week, and include "games, craft displays and sales, giveaway ceremonies, and other features, along with the main attraction, costumed dancing" (Lurie 1971:450). The Waccamaw powwow fits this description. It is held annually in October and, though members of other tribes attend and compete in the dance contests, the powwow is financed, organized, and sponsored by the Waccamaw alone. This kind of powwow, as Paredes (1965:1) points out, promotes community solidarity through participation in a uniquely Indian event. Whether locally sponsored or jointly sponsored by several Indian tribes and communities, powwows diffuse certain pan-Indian traditions, such as the dance costumes, but at the same time they can reinforce local Indian identity (Lurie 1917:450). In more acculturated communities, "they may be one of the very few open and explicit statements of Indianness" (Paredes 1965:1).

The Waccamaw powwow follows the Indian school as an important focus of community activity. The powwow is held on five acres of tribal

*Above:* Waccamaw Siouan catfish pond, ca. 1985. *Below:* Waccamaw Siouan workers harvest catfish, ca. 1985. *Opposite, top:* Waccamaw Siouan Aqua-Culture project truck, ca. 1985. *Opposite, center and bottom:* Waccamaw Siouan powwow dancers, ca. 1985. (Photos: Patricia Barker Lerch)

land located within the heart of Waccamaw territory. Doubling during the year as the parking lot for the offices of WSDA and a day care center, each October the tract is transformed into the dance grounds of the annual powwow. Preparations begin in early spring preceding each powwow when the board assigns tasks to the major standing committees: food, dance contest, princess pageant, powwow booklet, traders, games, parade.

The two events that highlight the powwow are the Indian princess contest and the competitive Indian dancing. A "little" Miss Waccamaw Sioux as well as a teenage Miss Waccamaw Sioux are chosen from among the young Indian girls. The older contestants compete in four areas: talent, street wear, formal wear, and Indian wear. The Indian wear, designed and made by the girls with the help of Indian seamstresses, generally conforms to a Plains Indian style of costume. The Indian-wear outfits are often the same ones used in the Indian dance competition, as many of the pageant contestants are also members of the dance team.

The regalia for dancing features both "traditional" and "fancy" or "war" dances. The traditional dances are those of the particular tribes represented at the powwow. In addition each dancer improvises and creates his or her own particular dance. Contestants are drawn to the powwow dances by the cash prizes, and dancers from other North Carolina Indian tribes, such as the Lumbee, Coharie, Haliwa-Saponi, and Tuscarora, are often present. Occasionally, dancers from Oklahoma or Florida tribes participate, as do the Cherokees of North Carolina. The dance competition thus is intertribal.

The dances performed at the powwow are described as "customary" or "Indian" in origin although not necessarily original to the Waccamaw specifically but rather to Indians generally. They feature pan-Indian dance traditions. The dance regalia also conforms to a pan-Indian style closely associated with Plains Indian culture (Thomas 1965). The women's dance costumes are white, tan, or dark brown suede and decorated with colored wooden beads attached to rows of fringe that hang down from the bust line front and back. A popular variation to the "square tail" skirt with an even hemline is the uneven hemline in which one side is cut higher than the other. Fringe lines the sleeves, back, and hem of the dress. All female dancers wear suede moccasins during the dancing, and some of the older women carry decorated shawls over their arms. The decorations may include shells, beads, acorns, dyed corn, colored feathers, and ankle bells. These ornaments are purchased at craft shops, and the entire costume is handmade by local Indian women for about forty dollars. The men's dance regalia is more expensive than the women's and averages around seventy-five dollars. The male dancers order their regalia materials from Cherokee, North Carolina, where there are Indian stores specializing in the manufacture of feathers, head roaches, and arm, shoulder, and rear bustles of feathers. Many male dancers wear choker necklaces, bone breastplates, breechclouts and leggings, knee bands with bells, and angora anklets and moccasins.

Participation in the powwow as an Indian dancer or as a contestant in the princess pageant demonstrates a high level of commitment to Indian heritage and ancestry. The symbols adopted may be pan-Indian and the regalia of Plains origin, but the Indian identity being celebrated is local (e.g., Waccamaw). The powwow activities provide a way for the tribal community to publicly demonstrate its own commitment to its Indian identity. The powwow is just one more variation of the articulatory theme carried throughout the early history of the community. The Waccamaw have adopted the powwow complex with its pan-Indian features as a way to communicate their presence to their neighbors but, as in the past, they have chosen to do so through the explicit expression of their image of themselves as Indian people.

# 4

# CONTEMPORARY NATIVE AMERICANS IN SOUTH CAROLINA

*Wesley DuRant Taukchiray* and *Alice Bee Kasakoff*
With Photographs by *Gene Joseph Crediford*

In recent years, the Indian communities of South Carolina have grown. They have sought public recognition as Indians, formed ties with each other and with Indian groups outside the state, and adopted markers of Indian identity. This chapter discusses the factors responsible for the persistence of Indian groups in South Carolina and their recent florescence. In the second part of the chapter, we describe three groups in detail: two in the Low Country, currently known as the Edistos and the Santees, and the Catawba.[1]

South Carolinians acknowledge the existence of the Catawba: most schoolchildren know at least that they are responsible for the state's irregular northern boundary. The Catawba tribe's state and federal recognition have guaranteed public recognition as well, but Indians without these legal guarantees are nearly invisible to the public, even to their neighbors. Most people are surprised to hear of their existence. This chapter, we hope, will make it clear that such groups exist and that they have had a long history. It should also shed some light on the reasons they are not better known.

All Indians in the state have been a third group in a biracial system, and they have all had to adopt similar strategies to avoid absorption into the two larger racial groups. The Catawba have had at least some legal guarantees that they will be treated as a separate "nation," however often these may have been ignored or subverted, so it has been easier for them to maintain an identity as Indian. The Low Country groups, on the other hand, have had to struggle to form such an identity and convince others of its validity.

The approach we take is largely historical, though we do provide basic information about the current situation for each of the three groups we discuss in detail.[2] Except where explicitly noted, our statements apply to the situation as it existed in 1986. We are interested in the forces that brought such communities into existence, maintain them, and, in some cases, led to their disappearance. These processes can only be observed over the long run.

Little has been written on the Low Country groups and what has been published recently has been in newspapers and magazines. Recently, however, Moore (1986) has compiled a bibliography that is quite useful. The one book-length treatment (Berry 1963), though by and large accurate, has offended the Indians because it uses racial epithets they regard as derogatory. Its coverage ends in 1963, and it is not based upon historical research. More information is available on the Catawba, and their history is well known,[3] but we are providing details that have not been published elsewhere, as well as information about more recent developments. Recently, Ferguson and Crediford (1986) collaborated on a useful introduction to the Indians currently in the state. The pamphlet locates the Indian communities, provides a brief history, and contains several photographs.

## The Indian Communities

## Our Definition of Indian Communities

A number of individuals with substantial Indian ancestry reside in the state. We, however, confine ourselves here to people who belong to full-fledged Indian communities. These groups have Indian churches, have had Indian schools in the past, and have or have had Indian bars, stores, and the like.

Moreover, we confine ourselves to groups that publicly maintain that they are Indian. We do not discuss groups that some outsiders have speculated have Indian ancestry, such as the Sumter Turks near Dalzell and the Buckhead community near Smoaks in Bamberg County. The Sumter Turks do not concur that they are Indian and have said that they consider themselves to be "white Turk Americans." We do not know what the people of Buckhead consider themselves to be.

Nor do we include scattered households of Indian descent that do not form full-fledged communities (unless they can be linked to the groups we do discuss). The Indians named Chavis between Salley and Neeses, though numerous, may fall into this category. They have largely entered the general white community.

We include only those groups that, according to our research, actually have Indian ancestry. Other groups in the state may assert Indian identity, but, if so, they have done it so far only within their local areas. We suspect they are descended from Indians but need to do more research to be completely convinced. Notable among these are the Indians of Crawl Creek near Pineville.

From the perspective of decades, Indian communities have been fluid. The special legal status the Catawbas had because of their federal and now state recognition, of course, made it easier for them to maintain their Indian identity, but even that did not prevent dispersal at several points in their history. Scattered Indian households are cited in historical records, and some of them eventually formed communities with their own stores, churches, and schools, but many have not. Several Indian schools were quite short lived, doubtless reflecting the communities they served; as one closed another opened elsewhere. Sometimes the children were taken into the white schools. There were, and are today, clusters of Indian households without separate community institutions that are in the process of becoming white. Nevertheless, over time, local communities have coalesced, a process we describe shortly, and today we are in the midst of a revival.

## Clusters of Communities

The Catawba are the best known Indians in the state. They have had a special status in the state since the Revolution, enjoying a reservation granted to them in 1842. In 1943 they were recognized by the federal government as Indian and enjoyed that status until 1962, when the vote that they took in 1959 to terminate their federal status took effect. Since then they have continued to have state recognition.

But other Indian communities exist in the state. Most of these are pockets of households, scattered among households of other ethnic groups. The Low Country groups are located in inaccessible areas, near swamps, down dirt roads. Each such pocket has been part of a larger cluster of local communities, spatially distinct from the other clusters and largely endogamous. Although they have existed for a long time, these clusters have neither federal, state, nor, until recently, public recognition as Indian.

Since the early 1970s, some of these clusters have actively sought to be recognized as Indian by the federal government and the rest of the state's citizenry. Three have joined together to form the Council of Native Americans of South Carolina. Each has adopted a name for itself from a nearby river—the names we use in this chapter—and now elects a chief. The two in the Low Country, the Edistos and the Santees, will be discussed in detail in the latter part of the chapter. Each consists of at least two communities of one to two hundred individuals. The Edistos probably came from a now extinct community called Osbourne and currently include two communities, Four Holes and Creeltown, plus other related groups. The Santees are located in Orangeburg and Berkeley counties. Their community of White Oak is the only one to actively pursue its Indian identity, but Indians living in Varnertown and other places belong to this cluster. Map 5 locates these clusters.

The third group in the council, the Pee Dee (the name comes from the Pee Dee River; the group is not descended from the Pee Dee Indians who formerly existed in the state), is the largest cluster in the state today. Accurate figures are not available but we think there are at least 2,000. They live south of the North Carolina line in Dillon, Marion, and Marlboro counties. The historical research on their origins is in its infancy, but they consist at least in part, and probably entirely, of Indians who moved there during the nineteenth century from Robeson County, North Carolina.

We call them Pee Dee for convenience but the group is divided geographically. Those near McColl in Marlboro County belong to the Pee Dee Indian Association (it belongs to the council). The Marion-Dillon Indian Association, formed recently, represents the Indians in those counties as well as the Sardis Indian community (centering near Latta).[4] The Lumbee Regional Development Association, which represents the North Carolina Lumbees, recognizes the genealogical links between the North Carolina Lumbees and those in South Carolina, but the latter have not so far received any services through this group.

Urban Indians from the Greenville-Spartanburg area have organized and recently joined the council, calling themselves Piedmont Indians. Recent arrivals in the state, some are members of the federally recognized Eastern Cherokee tribe. The group contains few if any migrants from the Indian communities within the state who, if they migrate to cities, tend to leave the state or go to Charleston, which is close enough to home for them to continue to participate in their own communities.

Some groups maintain a public identity as Indian but do not belong to the council. For example, there is a third Low Country cluster, which has not been politically active: Goins community, located two miles north of Greelyville, in Williamsburg County. In the 1870s this group split from the tribe now called the Smilings, who used to live in rural Sumter County in Privateer Township, north of Paxville and south of Manning. In 1800 the ancestral group obtained a small patch of land (1.8 square miles). In the 1870s some of the Goinses moved out and founded Goins community. In

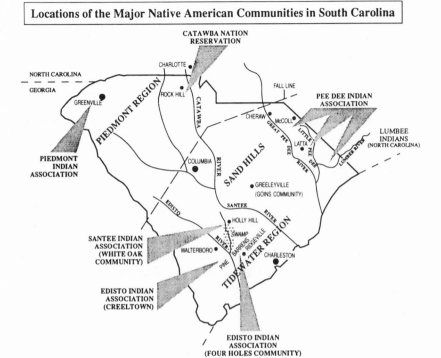

Locations of Modern South Carolina Indian Groups (Copyright 1990 The University of South Carolina. This map was produced by the Instructional Services Center of The University of South Carolina, Columbia, S.C., and is reproduced herein with the express permission of The University of South Carolina.)

1910 the federal census listed 126 American Indians in Privateer Township, and they correspond to the present-day Smilings.[5] By 1913 members of the community who had remained behind began moving to North Carolina in order to attend state Indian schools. By 1925 they had all left the state and are currently living in rural North Carolina between Maxton and Rowland, where they became known as the Smiling Indians. There are probably other groups besides Goins community that have yet to seek recognition as Indian from a wider public.

During the colonial period, disruption caused by white settlement and warfare led the different tribes to migrate and there was probably more interaction among the Indians in the state then than there has been since. Since 1980, some of the nonrecognized clusters have cooperated through the Council of Native Americans of South Carolina. But for the 200 years before the council was formed, the different clusters within the state did not interact to any significant degree. The two Low Country clusters are the single exception; they have ancestors in common, intermarried somewhat, and there was some migration from one cluster to the other. But we can document no contact between the Catawba and the Low Country groups, for example, from 1758 to 1972.

In 1988 the Catawba joined the council and since then the Indians have achieved a unity unprecedented in the state's history. The competition between groups with different legal statuses and different degrees or kinds of "Indianness" appears to have ended. Members of the state's Indian groups have been interacting and cooperating politically more than ever before.[6]

## Groups Covered

We have focused upon clusters with which Wesley Taukchiray is most familiar. He has been visiting Creeltown, Four Holes (both Edistos), White Oak (Santee), and the Catawbas since 1969. This chapter is based upon what he learned from those Indians and from archival research. Some communities with close connections to these communities are quite hostile to researchers (Varnertown, for example), and we know quite little about them. But we have included what we could to provide as full a picture as possible of each cluster. We have followed the wishes of the Indians in referring to them by the names they prefer.

## Factors Responsible for Persistence of Indians

### Racial System

The Indians owe their continued existence to the racial ideology of the region. When this ideology changed, so did the position of Indians. During the colonial period, some Indians were members of tribes that had made treaties with the colony or, later, the federal government. Over time, decimated by war and their lands taken by colonists, remnants of several of these groups joined the Catawba Nation. The last group to join the Catawba that we know of did so shortly before the Revolution. The Indians who joined the Catawba Nation all spoke Indian languages (though not all spoke Catawba). Thus, the nation was a haven for the more traditional Indians of the area. They were granted a reservation in 1763 in a treaty with the king of England.

Over a century of depopulation from disease and war in addition to the dislocation caused by the new settlers meant that many Indians were unable to maintain their languages (and cultures), even if they wanted to. Some Indians in the colony, mostly indigenous small tribes, were sometimes referred to as "settlement Indians" or "parched-corn Indians." By far the largest of the indigenous groups was the Ettowan, followed by the Kusso or Kussoo. After the colony-wide smallpox epidemic of 1760, these smaller groups were not mentioned in records as belonging to particular tribes. These more assimilated Indians probably would not have felt comfortable among the Catawba during the colonial period. Instead of joining them, they became "free persons of color" under the evolving racial system. During the antebellum period three groups held legal status that was clearly defined: free whites, black slaves, and "free persons of color." This last category included everyone who was neither white nor a slave. The category free persons of color included free blacks, but it also included people from India, Morocco, and the Moluccas along with the American Indians. Beginning in 1792, free persons of color between the ages of sixteen and fifty were assessed a capitation tax in addition to the taxes whites paid. If they could not pay, they were enslaved to raise the money.[7] This system ensured that members of this intermediate category paid their way in society.

As the system evolved, people looked for ways to escape this tax. If their ancestry was not black, they could escape it through filing affidavits attesting to their descent. Status was inherited through the mother, so if they could prove that their mothers were Indian, not black slaves, they could avoid the tax. The result was a distinction within the category of free persons of color between those descended from slave women who had been freed (or who had themselves been freed) and the rest. Descendants of black women who had been freed or people who had themselves been freed had no way to get out of paying the tax and were in more danger of returning to slavery, if poor. But even the wealthiest free persons of color in the Low Country obtained "affidavits of Indian descent," if they could qualify, to protect themselves from enslavement as the slave system became more repressive. (We don't want to exaggerate this distinction. Men who had been freed or whose free status came through their mothers had to marry free women or their children would be slaves.)

The Catawba were not part of this system. In many ways they were not really a part of the society at the time. True members of the society were taxed. Either they paid taxes themselves, in which case they were free (whites and free persons of color), or they had them paid for them (slaves). The Catawba were not taxed. They were not enumerated on the federal census until 1880 (other than for six off-reservation Catawbas in Chester and York counties in 1870).

We have examined more than 200 "affidavits of Indian descent" filed between 1775 and 1863. Only six of the many people who claimed to be Indian in these documents are ancestors of the Indians we know of today.[8] Such free persons and their children could "easily pass into White society without much ado" (Wikramanayake 1973:76). Even at the time of filing, many of the people were married to whites. A few were married to blacks and were considered black. Not all Indians in the state at the time filed such affidavits; those living in remote areas could probably avoid the tax collector. But on the basis of these records, descendants of most of the people claiming to be Indian in the past are probably now considered white. A much smaller number are probably considered black. In South Carolina, in the antebellum period at least, Indianness was not the enduring category it has become in the popular imagination. It was, rather, a way station to other identifications.

We reproduce here the text of an affidavit of Indian descent from just before the Civil War.[9]

John H. Martin      State of South Carolina
                              Personally appeared before me
Affidavits respecting him.
Robert Keith Payne who being sworn in due form of Law makes Oath and saith that he is well acquainted with a colored man named John Hozendorf Martin a tailor formerly residing in Charleston, now in Walterborough, he saith that the mother of the said Martin was the nurse of Deponent in his infancy and he was particularly well acquainted with her all her life and she was well known in his fathers family, he knew Martin as a boy, and from time of his very earliest recollection being frequently at the residence of his family and as the son of his nurse, her name was Sarah Martin, she was always reputed to be and so known and understood as of Indian descent and that was her reputation with every body, at the time—she was well known in the family, and his father and mother always so considered her and so spoke of her—Deponent always knew his father who was a carpenter and built a house at the farm of his deponent's father, near Charleston, he was of a dark reddish complexion and said to be Moor. Deponent saith that Martin has always been regarded in Charleston as of Indian Descent and deponent says that he is certain that none of the family ever paid taxes as colored persons of African descent.
      Sworn to before me this
      13th April 1852                                    Robt. K. Payne
      Thos. O. Elliott. Magistrate
      State of South Carolina
      Charleston District

This is followed in the records by a second one, in which Josiah S. Payne, brother of the first deponent, on 24 August 1852, swears that John Hozendorff Martin was "the son of a certain respectable Indian Woman who was a nurse in Charleston, knew her as a nurse in his fathers family, she had long black hair, Indian complexion, and was regarded as an Indian fully entitled to and enjoying White Laws, and belonging to that class of free colored persons who were entitled to the Laws of white people."

After the Civil War, the legal status of free persons of color disappeared. Some of the free persons of color cast their lot with blacks and were among the state's prominent black leaders of the time (Williamson 1975:316–17). Probably, however, these were people whose black ancestry could not be denied, many of them the "free persons of color" who could not obtain affidavits of Indian descent. Other free persons of color did not join the black community and were probably forced to form separate communities, some of them for the first time.[10] They remained scattered throughout the Low Country.

In the period after the Civil War, when laws were passed to keep the races separate, it was probably more difficult for Indians to be accepted as white than it was before. The coalescence of the Indian communities we now see in the Low Country accelerated during the late nineteenth and the early twentieth centuries. (We do not want to exclude the possibility that such communities existed there before the war, especially in view of the numerous gaps in the historical record; but we haven't found them.)

Prior to the Civil War no laws prohibited marriage between races. Those that were instituted later were not enforced as strictly in South Carolina as they were in North Carolina. This is reputed to have led Indians from Robeson County, North Carolina, who wanted to marry non-Indians to migrate to South Carolina, and to have been partially responsible for the establishment of the Indian communities in Dillon, Marlboro, and Marion counties.

After the war and up until segregation ended, Indians enjoyed many rights of the white population. They obtained the vote before blacks,[11] apparently because in some small communities there were so many they could swing local elections. Also those who served in the armed forces were usually accepted as white. Many of their schools, though serving only Indians, were listed as white in the state's records. Some children did attend white schools. Nevertheless they were never fully accepted by the majority of whites.

## Endogamy

In order to maintain an identity as Indian, community members often married among themselves or sometimes with groups, such as Filipinos, who also did not fit into the racial categories of the surrounding society. The extent to which they married out, and where they lived once they did so, was crucial to whether a particular community continued to survive and retain its identity as Indian.

Since World War II the Catawba have married out the most. They can afford to do so because their ethnicity is legally guaranteed now by their relationship to the state and in the past by their federal Indian status. Few Indian couples exist among the Catawba today.

The situation is different in the Low Country. In the communities that persist as Indian, the overwhelming majority of couples are Indian. If mixed couples do settle in the Indian communities, usually the wife is white, not the husband. Some of the people raised in these communities married whites and left, the children being raised as white. And we know of an area in Lincolnville where two Indian families who married each other formerly are now marrying whites. Other Indians expect that in a few generations the knowledge of their Indian ancestry will be lost.

We have much less information on people who marry blacks. Because blacks are not accepted as members of these Indian communities, these couples live elsewhere. The Catawba reservation has served as a line of defense against the black community. Persons of mixed Indian and black descent are not allowed to live on the reservation and they have never been listed on the tribal roll.

Indians also migrate as couples. When they do, they may seek to be accepted as white in other areas (see the case of the Platts discussed later in this chapter). Thus the communities we currently see as Indian are a residue of people who have stayed while their brothers and sisters left.

## Community Institutions

Each of the groups we discuss has a store and a church and some also have bars. These places are not necessarily frequented exclusively by Indians, but if others come there it is known they will be "hanging out" with Indians. The churches belong to different denominations from those of the surrounding communities, differences that reinforce their separate identity and especially their distinctness from blacks. The Catawbas are Mormon. Until recently Mormons did not allow blacks at the top levels of the church hierarchy. The Low Country groups are Church of God; to our knowledge no black Churches of God exist in South Carolina.[12]

In the past each of these communities had a separate Indian school. Most began as subscription schools, paid for by the parents of the pupils or by white sponsors, as a charity, rather than by the state. (The whites would not let the children attend their schools.) Sardis Indian School (near Latta) began in 1885, a one-room school operated by a local church. In that same year, a short distance away, the related Indians of Robeson County obtained state recognition from North Carolina. In 1913 the South Carolina Supreme Court ruled that even children who were "entitled to be classed as White" by the state (they had less than one-eighth Negro blood) could be segregated if the decision were "neither capricious nor arbitrary" and if the children were provided with equal facilities. The whites had taken their children out of the school (in Dillon County) (Berry 1963:119–22). The children in question were apparently non-Indian but the decision was also applied to Indians and provided a mandate for the establishment of Indian schools. Most of the Indian schools were eventually supported by the state. But only Charleston, Dillon, and Colleton counties identified these schools as Indian in their records. The rest are listed as white.[13] Some students did attend white schools, but it was at the discretion of the local school boards.

Indians were among the first nonwhites to have their own segregated schools closed and to then attend otherwise all-white schools. The Goins community school closed in 1949, having declined to three pupils from a peak enrollment of twenty pupils. Sardis Indian School in Dillon County (near Latta) closed in 1952. And in 1955, migrants from White Oak to Florida sued to have their children attend the white school in their new home. Three Indian schools closed with the advent of integration in 1966 (the Catawba school and the ones at Creeltown and White Oak). The last two Indian schools in the state closed in 1970: the Leland Grove Indian School (at Hamer, near the North Carolina line in Dillon County), and the school at Four Holes, after the Indians, in protest over the poor education they were receiving, set up a "Freedom School." The county had refused to allow the Indians to attend integrated schools.

The closing of these schools has been something of a mixed blessing. Indians can go further in the new system than they could before when the lack of Indian high schools meant they had to attend with blacks, which few if any chose to do. But few have finished high school since integration. Now Indian children have to struggle to assert their separate ethnic identity among their schoolmates. In 1977–78, Department of Education funds (Title IV, Part A) were used to create a display of American Indian aboriginal technique handmade goods from the South in two schools where children from Four Holes attend, in an attempt to make the pupils aware of the Indian heritage in this area. It is still there. But, with the exception of some Catawbas, who attend Mormon colleges in Utah, we know of only three people who have grown up in the state's Indian communities who have continued beyond high school, though there may be others.

## Economic Niche

People in several of these communities are quite poor (with the exception of many Catawbas and, in the past few years, some of the Santees). All of the Indians historically present in the state except the Catawbas were located in the pine barrens region, an area of low population density, where the sandy soil made farming unprofitable. The concentration of the Indians in the pine barrens probably came about after the Civil War, when the Indians found it advantageous to separate themselves from blacks, who were concentrated on the coast. Several Indians joined the Low Country communities from areas nearer the coast.[14]

Some men existed by hunting and fishing, but forest work seems to be preferred today. The chief in Creeltown has a successful stump-pulling business that employs other Indians. In the past some Indians made cypress paddles and splint-oak basketry, which they sold. These activities are not unique to these groups, but members of these communities trained others to carry on these traditions when Indians were no longer interested in carrying them on. In the past, the Catawba too were identified with forest work, which represents another way the Indians distinguish themselves from blacks, who farmed.

## Recent Florescence

## Population Growth

Census figures are, by and large, unreliable, but the 1980 census showed a near tripling of the state's Indian population, and from 1960 to 1970 the population doubled.[15] The increase is not only the result of population growth largely from natural increase but perhaps even more reflects the Indians' willingness to publicly identify themselves as Indian and to assert this identity to the census taker.

Population growth goes back to the midnineteenth century for most groups. Most of the current Indians are descended from small enclaves, some of which came together on the sites of the current local communities while others disappeared. One or more households we now know as Indian were listed in the censuses from 1830 to 1850 at each of the current sites of White Oak and Creeltown as well as at the now extinct community of Osbourne. By the first censuses in this century, the communities had grown to five or six households, and people had joined from other parts of the Low Country. It may have been the need for children to attend school and their desire to attend with other Indians that caused the communities to coalesce.[16]

Since the beginning of this century the communities have grown even more, especially within the last fifteen years. This growth may be the result of lower death rates due to improved health care, which in turn may have made it easier for young people to find spouses in their communities. During the last few years two of the Low Country communities have formed new churches.

The Catawba also have grown. The number on the roll has increased and so has the number living on the reservation. In 1889, with only 50 people in twelve households, they were probably the largest Indian concentration in the state (other than Lumbees in Dillon, Marlboro, and Marion counties). As late as the 1960 census, only some 350 Indians were living in York County. During the 1960s a slight increase occurred, but in the 1970s the number of Indians in York County tripled. Catawbas can vote in tribal elections only if they live within seventy-five miles of the reservation. The increased political activity of the tribe may have brought some of these people back.

However, at the same time these communities have grown others have disappeared. The Smilings settled in Robeson County, North Carolina, between Maxton and Rowland and have partially merged with the Lumbees, and Indian families who never affiliated themselves with any of the more clearly defined communities are marrying whites.

## Political Activity

In recent years all the state's Indians have become increasingly vocal and want greater recognition and more privileges as Indians. The first non-recognized group to become politically active was the community of Four Holes, as a result of the protest over schooling in 1969. Chief Robert Davidson was particularly important in pressing for public recognition of this community's needs. He, two of his brothers, and another man, all from Four Holes, were the only Indians from South Carolina at an early (1972) meeting of CENA (a national Indian organization, Coalition of Eastern Native Americans, no longer in existence). (The Catawba tribe joined shortly afterward.) Four Holes is the only community in the state, besides the Catawba, to obtain grants on its own. It was the first to join the council, followed by Creeltown in 1980; more recently White Oak has become more vocal. However, a sizable number of Indians live not many miles from these communities and interaction has occurred with those that have not joined in the movement for recognition and services. Several of these may become more active in the future. The Pee Dees are just beginning to organize, encouraged in part by the example of their North Carolina relations.

Since the late 1970s the governor's office has encouraged Indians to express their needs and has helped them obtain federal and state funds. From the administration of James Edwards (1975–78) onward, the Indians have benefited from several federal programs and block grants administered through the governor's office. (South Carolina is one of the few states where the governor must approve block grants. In the past, governors had encouraged Indians to apply for them.) Since 1976 the Indians have been receiving CETA funds (supplanted by JTPA—Job Training Partnership Act—funds in the 1980s), funneled through the governor's office, that support offices and secretaries in four communities: the Catawba, the Edistos (at Four Holes), the Santees (Holly Hill), and the Pee Dees (at Bennettsville).

In the late 1970s the governor's office assessed the needs of the state's Indians and published a report, which recognized four major groups in the state (Catawba, Edisto, Pee Dee, and Santee) and concluded that their main problem was isolation. In most of the Indian groups housing was substandard and communities in the Low Country had inadequate water systems. The report recommended that the groups apply for services available through various state and federal government agencies (Bryant 1979). A person within the governor's office has served as liaison with the Indians at least as far back as 1976.

The Council of Native Americans of South Carolina was organized in 1979 after two years of discussions among the Indian people, church sponsors, and the governor's office. It has been sponsored by the National Indian Lutheran Board and the United Methodist Church.[17] The organization has been spearheaded by Grace Lowry, a Lumbee from North Carolina who lived in Columbia and who in 1985 was named "Volunteer of the Year" for her work. Since her departure as director, the post has continued to be held by Lumbees from North Carolina, who thus are assuming a leadership role for the Indians of the state above the level of the local communities. The council has been advised by the United Indians of America, an organization headquartered in Washington, D.C.

The council began as an advocacy group but has become a program office that administers grants for the separate Indian groups it serves. In 1981 the council first sponsored a camp, which continued for several years, for Indian children in the state. In 1986 it received a grant from the Administration for Native Americans in the Department of Health and Human Services to encourage the development of small businesses among Indians.

The state's Indians have participated little in pan-Indian movements. What little influence these movements have had comes largely from contacts with North Carolina groups, especially the Lumbee. In 1970 five Indians from Four Holes attended the Coharie Indian powwow in North Carolina, the first time Indians from the Low Country had attended such an event. In 1979 Four Holes held its first powwow, an indication of this

*Left:* Gilbert Blue, Chief of Catawbas, at home in 1985. *Below:* Blondel Chavis and Yolanda Harris Scott in front of the former Leland Grove Indian School, the last Indian school in the state to close its doors. Now the Leland Grove Free Will Baptist Church (Indian), Dillon County, South Carolina, 1985. (Photos: Gene Joseph Crediford)

*Right:* Catawba Nola Campbell smoothing a pot with a cob, 1984 (Photo: Gene Joseph Crediford, courtesy Elizabeth D. Bernardin and Linda Kirszenbaum, University of South Carolina). *Below:* Edistos Georgia Davidson (tribal historian) and Matthew Creel (chief in 1989) at the Edisto powwow, 1983 (Photo: Gene Joseph Crediford)

*Above:* South Carolina Indians look on from the steps as North Carolina Indians dressed for a powwow entertain them on the last day of camp at Kings Mountain, South Carolina, 1985. *Below:* Home of Santee Utson Platt, at the center back, surrounded by those of his three children and their vegetable gardens; he is minister of the Church of God at White Oak. The road leads to the community. (Photos: Gene Joseph Crediford)

community's attempt to publicly proclaim its Indian ancestry. The pow-wow has become an annual event each May. Other groups now hold pow-wows as well, and one is held at the end of August each year, organized by the council at the conclusion of its camp. This is the only social event that brings the (non-Catawba) Indians of the state together regularly. These events often include fancy dancing and drummers from outside the state, but the state's Indians have been slow to participate in these pan-Indian activities themselves. We know of none with a complete costume and only a few even wear Indian jewelry, though Chief Davidson has an Indian bonnet. The few people who own such items wear them mainly at such powwows or other public events.

In 1979 and 1976, respectively, the Santees and the Edistos each ap-proached the BIA to obtain federal recognition. Since 1983 the council has tried to obtain state recognition for its members: the Pee Dees, the Edistos, the Santees, and the Piedmont Indians. They were assisted by W. J. Strick-land and Helen Schierbeck from United Indians of America. The first at-tempt, in 1983, failed, but in the spring of 1986 they introduced a new bill, which simply named the Indian groups. They wanted respect and visibility within the state and they hoped such a bill would help them qualify for federal funds earmarked for Indians who do not have federal recognition. The bill did not pass, but in 1986 the governor created an Indian commis-sion that has representatives from the Catawba, Pee Dees, Edistos, and Santees that are appointed by the governor.

As of 1989, the first priority of the council was to create a stronger Indian commission. In 1988 a bill was introduced into the legislature that would provide for an ongoing executive director and would make the rep-resentatives from each Indian community elected by each community rather than appointed by the governor. While funds were appropriated for the newly structured commission in 1988, the legislation itself was not passed due to the reluctance of the legislature to become involved in Indian matters while a Catawba suit was still pending. Instead a committee was appointed by the governor to study how such a commission might affect the Catawba land claim.[18]

The aforementioned Catawba suit (still ongoing as of 1990) to regain land lost in 1840 is another example of the increased Indian political ac-tivity. The Catawba voted to terminate their federal status in 1959, retain-ing a small state reservation when this vote came into effect in 1962. But in 1973 Gilbert Blue reorganized a council and became chief. He has worked to revitalize the Indian community and its culture.

In 1975 some Catawba decided to go forward with a suit stemming from the state's alleged violation of the Non-Intercourse Act. In April 1977 the tribe voted to pursue it and is currently represented by attorneys from the Native American Rights Fund. Passed in 1790, this federal act held that states had to obtain congressional approval before taking Indian land. In 1840 their 144,000-acre reservation was taken by the state, on the understanding the Catawba would be relocated among the Cherokee of North Carolina and compensated monetarily as well. The promised relocation never occurred, nor were they given money for their reservation, and the federal government has never approved the action. The only "compensation" Catawbas obtained was their current state reservation of only 630 acres.

The state and 27,000 people holding title to the contested land convinced the lowest court that termination invalidated the Catawba claim under the Non-Intercourse Act. But, in 1983, the appeals court held that the termination decision did not affect the claim. The case was heard by the U.S. Supreme Court in December 1985 but was remanded to a lower court in June 1986. It was heard in Richmond, Virginia, in December 1986. The tribe voted in 1959 to terminate their federal Indian status, which meant that the laws of the state of South Carolina would apply to them as they do to other citizens. The Catawba were assured, verbally, when they voted for termination, that their vote would not affect future land claims. The court held that the state's statute of limitations on land claims of ten years applies to this case but left it to a lower court to decide exactly how it applies.[19]

The tribe has been split over the kinds of benefits to pursue. Many who had left the reservation wanted to settle for money, while many who remained on the reservation wanted to press for land. In June 1978 they reached a compromise and decided to ask for a combination of money and land. As part of the suit they are also asking that their federal recognition be restored.[20]

Because the Catawba were federally recognized and enjoyed a great deal of public recognition as Indians, their interests have diverged from Indians that are not recognized. They applied to join USET (United Southeastern Tribes now United South and Eastern Tribes), which does not admit nonrecognized groups. And, while the Catawba have been asked repeatedly to join the Council of Native Americans of South Carolina, they did not accept the invitation until 1988. As a result of the Catawba suit, the interests of the Catawba and the nonrecognized Indians have moved further apart. Because whites in the communities surrounding the Catawba have organized to oppose the suit and some of their leaders are state representatives, the nonrecognized Indians have been unable to get support for their interests in the state legislature. The legislature is afraid that recognition will make it easier for these groups to claim land as well.

In what follows we discuss the Edistos, Santees, and then the Catawba in detail.

## Edistos

## Osbourne

Most of the present-day Edistos came from a community called Osbourne, which no longer exists. It, in turn, can be traced to some Indians who lived in its vicinity in the eighteenth century. In February 1747, by the modern calendar, fifty Natchez Indians (originally from what is now Louisiana) who had been living among the Upper Cherokees (i.e., in what is now extreme western North Carolina or eastern Tennessee) asked the colonial government in Charleston if they might be allowed to become settlement Indians. They wished to be allied to the English rather than to the French. The governor of South Carolina told them they could live "at Edisto" and gave them twelve axes, three guns, and twelve kettles to make them feel welcome.

This group is extremely well documented from 1747 to 1763. It seems to have centered at the point some six and a half miles south of present-day Walterboro, Colleton County, where Highway 64 crosses Chessey Creek. Here there was a pair of tiny bridges that formerly bore the name of Ebersons Causeway. The group lived from that spot eastward to the Edisto River. Over an eight-year period beginning in 1748, French-allied Indians from the present state of Indiana severely decimated this already very small group.

The Indians now living in the Edisto River area first appear in the federal census in 1830 as one household, that of Daniel and Nancy Windham, who seem to have lived on the present Highway 64 about five and a half miles south from Ebersons Causeway, well within the range of the earlier group. The Windhams' Indian descendants today claim a connection.

By 1840 this one household had moved to St. Paul's parish, on the other side of Edisto River, and by 1850 lived in the vicinity of Sand Hill Church (still in that parish) on upper Drayton Swamp. The Indian community that grew up around this one household remained in about that same spot for the rest of its existence. It was about three miles south of a former reservation, mentioned in 1711 as "land laid out to the Cussow Indians."[21]

In 1900 the community near Sand Hill Church appeared as thirty-three Windhams, Davidsons, Winninghams, and Mucklevaneys in seven households. As late as 1927 the community, called Osbourne, consisted of a few hundred Indians and encompassed the present Highway 163 from Edisto River and Highway 137 east-northeast to Highway 84 in far southern Dorchester County very near the Charleston County line. By this time the community had its own Indian school, taught by Lou Berta Davidson, an Indian who lived there. This school was never state supported.

Osbourne has now utterly dispersed—the houses are gone; no one lives on the site. Older community members know of its existence and at least one older resident of Creeltown can point out the Indian graveyard and the site of the house of Reuben Austin (Aus) Davidson, who is the only Indian listed in the 1880 census who could read and write, the first literate Indian on the Edisto River.

## The Diaspora from Osbourne

In the 1940s on Edisto Island there was an Indian school that was not state supported. Sixteen children attended (their surnames were Davidson, Russel, and Mucklevaney). They came from Osbourne. This small community has dispersed to Four Holes and Creeltown, though at least one or two individuals remain on Edisto Island.

Another group is located along the east bank of the Edisto River from Jellico, at Alternate 17 in Dorchester County, downstream to old Highway 17 in Charleston County. These Indians are named Reeves, Harrison, Willis, and Friendly. So far they have not pressed the state for legal recognition with the rest of the Edistos. There are also some Indians in Jacksonboro on the opposite, west bank, which is Colleton County, who belong to this group.

A number of now elderly Indians living at Four Holes and Creeltown, with many descendants there, were born at Osbourne. A few others are scattered at Megget and Hollywood and below Parkers Ferry, in the adjacent portion of Charleston County.

Other communities that probably came originally from Osbourne are Miller Bay or Miller Indian School, which was state supported at Ravenel from 1932 to 1942 and listed in the published state school directories along with the white schools but with the word "Indian" in parentheses following the name of the school. Peak enrollment was twenty students; the surnames were Miller and Reeves. Possibly also from Osbourne were the pupils attending Pine View School, which operated somewhere in North Charleston as a state-supported Indian school from 1934 to 1938. Pine View never had more than seven pupils. It was also listed as white but with the word "Indian" in parentheses after the name of the school in the published state school directories.

## Creeltown

The Indian community known variously as Creeltown, Rock Hill, or Little Rock first appears on the federal census in 1850 in Sheridan Township, the northeasternmost township in St. Bartholomew's parish, Colleton County. This is also the present location of the community, which lies at the junction of Highways 61 and 651 six to seven miles north of Cottageville, South Carolina, a short walk through the woods from the Edisto River. In 1850 the community consisted of only two households. One was that of William Bartholomew ("Bart") Creel, who was born about 1816 and is remembered by his descendants to have been Indian; his wife, said to have been Italian; and their seven children. The house stood at "the old Bart Field," between Deed Creek and Highway 46. This was the only large cleared area for several miles and served as a local landmark. After 1850 the Creels had six more children. Of the thirteen, three sons remained in the community, as did one of their nephews; all of the other children left. The second household in 1850 was that of Isaac Davidson, age seventeen, and his older brother George. Isaac Davidson remained among the Edistos, marrying an Indian from the Osbourne section and living at first in Creeltown and later in the Osbourne Indian community.

Eight of the grandsons of Bart Creel married six of his granddaughters (their first cousins) and two of his great-granddaughters. Their many children are the core of Creeltown, which, however, appears in the 1880 census to have only twenty acknowledged Indian residents (in five households headed by Creels). A few Davidsons returned from Osbourne. By 1900 a man from the county seat, Walterboro, named Hosea Martin, had moved to Creeltown with his white wife.[22]

White oak–splint basketry was produced in Creeltown until the death of the last weaver, Henry Creel, in 1939. The community had no school of its own until the 1940s and it was not state supported until 1956. It is listed in state school directories from 1956 to 1964 as Indian Rock Hill Elementary. Enrollment peaked at thirty-two pupils. It closed in 1966. Beginning in the summer of 1966, the First Baptist Church in Walterboro instituted the Indian Rock Hill Vacation Bible School for the children and adults of Creeltown.[23]

In February 1980 the community consisted of 117 resident members (108 Indians, 1 Polish man who had married an Indian woman, 3 white women who had married Indian men, and 5 white stepchildren). The members of the community have for many years maintained their own, predominantly Indian, Church of God. The community occupies one large continuous block of land, unbroken except for the presence of Maple Cane Church, which is white. The old Indian school is kept up as a community center. Creeltown has had a day care center since before 1981, funded by the Native American Division of Save the Children. In August 1986 a sewage and water system was completed, funded by the state. As far as we know, this is the last Indian community in the state to obtain running water.

## Four Holes

Four Holes Indian community branched off from Creeltown between 1900 and 1910. As Walter Creel states, "Creeltown is the mother of Four Holes." This community is located along Highway 386; it is four miles southwest of Ridgeville, South Carolina, and just north of Givhans State Park. No Indians lived there in 1900, but the community appears in the 1910 census as about twenty-five people in five households, clearly distinguishable to anyone familiar with the genealogies. The main surname, Mucklevaney, came from Osbourne. (The Mucklevaneys first appear as a single household at Canadys Crossroads in Colleton County, on the south bank of Edisto River about six miles west of Creeltown, in the 1870 and 1880 censuses. By 1900 they lived at Osbourne). Today, Four Holes and Creeltown are about six miles apart. Four Holes came into existence simply because of the population increase at Creeltown.

In 1925 there were five households.[24] An Indian school existed there by the early to mid-1920s, the first classes being held in "the Old Muck Church," an Indian church. This school was state supported from 1938 to 1970, always listed as white, with an enrollment peaking at more than eighty. The state highway department maps of Dorchester County show the Four Holes Church, successor to the Old Muck Church, from 1938 forward, on all revisions, as "Special," meaning Indian. Currently, Four Holes Church is Church of God.

In 1959 there were eighteen households.[25] A careful census done by Taukchiray, Georgia Davidson, and Four Holes Freedom School on 1 October, 1969 found 275 people there in fifty-seven households, all Indian except for 1 white wife (from Florida) and her 3 white children by earlier marriages. Of the Indians, 20 adults came from White Oak and 9 adults came from "Summerville," meaning the diffuse Indian community stretching from Lincolnville and Summerville to Moncks Corner. Of these last, a man and a woman (first cousins) came from Varnertown, the one distinct Indian settlement in that area. Otherwise, everyone came from Creeltown either directly or by way of at least one parent or grandparent from Creeltown. Seven adults remained alive of the first generation of Indians born at Four Holes. One man (John Muckenfuss, Sr., 1916–73) hunted

and fished full-time, and two others (Robert Wilder and Prentice Davidson) did so part-time. (Muckenfuss and Wilder were of the first generation
of Indians born at Four Holes; Davidson came from Osbourne.) The
cypress boat paddles carved on very rare occasions by John Muckenfuss,
Sr., were the only handmade goods produced in the community, and his
son John Muckenfuss (born in 1941) continues to make them. In 1969 the
community included an Indian church, two Indian stores, and two Indian
bars.

Dissatisfaction with the Indian school led to intensive political activity
in August 1969 that has continued to the present. Today Four Holes includes two Indian churches—both Church of God—one Indian store, and
one Indian bar, plus a community center; and there is a festival every May.
Robert Davidson (born on Edisto Island) was chief from 1973 to 1982,
succeeded by Eddie Leroy Martin. Johnny Creel was chief in both Four
Holes and Creeltown in 1986 but has since been succeeded by Matthew
Creel. Four Holes and Creeltown together are pressing for state recognition as the Edisto Natchez Kusso Indians.

## Santees

## White Oak

The White Oak Indian community first appears in the federal census
records in 1850 in the northern end of the old parish of St. James Goose
Creek, which is also the present location of the community. It lies mostly
on Highway 1376 (Fire Tower Road) about a mile and a half north of
Holly Hill in the eastern part of what is now Orangeburg County, South
Carolina. In 1850, the community seems to have consisted of a few households of Russels and Sweats.[26]

By 1922 the community had its own segregated, state-supported school.
Jesse Steiner's *American Community in Action* has a chapter on this com-
munity, based on the term paper of one of his students (a very prejudiced
student) at the University of North Carolina at Chapel Hill (Steiner 1928).
But it was not until 1930, apparently, that the people of White Oak were
called Indian on the federal census, which lists 134 Indians in Orangeburg
County. State highway department maps show the "Indian Church" on
Fire Tower Road north of Holly Hill in the eastern end of Orangeburg
County on all revisions from 1938 to the present. It is now Church of God.
In 1954 one household from this community, that of Allen Platt and Laura
Dangerfield Platt, gained national prominence due to persecution by the
high sheriff, so-called, of Lake County, Florida, who would not let their

children attend the white school in that county. The Platts contended that they were of Cherokee and Irish descent. (Articles on this issue appeared in *Time* and *Life* magazines and other places.[27]) The state-supported, segregated school closed in 1966. More than eighty pupils were then enrolled, but the school had been listed as a white school in every one of the state school directories.

The people in this community have a way of speaking English among themselves that is difficult for outsiders to understand. The community has a membership roll. Oscar Pratt is chief, Jimmy Pratt is assistant chief, and Hudson Crummie is the one former chief still living. The people call themselves Santees, from the name of the nearby river. Several articles have appeared in the Columbia newspapers recognizing the people as Indians. They are currently pressing for state recognition through the Native American council in Columbia. A second Church of God has been organized in the past few years. This community has had and continues to have great problems with poverty, lack of formal education, job discrimination, and poor health.

## Varnertown

A great many Indians live from Summerville and Lincolnville to Moncks Corner. But the other Low Country groups know of only one distinct settlement, a part of this bloc, that is called Varnertown, which in 1977 consisted of a long dirt road and a short dirt road, paralleling each other, to the right off Alternate 17 just past Carnes Crossroads on the way to Moncks Corner. This is in Berkeley County in what was once the parish of St. James Goose Creek. The Indians from Summerville and Lincolnville to Moncks Corner have never been interested in recognition as Indian. They are hostile to outside investigators unless they are of American Indian descent. The White Oak Indians have claimed jurisdiction over all Indians in Berkeley County, and a few of those at Varnertown have enrolled at White Oak.

Varnertown appears in the federal census at least as early as 1900 in the form of the household of William and Mamie (or Mary) Varner, according to present research, but this research remains in its infancy. Varnertown appears as a sizable community on the 1910 census. Marion Post Wolcott took photographs of Indians in this community in December 1938.[28] A state-supported Indian school, the Varner School, existed at Varnertown from 1939 to 1962, when it closed. Its enrollment varied from eleven to twenty-seven pupils, and it was always listed as a white school. Filipinos who had come to South Carolina by way of the Charleston Navy Yard began to marry into Varnertown around 1935 or 1946 (according to varying estimates), bringing in the surnames of Alfaro, Garcia, Ricafrenti, Blas, Bugasian (pronounced Bugeweezer), and others. Filipinos in Charleston recognize the people of Varnertown as Indian. The very small amount of Filipino ancestry at Four Holes and Creeltown comes from Varnertown.

Two Indian surnames are associated with Varnertown: Dangerfield and Clark. The Dangerfields descend from four brothers, John, James, William, and Morton Dangerfield, born between about 1815 and 1828, whose parents were a white man named Dangerfield (died 1852) and an Indian woman named Hannah (died 1857 in the parish of St. Johns Berkeley). According to an affidavit of Indian descent, her parents were a white man (William Elliot Edings of Edisto Island, who was still living in 1797) and "Indian Mary" of Edisto Island. Another affidavit mentions a William Clark whose two grandmothers were said to be, respectively, a "native Indian woman" in that parish and a Catawba Indian woman in the city of Charleston. A connection may exist between him and the present-day Clarks in that parish, including some at White Oak, who are Indians.[29]

## Other Indian Schools _____

Indians have mentioned the following Indian schools in addition to those we have already mentioned. One school near Moncks Corner closed about 1937 or 1938. Another, the Ridge School between Varner School and Summerville, was state supported and closed in 1954 with an enrollment of more than eighty pupils. Finally, the Red School stood at the site of the present Citizens and Southern Bank at the junction of Highways 78 and Alternate 17. Altogether at least four Indian schools stood along Alternate 17 from Moncks Corner to Summerville.

## The Catawba Nation _____

What follows is not intended to be an exhaustive account. The historical material supplements what Merrell has recently published (1984a, 1984b, 1989) but is not included in his work. The information on the modern Catawba supplements Hudson's book (1970), which concentrates on the years from 1932 to 1970.

## Historical Background

An amalgam of several Indian tribes, the Catawba Nation was a very fluid group before the Revolution. Beginning about 1716 (the end of the Yamasee War), other declining nations of Indians began to take refuge in the Catawba Nation, at first as separate towns within the nation. One of the first was the Wateree Indians, who had had only 40 men in 1715. They came in as early as 1716, left again in 1733, and returned in 1736, this time with the remnant of the Congaree Indians living among them. Some of the Saraw (Cheraw) Indians already lived in the Catawba Nation by 1724 and some of the Waccamaw Indians lived there, half a mile from the main Catawba town, by 1727. The rest of the Waccamaws seem to have come in 1733 or 1734; more Cheraws came in 1737 or 1738. The Saponi Indians at Fort Christanna in Virginia migrated to the Catawbas in 1729, but part of them left and went north in 1732 and another part did so in 1753, for what amounted to reasons of business and trade. We are gradually beginning to understand these comings and goings. Twenty Indian languages were spoken by the 400 Catawba warriors in 1743.

Before the Revolution, the Catawba population fluctuated. The (Charleston) *South Carolina Gazette* for 3 May 1760 states that seventy years earlier the population of the Catawba Nation had stood at 4,000. In 1712 Colonel John Barnwell estimated 970 Catawba warriors and 1,500 women and children in nine towns. Maps from 1712 to 1756 show these towns from the headwaters of Big Allison Creek on the west bank of the Catawba River, downstream to the mouth of Sugar (in Catawba, Sookiree) Creek on the north bank, with the biggest town, Eeswa or Neeswa, on the north bank near Nations Ford. This is in York County, South Carolina, near the present Fort Mill, and further upstream.

A severe smallpox epidemic decimated the Catawba in December 1759, much to the consternation of their English allies, who saw them as a buffer against the French and their Indians. By 1768 the nation consisted of only 100 Catawbas in twenty or thirty families, and 50 or 60 other Indians (called "Cheraws" by the traders, but made up of the remnants of many former nations). The comings and goings were not over yet; a part of the Saponi seem to have rejoined by 1775.

The Catawbas have lived in the same main village since 1781, corresponding to a small reservation of scarcely more than a square mile since 1842. The earliest census giving names and ages is the fall of 1849, but the reservation does not appear on the federal census until 1880, when the recognized Catawbas consisted of sixty people on the reservation and nineteen others in adjoining counties of North and South Carolina. In

1889 James Mooney found the reservation population to consist of fifty Catawbas in a dozen houses; the present tribe stems from this remnant.

## Cultural Persistence

The last two speakers of the Catawba language on the reservation were Sally Brown Gordon (1863–1952) and her half-brother, Sam Blue (1873–1959). Between themselves they spoke Catawba exclusively. Their mother, Margaret Ayers Harris (1831–1922), seems to have been the last Indian in South Carolina to teach her children an American Indian language. Nevertheless, the language has become an important Indian symbol and Chief Gilbert Blue, the current chief, is trying to reestablish it as part of the movement to revive the culture.[30]

M. R. Harrington found two baskets of split Arundinaria cane (an art form of the Indians of the South) on the reservation in 1908, and Frank G. Speck found four in 1919. No more have been seen. Several collections contain an example of white-oak basketry from the Catawba reservation. For example, the museum on the Alabama-Coushatta Reservation, in Livingston, Texas, has one.

However, the ability to make pottery has become an important marker of Catawba Indian identity for women. Passed from woman to woman, usually mother to daughter (the only current example of matrilineality we know of in this community), the number of potters working within the "traditional" style has grown. In 1969 the nation had thirty-five including both the active and the inactive. The location of the clay mines remains a Catawba secret, and knowledge is not given to outsiders, who thus cannot make pots. The best of the pottery includes pot drums, smoking pipes, and lidded pots suitable for cooking meals, though these last are very rarely produced.

Marriage outside the tribe has increased dramatically in the last fifty years. In 1944 the tribe included 69 households, over half (40) headed by a Catawba man married to a Catawba woman. Fourteen years later there were 123 households, but only a third (42) were headed by a Catawba man married to a Catawba woman. The out-marriages were with whites. The present enrollment of twelve to fourteen hundred may include no Catawbas married to Catawbas other than couples whose own grown children have married whites. There is however a small but growing trend toward marriages with Indians of federally recognized tribes.

The distinction between fullbloods and the rest is an important one that continues to be made not only by outsiders but by the Catawba themselves. The last reputed fullblood Indian in the tribe, Mrs. Hester Louisa Jean Cantey Blue (December 1880–July 1963), was the wife of Sam Blue. The last generation of reputed fullbloods consisted of fifteen or more members, all born before 1881.

The community is currently undergoing a revival. The state-supported elementary school closed in 1966, and only about 50 Indians were living on the reservation in 1969. But in July 1986 thirty households were there, all Catawba. The reservation is not big enough, so about forty-two Catawba households are situated adjacent to the reservation on George Dunn Road, Reservation Road, Shadow Road, and Old Friendship Road. The 1980 census lists some 1,200 Indians living in York County. Most are Catawba with a few Lumbee. Since their first contact with the Church of Jesus Christ of Latter Day Saints in 1883, most of the Catawbas have been Mormon, and a new Mormon church stands next to the reservation.

Gilbert Blue, a grandson of Sam Blue, has been chief since 1973. The tribe is governed by a community council of ten men. Chief Blue's goal is to revive some of the old culture and combine it with a program of economic development, which is to be financed by the land claims settlement. He also wishes to regain federal Indian status for the tribe.

## Conclusions

Contrary to what the public may believe, "the Indian" has not persisted from time immemorial unchanged. When the ideas underlying the system of racial categories changed, so did the idea of what was "Indian," and as the way the different groups were treated changed, the Indians developed new ways of coping with the situation.

In the Low Country, a stage of relative fluidity—when the Indian was a free person of color who could often pass for white—gave way to more rigid racial categories after the Civil War, a system in which the races had to be kept separate. The tiny pockets of Indians left in the Low Country had to come together, many for the first time. Finally, when racial segregation ended, the Indians had to adopt a new mode of political action and a search for "history," a history made necessary by the public's definition of Indian, a person whose identity comes entirely from the past.

Even though the Catawba have been legally recognized as Indians and others in South Carolina have not, they have moved through similar stages, doubtless because they have had to operate within the same system of ethnic groups. The Catawba too have recently moved from an integrationist stand to one that emphasizes their separate ethnic identity and their distinct Indian past.

Because the Indians do not fit into the accepted racial categories, they are more difficult to study than the blacks and the whites and more apt to be ignored by the larger society. Some communities resist being studied. The system of racial classification and interaction in our society cannot be understood just by studying the major groups. The smaller ones, those who have had to work to "fit in," show us that the matter of race is not cut and dried. Systems of racial stratification are not given by biology, as our culture so often tells us, but are determined by society and are, at least for some groups, open to negotiation.

The Indians' experiences illuminate the system of rules by which we all operate, whether white, black, or Indian. To understand such a system we need to follow people from groups that identify themselves as Indian as they move in and out of groups that identify themselves as white or as black. To do so would expose their descendants to a full knowledge of their racial origins; thus it remains an extremely sensitive issue in South Carolina, perhaps more so for the Indians than for any other ethnic group. Yet without this knowledge, we will never learn how such systems evolve and why they persist today. Nor will we learn how, or even if, social systems that severely disadvantage certain ethnic groups, at the expense of others, can be eliminated.

# 5

# SEMINOLES AND MICCOSUKEES: A CENTURY IN RETROSPECTIVE

*Harry A. Kersey, Jr.*

## Prologue

The year was 1983, and the evening was typical of June in Florida: oppressively hot and muggy. My clothing was soaked with perspiration after only a short walk from the parking garage to the terminal building at Miami International Airport. Waiting there was a young Miccosukee Indian friend, as well as two staff members from the Florida Governor's Council on Indian Affairs who had just arrived on a flight from the state capital. The occasion for our rendezvous was to attend the sacred busk ritual held by traditional Indians in south Florida, the Green Corn Dance. The Indian and I had spent all of our lives in this heat and humidity; we wondered how it would affect the others when we got into the Everglades.

It was almost midnight when we left the city and drove westward some forty miles to the Miccosukee Reservation located on the edge of Everglades National Park. By the time we arrived at the village a late rising new moon bathed the homes in a pale silver glow. The village was dark and seemed deserted; only the occasional barking of a dog broke the silence. We paused at an Indian home just long enough to change into woods clothing and boots and to apply insect repellent; then we were on the move again, heading along the Tamiami Trail, a cross-state highway bisecting the Everglades. Within half an hour our car slowed and pulled off at a spot where the shoulders of the road widened and several Indian vehicles were parked. Figures in the shadows—the perimeter guards—issued a muffled greeting in *ilaponki*, as the Miccosukees call their own language. From that point it was only a half-mile walk to the dance site. Numerous large chickees ringed the busk ground, their steeply pitched thatched roofs sil-houetted against the treeline of a cypress stand. The clans were arrayed in the traditional manner, each having a camp facing the dance area. That evening we were to be guests of the Bird Clan.

The night passed slowly and uncomfortably, accentuated by steamy rain showers, gnats, mosquitoes, and not a few inebriated brawlers who were quickly subdued by the elders. It must have been nearly 2 A.M. when an exhorter appeared before the massive fire on the dance ground and called for a traditional stomp dance. Immediately a group of some thirty Indians, including both genders and a variety of ages, formed pairs and began a monotonal rhythmic chant as they danced in a deliberately executed cir-cuit around the fire. Most of the men wore modern clothing—jeans, boots, and denim work shirts or patchwork shirts; however, a number of the older women and younger girls wore traditional patchwork skirts and short capes. Several of the dancers had colorful rattles fastened to their legs; these were fashioned from the shell of the box turtle and filled with canna seed—often called Indian shot—and their staccato sound punctu-ated the dance rhythm.

As the figures circled the fire, dancing in a line of pairs, the event I had really come to observe took place. From a small structure at the side of the dance ground, almost obscured in the shadows, a stooped, frail figure ap-peared. He was only slightly above five feet in height, and white hair fringed the high turban he wore; his colorful garb sparkled in the reflected glow of the flames while he briefly prayed aloud, then abruptly returned to the seclusion of his shelter. This was Ingraham Billie, ninety-three years of age, the last of the great medicine men functioning among the Seminole and Miccosukee people. He presided over the several-day ceremony with great dignity and energy. However, we had correctly assumed that the old man would not be conducting many more Green Corn Dances, and with his demise would come the end of an era. A year later, while I was teaching in Africa, the news of his death reached me.[1]

Ingraham Billie's life had coincided with a century of unparalleled changes in the culture of the Florida Indians. Born in the Big Cypress ca. 1890, he was a member of the Panther Clan, which traditionally provided the medicine men for the Mikasuki-speaking Seminoles. The Billie family was historically prominent (MacCauley 1887:492–94, 527–28; Sturte-vant 1956). His father Little Billie, also called Billy Conapatchee, was the first Seminole known to have attended school in Florida in the 1870s. Two of his uncles, Billy Fewel or "Key West Billy" and Miami Billy, appear frequently in ethnohistorical accounts of life on the Florida frontier at the turn of the century. An older brother, Josie Billie, was also a famous medicine man before converting to Christianity during the 1940s. In sum, the Billies represented a prototypical Indian family of the period: they observed the traditional religious and cultural values; made their living primarily from hunting, trapping, and subsistence farming; had limited contacts with the outside world except for white traders; and generally led a very self-sufficient, independent existence. By the time of Ingraham Billie's death the tranquil world of his youth had long since disappeared to be replaced by a modern Seminole/Miccosukee life-style.

Today two Indian tribes are federally recognized in Florida: the Seminole Tribe of Florida dates its organization from 1957, while the Miccosukee Tribe of Indians came into being in 1961. (*Editor's note*: The federally recognized Poarch Band of Creeks [see next chapter], although headquartered in Alabama, has some of its members, a portion of its tribal services area, and one acre of its trust land located in extreme northwestern Florida.) The Seminole and Miccosukee tribes, closely linked through kinship, language, and cultural ties, nevertheless present striking contrasts in socioeconomic development and acculturation. It should be noted that language provides the most common bond between the communities at present. Ethnolinguistically, all members of the Miccosukee Tribe speak a Hitchiti tongue known as Mikasuki (traditional anthropological usage), as do two-thirds of the Seminole Tribe; the remaining Seminoles speak the Muskogee (often used synonymously with Creek) language. Communication among the Florida tribes, therefore, required fluency in both native languages as well as English.

The Seminoles are by far the best known of the two groups, primarily because of their historical role as one of the Five Civilized Tribes in the Southeast that resisted the federal removal policy in the 1830s and fought three futile wars to remain in their homeland. These Indians can trace their ancestry to a remnant group that evaded removal at the conclusion of the Third Seminole War (1855–58) and remained in the Everglades of Florida (Covington 1982). By the present century the tribe has become a widely recognized and colorful aspect of Florida life that was prominently featured in the state's tourism advertising. Even so, the Seminoles narrowly averted political termination by the federal government in the 1950s. They then sought formal recognition under the Indian Reorganization Act.

The Wheeler-Howard Bill of 1934, more commonly known as the Indian Reorganization Act (IRA), was the linchpin of the Roosevelt administration's New Deal for American Indians (Deloria and Lytle 1984; Kelly 1983; Philp 1977). The IRA provided for the revitalization of virtually every aspect of Indian life, including health services, education, and tribal self-governance. In addition, it mandated the preservation of tribal lands in a perpetual trust status administered by the federal government, with exemption from both state and local taxation. To facilitate economic development, the tribes received authorization to incorporate and conduct their own business affairs. Furthermore, the Indian tribal councils were vested with rights to negotiate with federal, state, and local governments. One interesting section of the IRA provided that a tribe would automatically be covered unless a majority of the adult members specifically voted to exclude their people from its provisions. All tribes had to make this choice within one year following congressional approval of the bill. In 1935, a month prior to the scheduled IRA vote in Florida, Commissioner of Indian Affairs John Collier made his first official visit to the Florida Seminoles (Collier 1935). He inspected Indian camps and met with a large delegation at West Palm Beach to urge their support for the measure. These efforts were to no avail; the Seminoles of Florida, like most traditional Indians in other parts of the country, generally boycotted the government-sponsored balloting. However, by a convoluted bureaucratic logic, the Seminoles were recorded as having approved the IRA even though only 21 (in a population of over 500) cast votes, all favorable. In the long run this proved to be a most fortuitous turn of events; however, another twenty-two years would pass before the tribe sought formal recognition.

Although federal authorities had begun to establish a land base for the Seminole people during the last decade of the nineteenth century, it was extremely difficult to convince the Indians to move to these enclaves. There was no control over the widely scattered Seminole camps. Most Seminoles were distrustful of virtually anything having to do with the federal government; moreover, their traditional leaders counseled against accepting the white man's medicine and schooling. During the intensive trading period from 1870 to 1930 the Seminoles derived a substantial cash income from selling pelts, plumes, and hides to trading post operators (Kersey 1975). With this money they purchased a variety of articles that radically altered their material culture. The drainage of the Everglades beginning in 1906, coupled with the collapse of the international fashion market at the onset of World War I, brought an end to the trading and left Indians in a near destitute condition. Furthermore, the rapid settlement of south Florida after the railroad arrived in 1896 forced the Seminoles from many of their traditional hunting and camping grounds.

It was not until the depression years of the 1930s that the Seminoles began to move in any appreciable numbers to the reservations. Initially, a few families that had been displaced from their campsites along the lower east coast came to the Dania Reservation southwest of Fort Lauderdale. This site was opened in 1926 as a camp for "sick and indigent Indians" from throughout the state, but it soon became home almost exclusively to the east coast band (Nash 1931:70). The federal agent erected homes, a school, and employed adults in agricultural projects designed to make them economically self-sufficient. Apparently most of the Indians preferred to work for government wages clearing the land rather than cultivate the small farm plots assigned to each family. As the United States entered the depths of the Great Depression, federal relief programs for Seminole Indians in Florida were centered at the Dania Reservation. The New Deal had spun off an Indian counterpart to the Civilian Conservation Corps known as the Indian Emergency Relief Work, which employed Seminoles in a variety of reclamation, road construction, and housing construction projects (Parman 1975:127–45; Covington 1981). This was a period in which many Seminoles initially entered the wage-labor economy both on and off the reservations. Actually, in the early years of the depression era prior to the advent of federal programs, many Seminoles were already engaged in some form of seasonal agricultural work (Kersey 1989a). A few Indian families also resided part of the year at commercial "tourist villages" in Miami and other resort areas (West 1981).

The decade of the 1940s brought World War II, but it had a limited impact on the Seminole people of Florida. Indian males had little inclination to register for the draft or join the military voluntarily, and the local draft boards opted not to enforce the Selective Service rules that technically applied to Seminoles as citizens of the United States. Even so, it is doubtful that a large number of them would have passed the minimal educational and medical requirements for military service if strictly administered. Only three Seminoles are known to have volunteered for military duty, and one of them served with distinction as a marine in the Pacific (Covington 1979). A few Indians living in the vicinity of Miami were employed in war-related industries such as boat building and light aircraft manufacturing, but for the most part there was little interest in relocating to urban areas and seeking employment, as was the case with many other tribal peoples. Many Indian families were content to remain on the reservations where they engaged in federally subsidized employment or worked as agricultural day laborers at nearby farms and ranches. Also, their children attended day schools, and a public health clinic was available. Throughout the period an increasing number of Indians gradually deserted their Everglades camps and moved to reservations, so that by the 1950s a majority of the Florida Seminoles were living on federal trust lands.

In 1953 the 83d Congress passed House Concurrent Resolution 108, which mandated the termination of federal services and the disposal of trust lands for a number of Indian tribes. This misguided policy, initiated as part of a conservative effort to cut federal expenses, was abetted by the long-standing assimilationist impulse to detribalize Indians. The Florida Seminoles were listed as one of the groups to be terminated—much to the dismay of the Seminoles and their non-Indian supporters (Kersey 1989b). At that time there was no tribal government or business organization and virtually no leadership cadre, as fewer than a dozen Seminoles had attained a high school education. The tribe was totally dependent on the Bureau of Indian Affairs to provide every aspect of health services, education, land management, and road maintenance on the reservations. In addition, the government was still a major permanent employer of Indian adults. In no way could these Indians have reasonably been considered capable of managing their own affairs; thus they were not good candidates for termination of services. This was made clear in a series of congressional hearings conducted in Washington, D.C., and Florida during 1954–55 (U.S. Congress 1954, 1955). Testimony by numerous Indian and non-Indian witnesses emphasized the need for at least a twenty-five-year period of continued federal supervision during which the Seminoles could prepare themselves to assume control of their reservations and a nascent cattle enterprise. Many longtime friends of the Indians spoke eloquently of the need to retain the Seminole lands and culture. Only the representatives of those ultraconservative Mikasuki-speaking Seminoles who lived in the Everglades and rejected any manner of interaction with the government spoke in favor of the general principle of terminating all federal supervision over Indian peoples. Responding to the pressure from their influential constituents, as well as the obvious lack of Seminole preparedness to run their own affairs, the Florida congressional delegation had the Seminole termination bill killed in committee. Thus the Seminoles averted the economic and social disaster that befell some few other tribes who were not as fortunate and became the victims of federal termination policy, for example, the Menominee of Wisconsin.

In 1957 the Florida Seminoles exercised their rights under Section 16 of the Indian Reorganization Act to establish limited tribal self-government through the adoption of a constitution and bylaws. A committee of representative tribal members worked with an official of the Bureau of Indian Affairs to draft the necessary documents. The key government figure in this process, Rex Quinn, was himself an Indian; he would later return to Florida and serve as Seminole agent for a time during the 1960s (Seminole Tribe of Florida 1977). Prominent among the Seminoles was Bill Osceola, chairman of the constitutional committee, who would serve as chief elected officer of the newly organized tribe. The constitution and bylaws they developed were adopted in August 1957 by a vote of 241 to 5, thereby far exceeding the simple majority vote required by the IRA (U.S. Department of the Interior 1957). Similarly, a corporate charter was adopted by the Seminoles at the same balloting. The only sizable element within the tribe to boycott the voting was the conservative Mikasuki speakers who lived near the Tamiami Trail. These people would form the nucleus for a separate polity based on tenacious retention of traditional cultural and religious values, and they later received federal recognition as the Miccosukee Tribe of Indians.

The constitution and bylaws, which were amended in 1963 to reflect changed sociopolitical conditions, spell out the grounds for membership in the Seminole Tribe (those registered on the tribal roll or proving blood quantum of one-fourth or more), qualifications of electors (age eighteen), and regulations for conducting tribal elections and revising the fundamental documents of the tribe. The constitution provided for a tribal council. It is headed by a chairman chosen at large by the people of the reservations to serve a four-year term. Each reservation elects its own representatives to the tribal council for two-year terms. A secretary and a treasurer are appointed to serve at the discretion of the council. The council is empowered to function as a legislative branch charged with overall conduct of tribal affairs. The tribal chairman serves as chief executive supervising the tribal bureaucracy. A separate corporate arm known as the Seminole Tribe of Florida, Inc., is headed by a president elected at large by the reservation residents, while members of the board of directors are selected from each reservation. This board is responsible for initiating and conducting the business enterprises of the Seminole Tribe. To ensure coordination and cooperation between the entities, the tribal chairman sits ex officio on the board of directors, while the president serves ex officio on the tribal council.

Tribal economic development was virtually nonexistent for almost a decade. Three federal reservations, plus a state reservation, provided the Seminoles with a land base of nearly 200,000 acres; however, much of the land was submarginal and unproductive. A beef cattle industry had begun on the Brighton Reservation in the 1930s and was extended to the Big Cypress Reservation after World War II. Only a few Indian families benefited from this enterprise, and they formed an economic and political elite within the tribe for many years (Garbarino 1966:105–20). The tribe also rented several thousand acres of land to commercial citrus growers and truck farmers, but this action provided minimal economic returns. At the urban Hollywood Reservation a valuable asset was also squandered in the 1960s when the cash-starved tribe entered into extended leases on commercial properties at unfavorable terms (Ammidown 1981). Throughout this period an attempt was made to continue operating the tribal "tourist center" and the sale of handicrafts to visitors; these proved equally unprofitable. Also, only a few tribal members possessed the education or requisite skills for employment away from the reservations where federal "Great Society" programs were the main employer. Clearly, the Seminoles needed to develop business enterprises that would provide employment opportunities for the people and a high-yield cash flow for the tribal coffers. They would have to break with the old views on "acceptable" Indian development projects—tourism, handicrafts, and the like—which the Bureau of Indian Affairs had encouraged and supported over the years. In the 1970s the Seminoles elected their first economically aggressive chairman, Howard Tommie; taking a cue from western tribes and exercising its right of sovereignty, the tribe began selling state tax–free cigarettes on the reservations in south Florida (Dorschner 1979).

The operation of "smoke shops" on the reservation was an immediate financial success for the Seminole owners and their non-Indian backers and was a boon as well to the tribal treasury. The ability of the Seminoles to sell cigarettes sans Florida sales tax gave them a tremendous advantage over local merchants, and it was not long before a legal challenge was mounted. In 1953 Congress had passed Public Law 280, which granted the states civil and criminal jurisdiction over offenses committed by or against Indians; however, P.L. 280 specified that this legislation did not authorize state taxation or regulation of Indian property. Nevertheless, in *Vending Unlimited, Inc., v. State of Florida*, in 1978, the sheriff of Broward County, venue of the Hollywood Reservation, in his individual capacity as a citizen and taxpayer sued to require the imposition of state taxes on transactions involving the sale of cigarettes to and by Seminoles doing business on the reservation. A circuit court ruled that the sale of cigarettes to and by one whose place of business was located on an Indian reservation within state boundaries was not taxable by the state. This ruling was affirmed by the First District Court of Appeal of Florida (364 So. 2d 548). This decision settled the issue of the Seminole Tribe's right to operate "smoke shops." However, subsequent contradictory rulings by federal courts in similar cases involving Indian cigarette businesses cast some doubt on the continuation of sales to non-Indians; therefore the tribe moved in another direction. The tribal attorney was an extraordinarily adroit negotiator, and the tribe became directly involved in support of political candidates. In 1979, following an intensive lobbying effort by the Seminoles and their backers, the Florida legislature passed a bill that permitted the tribe to continue the sale of tax-free cigarettes on the reservations (Florida Statutes, 210.05, 1985). This act has been challenged in virtually every succeeding legislative session, but it has been successfully defended on the grounds that revenues from "smoke shops" operated by the Seminole Tribe help to assure a continuing economic independence for the Indian people of Florida. Under the leadership of another dynamic chairman, James Billie, the Seminoles would soon expand their income through an even more controversial business scheme.

The year 1979 marked an economic watershed for the Seminole Tribe with the introduction of an unregulated high-stakes bingo game at the Hollywood Reservation. Prior to this time the tribal government had realized limited revenues from a tax imposed on cigarette sales and other fees associated with that business—in fact, the charge most often levied against the "smoke shops" was that the non-Indian partners were taking away the major profits. With the introduction of bingo run under contract by a private management firm, the Seminole Tribe became the major beneficiary of a financial bonanza. Operating virtually every night of the week and offering jackpots exceeding $10,000, as well as prizes of cars and trips, Seminole bingo became immensely profitable. Within two years the tribe was realizing over $5 million annually and soon opened a satellite bingo hall on the rural Brighton Reservation. In 1982 the Seminole Tribe acquired a small parcel of land in the metropolitan Tampa area, ostensibly to build a museum and create a burial site for Indian remains uncovered at a construction site. The land was quickly placed into federal trust status as a part of the Seminole reservation holdings and became the location of lucrative "smoke shop" and bingo operations. These aggressive entrepreneurial activities triggered a furious political backlash both in Florida and in the nation's capital.

Florida law restricted the conduct of bingo games to charitable, non-profit, or veterans' organizations; they could operate only two days per week and could offer no jackpots exceeding $250 per session. Operators of these games claimed that the Indians were cutting into their business severely, even busing clients hundreds of miles on bingo excursions. They organized a strong anti-Seminole bingo lobby and were supported by local law enforcement officials who darkly hinted at underworld involvement in the operation. In 1980 another landmark case tested the federal protection afforded to Indian lands. In *Seminole Tribe of Florida v. Butterworth* the Seminole Tribe of Florida requested the federal district court to permanently enjoin the sheriff of Broward County from enforcing Florida's bingo statute on Indian land. In essence, the decision hinged on whether the Florida law was found to be criminal/prohibitory or civil/regulatory; the court found it to be the latter. It held that Congress had not authorized Florida to impose its civil regulatory schemes on Indian lands. The court granted injunctive relief, finding that "in view of the Congressional policy enunciated in Public Law 280, the court must resolve a close question in favor of Indian sovereignty" (491 F. Supp. 1015). In 1981, the U.S. Court of Appeals Fifth Circuit (5 October 1981, No. 80–5496) affirmed the lower court decision, thus paving the way for further expansion of Seminole bingo (658 F. 2d 310).

Meanwhile in Washington the spread of bingo to federal reservations

*Above, left:* Author Harry Kersey (at left) and Seminole friend on Tamiami Trail, 1939 (Courtesy Kersey Family Collection). *Above right:* Ingraham Billie, Tamiami Trail, ca. 1943 (W. Stanley Hanson Collection, Courtesy the Seminole/Miccosukee Photographic Archive, Fort Lauderdale, Florida). *Below:* Seminole tribal police car, ca. 1980. Note "Indian Plaza Tobacco Shop" sign partially shown in background. (Photo: Harry Kersey)

across the nation had triggered a congressional investigation and the introduction of stringent regulatory legislation. Naturally, such regulation was vigorously opposed by Indian tribes that looked to bingo as a major existing or potential source of income. The Seminole Tribe itself at one point had a financial interest in the bingo operations of tribes in five states. Nevertheless, an immediate outcome of the "Tampa affair" appears to have been a Bureau of Indian Affairs moratorium on approval of bingo halls erected on newly acquired tribal lands; as a case in point, the Seminoles were denied in their application to federalize a parcel they had purchased near Melbourne, Florida. This ruling imposed a potentially severe hardship on smaller tribes that desperately need bingo revenues yet whose base reservations are located in remote areas far removed from urban population centers and high-volume tourist traffic.

Presently, most of the more than 1,600 enrolled members of the Seminole Tribe live on five reservations in the south Florida region. These include the three major tracts established as federal trust lands earlier in the century plus two smaller parcels that have been added within the last decade. All of these diverse constituencies are now represented in the tribal council. The largest and most remote of these reservations is Big Cypress, situated on the western edge of the Everglades. Although the government began acquiring the land during the last century and it was designated a federal reservation in 1911, the Mikasuki-speaking Seminoles of the region did not begin moving there until the depression years of the 1930s. Even then only a few families relocated their camps permanently to federal land, preferring to remain in the Everglades. To this day the residents of this reservation remain the most linguistically and culturally traditional element among the Seminole people, and many are closely related by family ties to members of the nearby Miccosukee Tribe. Only within the last few years have the residents of Big Cypress fully accepted the benefits of modern housing, health care facilities, and education that the other reservations enjoy (Garbarino 1966:30–48). In this rugged 40,000-acre setting, most Indians are employed in cattle herding, agricultural production, or maintaining the reservation as either tribal or BIA employees. Recently the tribe's largest bingo facility was built on the Big Cypress Reservation.

The Brighton Reservation is another large rural preserve located northwest of Lake Okeechobee. It is home to the Creek-speaking faction among the Seminole people. This site was acquired in the 1930s through the joint efforts of the Bureau of Indian Affairs and the Resettlement Administration, a New Deal agency specializing in submarginal lands (Covington 1976: 57–58). Occupying over 30,000 acres of savanna known as "Indian Prairie," it was an ideal location for raising cattle. The federal government provided a herd of 1,200 cattle brought in from the drought-stricken western states, and this herd became the nucleus of a thriving Seminole cattle industry (Glenn 1982:32). In 1939 the Seminoles selected three trustees to supervise the tribal cattle program. After about a decade the common herd was divided among individual owners who assumed mortgages and bought their livestock. A cattlemen's association was formed to represent the interests of these owners in dealing with the federal government and later with the newly formed tribal government. The success of the Brighton cattle venture led to the initiation of a similar program at Big Cypress in the late 1940s. Brighton Seminoles were apparently successful not only with cattle but also in other employment both on and off the reservation. Also, because this group had been in sustained contact with non-Indians for decades, they were more acculturated and easily adapted to government efforts to improve housing, health, and education. In the 1950s the Brighton people opted to close their own government school and send their children to public schools in a town near the reservation (Kersey 1970:31–32). The first Seminole to graduate from a public high school in Florida came from the Brighton Reservation, and this group supplied a disproportionate number of tribal government leaders during the first two decades of its existence.

When the Dania Reservation was opened in 1926 it was located in a rural area southwest of Fort Lauderdale. Today, this 500-acre tract is totally engulfed by the urban sprawl of the lower east coast of Florida. In the 1960s the tribe renamed it the Hollywood Reservation to reflect more accurately its geographic location adjacent to the city of Hollywood. The Seminole families who reside there are the most acculturated and affluent members of the tribe. Most work in some capacity for the tribal government or Bureau of Indian Affairs, but a number are also engaged in entrepreneurial ventures such as the "smoke shops" or tribal bingo halls— although these operations have employed disappointingly few Seminoles and at low skill level jobs. Relatively few Seminoles are employed in the private-sector work force, preferring association with other Indians as co-workers. The tribal government still employs a great number of non-Indians in key technical positions that Seminoles are slowly preparing to assume. This opportunity to work for the tribe at competitive salaries has probably kept many capable Seminoles from attempting to assimilate economically in the local community. However, they do send their children to nearby public schools and generally participate in the social life of the area.

A small Seminole settlement had existed near the town of Immokalee since a mission station was established there in the 1890s by the Women's National Indian Association (Kersey and Pullease 1973). The families who had camps there in this century were among the most poverty-stricken members of the tribe. Their living conditions were deplorable with sub-standard housing and a general lack of hygiene that exacerbated the poor health of the inhabitants. The Indians there were generally employed in low-paying seasonal agricultural labor on nearby farms and often found themselves dependent on public assistance. In the 1980s this plot of land was transferred to the Seminole Tribe and placed in federal trust status. Following that action tribal funds were expended to upgrade the living area, while a whole array of medical and social services were provided for the people.

Only a few Seminoles make their permanent residence at the small Tampa Reservation. They are employed in some phase of the tribally oper-ated bingo hall, "smoke shop," and tourist village operations. The strained relations between the tribe and Tampa municipal government as a result of federalizing this property does not appear to have translated into general hostility toward Indians per se, judging by the profitability of the enter-prises. At present the prevailing political climate is one of peaceful, albeit suspicious, coexistence between the parties.

The income derived from bingo has been used by the tribe to improve the quality of life on the reservations by upgrading housing, health, and recreation facilities. Through a contract with the Indian Health Service, clinics and medical care are provided on all reservations. Gymnasiums, swimming pools, and ball fields are available to even the most isolated Indian communities. The tribe also provides its own police and fire protec-tion at a cost of approximately $1 million annually. Cutbacks in federal funding for programs such as care for the elderly have placed additional demands on bingo revenues to cover the shortfall. In the foreseeable future the tribal leadership will have to produce revenues over and above those generated by bingo if essential services for the people are to be sustained at current levels.

A major thrust of tribal leadership during the last decade has been in the field of education. The children from the Hollywood, Brighton, and Im-mokalee reservations attend public school beginning in kindergarten, while a Head Start program is available at each location. At the remote Big Cypress Reservation the tribe operates the Ahfachkee Day School for grades K–8, after which the students are bused some thirty-five miles to the nearest public school to complete their education. The Ahfachkee school has been operated under a contract from the federal government since 1982, when the tribe voted to assume operational control. Presently there are several hundred high school graduates, while more than thirty Semi-noles hold college degrees; the school drop-out rate of 30 percent is near the national average. The tribal education department has initiated a number of programs to combat the drop-out problem, including early intervention and participation in a summer high school retention program for Indian youths that is held at Florida State University. In addition, many of the Seminoles who have completed college are now employed by the tribe and provide positive role models. For example, the current tribal attorney overcame sight impairment to become the first Seminole to receive a doctor of jurisprudence degree. The Seminole Tribe has a long tradition of selecting its best-educated members for positions of leadership within tribal government and business enterprises. As early as the 1960s the tribe elected a woman who was one of the first Florida Seminoles to complete a secondary education, Betty Mae Jumper, to a term as chairman of the tribal council (Kersey 1970:27–28, 33).

A substantial body of Florida statutes spells out the relationship of the Seminole and Miccosukee polities to the state. Historically, the Seminoles were first officially recognized in the 1868 Florida constitution, when two seats were set aside for Indians; this provision was subsequently deleted from the constitution of 1885. In 1917 the Florida legislature designated 100,000 acres in Monroe County as a state Indian reservation (Laws of Florida, chap. 7310, 1917). In the 1930s this reservation was relocated to Broward and Palm Beach counties, and the land was later divided between the two tribes, with the Seminoles controlling approximately 28,000 acres. This land will ultimately be added to the federal Big Cypress Reservation under provisions of the Seminole Land Claims Settlement Act of 1987 (101 Stat. 1556).

The sovereignty accorded Seminole reservations places them in a unique status vis à vis local governments. While the Indian communities are generally dependent on the local authorities for utilities, refuse collection, and schooling, they provide their own police and fire protection. Under Florida Statute 285.18 pursuant to P.L. 280, the Seminole police department is authorized to enforce all county ordinances, state laws, and United States codes, as well as tribal ordinances, on the reservations (Florida Statutes, chap. 285.18, 1985). Tribal ordinances, of course, cannot be enforced on non-Indians. Conversely, instances have occurred in which attempts by officials to apply state laws on the reservations have been held to be illegal. Perhaps the most highly publicized of these recent cases was that in which the chairman of the Seminole Tribe, James Billie, was brought to trial for killing a panther on tribal lands. A local court initially declined jurisdiction over actions occurring on an Indian reservation and dismissed the case. However, Billie was subsequently prosecuted in both federal and state courts for violating statutes protecting endangered species. In both instances the Seminole leader was exonerated (*United States v. Billie*, 87-8038-Cr-Paine, 1987; *State of Florida v. Billie*, 2d District Court of Appeals, Case No. 85-1539, 1987).

Many of the 400+ members of the Miccosukee Tribe of Indians are closely related to the Seminoles through ties of culture, language, clan, and kinship—actually, some Indian extended families have had some members enrolled in one tribe and some in the other tribe. Yet, equally significant differences separate the two groups and led to the formation of a second tribe. Today the most striking of these differences is the economic disparity that exists between Seminoles and Miccosukees. The Miccosukees have developed nothing even approximating the integrated business enterprises and highly productive land base of the Seminoles. In fact, until very recently the newer tribe did not even possess a reservation. Since shortly after its founding the Miccosukee Tribe has had headquarters and a residential area located on a strip of land some five miles long and a few hundred feet wide bordering the northern boundary of the Everglades National Park, an area that was leased from the National Park Service. In 1965 the Florida legislature divided the former state Indian reservation and the Miccosukees gained title to approximately 72,000 acres that became eligible for federal trust status.

The Miccosukee Tribe had its origin in a sociopolitical schism among the Seminoles dating back to the 1930s (Sturtevant 1971:118–20). The so-called Trail Indians, those Mikasuki speakers who had camps in the vicinity of the Tamiami Trail, represented the most conservative culture element among the Florida Indian people. They maintained the traditional ways of camp life, dress, language, and religion; at that time none had accepted Christianity while a small number of Seminoles were at least nominally Baptist converts. Furthermore, the Miccosukees claimed a separate cultural origin and identity from the Seminoles, based on differentiations existing in the Creek Confederacy of the 1700s. There appears to be ample historical and linguistic evidence to support this claim in the period prior to the Second Seminole War (1835–42), but such distinctions became blurred in the late nineteenth century. Although one former medicine man of the "Trail Indians" did lead his followers to the reservation in the 1930s and later accepted Christianity, he was an exception. When the Seminole Tribe organized in 1957, there did not appear to be a role for these hard-core traditionalists who were unwilling to move to the federal reservations and enroll as Seminoles (Freeman 1960:249–51). Instead they followed a dynamic young leader named Buffalo Tiger, a long-time spokesman for the council of elders, in seeking their own tribal identity. Initially, the Bureau of Indian Affairs was reluctant to grant recognition to what is considered to be just a dissident group of Seminoles. The group enlisted the assistance of an attorney and adopted some aggressive tactics to gain attention—such as having a delegation visit Cuba to seek recognition from Fidel Castro (Wilson 1960:270–72). In the face of such pressure, and accepting the dramatic cultural differences that existed between the groups, the secretary of the interior relented and granted the Miccosukee Tribe a constitution and a corporate charter in 1961 (U.S. Dept. of the Interior 1965). Like the Seminoles they have an elected council and chairman to make tribal decisions; unlike the Seminoles, the Miccosukees do not have a separate board of directors to conduct business affairs. The Miccosukees also differ from the Seminoles in that they divested themselves of a federal Indian agency as early as 1971 and became one of the first tribes in the nation to contract directly with the BIA for essential services. Unfortunately, the tribal budget is still very heavily dependent upon funding from the Bureau of Indian Affairs.

Although the official enrollment for the Miccosukee Tribe is low, it provides medical and educational services for a number of nonenrolled Mikasuki speakers living in the region who still maintain their independent existence. At the headquarters complex on the Tamiami Trail the tribe maintains a modern K–12 school system, a clinic funded by the Indian Health Service, and various social service units. Because these Indians have opted to remain socially and geographically isolated for so many years, limited educational progress has occurred. Yet, the Miccosukees were among the first tribes to choose to direct their own schools by contracting with the federal authorities (Kersey 1973). For nearly two decades the Miccosukee schools have utilized federal funds in developing a bilingual program to ease the transition to English, but with uncertain results (Lefley 1976). At present, education is a major concern of the tribal leadership. As with the Seminoles, emphasis is placed on early intervention to keep Indian youngsters in school, and a state Indian scholarship fund is available to assist those who are qualified to pursue higher education. Several Miccosukees are enrolled in community colleges and a few have completed college-level programs.

Nothing more clearly reveals the difference in degree of acculturation between the tribes than their political styles and governmental operations. When the Seminoles began their experiment in self-governance over three decades ago, the tribal council was a consensual deliberative body that conducted virtually all of its business in the native languages. Great care was taken to avoid or resolve conflicts in the process of decision making, and great deference was shown to elders even though they might not hold official positions in the government. Indian politicians were closely attuned to the sociocultural values and economic needs of their particular reservations, while candidates for tribal chairman were forced to wage a trilingual campaign without offending any particular constituency. Leadership was perceived as merely echoing the wishes of constituents rather than exercising independent judgment on issues affecting the total tribe.

Today, Seminole government has become enormously complex and far less parochial, reflecting the scope of the tribe's involvement in economic and political matters at the state and national levels. For example, the Seminoles have played a leading role in making United South and Eastern Tribes (USET) a major lobbying and service agency for tribes from Maine to Texas. The tribal council has become a fast-paced decision-making body, with meetings conducted primarily in English to facilitate communication with a predominantly non-Indian professional staff. The leadership is aware that it now represents a multireservation, socially stratified, and economically varied constituency; thus decisions promoting the well-being of the total tribe take precedence over narrow reservation interests.

Political life among the Miccosukees, on the other hand, tends to remain closely tied to family and clan relationships due to their smaller numbers and the close residential proximity of the population. Although social changes are taking place rapidly among the Miccosukees and the material culture has undergone an equally striking transformation, the old value structure still persists and politicians can ignore it only at their peril. As recently as the 1970s a study of Indian politics in Florida maintained that selection of leaders among both the Seminoles and the Miccosukees was still largely determined by clan membership (King 1976). Evidence was cited that ostensibly supported the thesis that most tribal officials selected by the people in democratically contested elections were nevertheless members of clans that had historically provided the political leaders for the old town structure in the Creek Confederacy, from whence came the Florida tribes. While it would be difficult to isolate clan affiliation as the most significant leadership variable among the Seminole, there can be little question that clan membership has a strong bearing on the selection of Miccosukee leaders—although not necessarily in the historically ascribed pattern imputed to it. A Miccosukee political leader appears to have little latitude in deviating from community cultural norms in pursuit of economic advancement for the tribe. To do so is to run the risk of being seen as "too progressive" or as a "big shot" by traditionalists who can rally support across clans to oust incumbents.

The single greatest concern for Miccosukee leaders at this time is the development of an economic structure that will generate income for the tribe and make it less dependent on government funding. Most of the people are presently employed in low-income tourism-related occupations, such as the Miccosukee cultural center and gift shop or at the tribally owned Miccosukee Restaurant on the Tamiami Trail. Others operate airboat rides or operate their own small gift shops nearby. The best-paying jobs are those in the tribal government, but these appointments are limited in number and subject to changing political fortunes. For example, the chairman of the Miccosukee Tribe who had served in that capacity since 1961 and had become a national figure in Indian affairs was recently voted out of office. A period of uncertain political transition is now at hand, although continuity does occur in the council membership. Initially, it appears that the new leaders are committed to the same general long-range goals and policies as their predecessors.

Within the last few years the Miccosukee Tribe has emerged from the shadow of its larger Seminole cousin and has received greater political recognition at both state and federal levels. In 1965 the Florida legislature divided the former state Indian reservation, awarding three-quarters of the acreage to the Miccosukees because they had no federal reservation (Florida Statutes, chap. 285.61, 1985). The tribe is also covered by all the statutes delineating the rights and privileges of Indians in Florida. Recently, because of new administration policies, tribal relations with Washington have become more ambivalent. The Miccosukees still receive virtually all of their operating income from the federal government, which leaves them in a very vulnerable political position. Although they sought to promote a revenue-producing enterprise such as a bingo hall, their reservation site is too distant from an urban population center to attract players; until recently, the federal authorities had denied their request to operate a bingo hall and tax-exempt cigarette sales center on a satellite property in the metropolitan Miami area. On the other hand, Congress enacted the Florida Indian Land Claims Settlement Act of 1982 (96 Stat. 2012). This significant legislation placed in federal trust status the Miccosukee portion of the former state Indian reservation; it also approved a large monetary settlement with the tribe and granted the Miccosukees perpetual lease control of more than 189,000 acres within a huge water impoundment preserve lying west of Miami known as Conservation Area Three. Although under the terms of the federal act both bingo and tax-exempt cigarette sales are effectively prohibited in all of these newly acquired Miccosukee lands, it makes little practical difference. Most of this remote wilderness area remains virtually the same as it was at the turn of the century, and the Indians are committed to preserving it as a hunting, fishing, and recreation area as well as a cultural link with their past. I believe that the old medicine man Ingraham Billie would have been pleased with this outcome.

# 6

# FEDERAL RECOGNITION AND THE POARCH CREEK INDIANS

## J. Anthony Paredes

A brief account of the Poarch Creek Indians written by one of the first missionaries to the group in modern times and published in the *Alabama Historical Quarterly* in 1930 (Macy 1930) is the earliest known scholarly work on these Indians. Frank Speck made a brief visit in 1941 and published the first, albeit very brief, anthropological reports on the Poarch Creeks (Speck 1947, 1949). Afterward, a few other scholars made short visits to the group, located near Atmore, Alabama, but no further works on the Poarch Creeks appeared in the scholarly literature until publication of my paper (Paredes 1974), first presented to the Southern Anthropological Society in 1973. Since 1974 I have published a variety of papers dealing with aspects of Poarch Creek history, culture, and social change (Paredes 1975, 1976a, 1976b, 1979, 1980; Paredes and Joos 1980).[1] The purpose of this essay, however, is to present in broad outline the 1980s outcomes of the further unfolding of changes among the Poarch Creeks foreshadowed in the 1973 paper. Before proceeding, however, a brief overview of earlier Poarch Creek history will serve to orient the reader unfamiliar with previous work.

The Poarch Creeks are descendants of some of the "Friendly Creek Indians" living in southwestern Alabama at the close of the Creek War of 1813–14. Many of these remained in their homeland after the Creek Removal of 1836 (indeed some served as interpreters for the removal), some with allotments dating to the 1815 Treaty of Fort Jackson. Over time some of the mixed-blood Creeks remaining in Alabama, including some descendants of the famous "hostile" Creek War leader William Weatherford, intermarried increasingly with whites, obtained free titles to their treaty allotments, and were assimilated into the general population, some becoming prominent citizens. Conversely, many of the poorer (and perhaps more "Indian-looking") unremoved Creeks—especially McGhees, Rolins, Colberts, and Adamses—married principally among themselves and remained a separate, distinct community locally recognized as "Indian." The principal anchorpoint for the Indian community was a tract of 1815 treaty allotment land near the head of the Perdido River at a locality white settlers of the 1880s and 1890s later would name "Poarch" (the derivation of the placename Poarch is uncertain, though it is known to be an uncommon, non-Indian surname in other areas of Alabama and Georgia). Although the federal government held the Poarch Creek allotment in trust until 1924, the Indians received no federal services. Other lands were secured by some Indian families in the late nineteenth century by filing ordinary homestead applications on lands they had occupied as squatters since as early as 1850 in at least one case.

Until about the time of the turn of the twentieth century the Poarch Creeks enjoyed a considerable degree of isolation and independence. Although troops had passed through the Creek Indians' area during the Civil War (and a number of Poarch Creek ancestors served in the Confederate army), extensive white settlement of this out-of-the-way corner of south Alabama did not begin on a large scale until the late 1880s. It is at about this time, also, that the last fluent speakers of the native language were entering middle age. By the 1970s only a few isolated Muskogean vocabulary items survived among a small number of Poarch Creeks, and only the most elderly—born around 1890—could remember when there were fluent speakers of the native language. A few other, humble elements of native culture (e.g., fish stupefaction, herb medicines, and *sofkee* making) survived considerably longer. By the beginning of the twentieth century the Poarch Creeks were highly acculturated but remained a distinct and growing community, numbering some 150 in the 1900 census. Moreover, as Stevens (1983) has shown, in 1900 the Poarch Creeks as a census cohort were clearly distinct from their non-Indian neighbors on a number of demographic and socioeconomic variables.

The first four decades of the twentieth century were marked by pronounced, bitterly remembered discrimination against the Poarch Creeks. They attended separate, county-run schools explicitly designated as Indian and were denied the public transportation to high schools provided to whites in the Poarch area. Reportedly during this era many Creeks were cheated out of much of their lands and thus were relegated to sharecropping and subjected to indignities of many kinds, including second-class status in the largest, white-controlled church in their vicinity. But this was also the era in which the Poarch Creeks firmly established their own churches—first Free Will Baptist in the 1910s, served by itinerant preachers, then Episcopal and Holiness congregations in the 1920s and 1930s, served with regular clergy. The Episcopal missionaries were very active in seeking educational and medical improvements for the Poarch Creeks as well as ministering to the spiritual needs, as they say, of the local Indians.

Through the institution of Indian churches and, to a lesser extent, the "Indian schools" came some formalization of leadership roles among the Poarch Creeks. Until this time, Poarch Creeks leadership was informal, relying upon the character and forcefulness of a few notable individuals in each generation.

By the end of World War II, a number of the Poarch Creeks had become keenly aware of their deprived condition while at the same time realizing new aspirations through military service, work outside the area, and the earlier missionary influences. The stage was set for revolutionary change in the Creek Indian community of southwestern Alabama that by then had a population nearing 400.

My 1973 paper described developments in the Poarch Creek community since World War II as conforming to Anthony F. C. Wallace's model (1961) of revitalization movements. By 1973 the Poarch Creeks had just completed a phase of such a movement marked by the establishment of equal educational opportunity for their children, successful completion of lengthy land claims litigation against the United States government, and development of an annual powwow on Thanksgiving Day. All of these things had been done through volunteer political activism—including a school boycott, direct confrontation, and lawsuits—financially supported largely by small donations from the local community. Dominating the course of events from the late 1940s to 1970 was the charismatic leadership of one man, Calvin W. McGhee, who was supported by a variety of close associates.

By the time I began field research on the Creeks in 1971, a year after McGhee's death, leadership had been assumed by a close-knit group of young men and women, including some of the Poarch Creeks' first high school graduates, who had been recently added to "the council." A formal council had first been established in 1950, with McGhee as its chairman, to press the land claims against the federal government. By 1973 the new cadre of younger leaders, though still serving on a volunteer basis without any significant corporate assets (or even a corporate address), were enthusiastically pursuing a variety of new avenues of community development. By 1986 their efforts were to complete a dramatic, visible cultural transformation of the people from their humble beginnings as an isolated, infor-

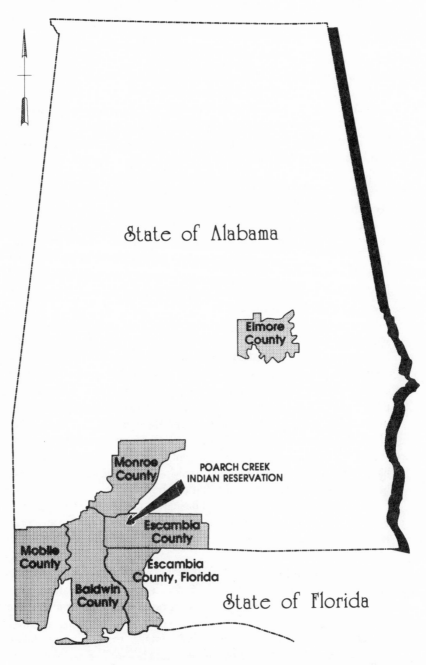

State of Alabama

Elmore County

Monroe County

POARCH CREEK INDIAN RESERVATION

Escambia County

Mobile County

Escambia County, Florida

Baldwin County

State of Florida

Gulf of Mexico

"The Poarch Indian Sphere of Influence" (taken from the back cover of a meeting folder by permission of the Poarch Band of Creeks). Counties indicated are those in which the band has landholdings and/or are included in the "tribal services area," that is, counties in which band members may reside and be eligible for such services as medical care from the U.S. Indian Health Service.

mally organized rural community of mixed-blood Friendly Creek Indian descendants in south Alabama to their present status as a formally constituted, federally recognized Indian tribe: the Poarch Band of Creek Indians. The band has approximately 1,850 enrolled members and is governed by a nine-member tribal council elected under the terms of a constitution adopted in 1985 pursuant to provisions of the national Indian Reorganization Act of 1934. Today the tribal administration provides band members services and opportunities that were at best only dimly perceived by even the most optimistic community leaders in the early 1970s.

In the published version of my 1973 paper (Paredes 1974:76) I observed that "The Indian movement clearly has entered a very complex, fast-paced, and vibrant era, and it is difficult to predict the specific developments of the months and years ahead." Now, with the benefit of hindsight it is possible to describe those developments and their relationship to the present conditions of the band.

Over the years many social actors have participated in developments within the Poarch Band of Creek Indians. Certain individuals, however, have distinguished themselves by their public visibility and their tenacious commitment to the cause. Especially noteworthy in this regard are the current tribal chairman, Eddie Tullis, and Buford Rolin, who has served the band in a variety of capacities. Many others have provided continuity or served at critical junctures and in specific activities in the flow of complicated events over the past twenty years. Along the way organizational shifts, false starts, political realignments, personnel changes, and schisms have occurred in the process of tribal institutionalization, a process that has sometimes moved at a pace that can be described as dizzying, as much for myself as for the participants. I hasten to add that at some points I have been myself as much participant as observer, especially in my role as a researcher-consultant in the development of the band's petition for federal recognition.

Fully unraveling in an analytical manner the details of the process of Poarch Creek tribal formalization and cultural transformation is beyond the scope of this chapter and must await book-length treatment. Presented here is a historical overview, though not necessarily always in chronological order, indicating some of the major turning points in Poarch Creek developments during the fifteen years before 1987. For convenience these changes are treated under three categories labeled "economic," "political," and—for lack of a better term—"public relations," even while recognizing that the actual events are more often than not intertwined among these analytical categories in exceedingly complicated ways. In all three areas—economic, political, and public relations—the Poarch Band has operated on at least three levels of administrative structure: local, state, and national.

## Public Relations

The most visible expression of the distinctiveness of the Poarch Creek Indian community over the years has been its annual Thanksgiving Homecoming Powwow initiated in 1970. Indeed, the powwow serves as a convenient barometer of the changes that have occurred in the band. During the early 1970s the powwow was the principal organized activity of the band and practically its only source of revenues. During those years, and afterward, one of the most dedicated leaders of this and related "Indian doings" was Calvin McGhee's son, Houston, along with other close kinsmen and associates, especially Evelyn McGhee Davidson Akins and Dewey and Olivette McGhee. Houston served as "chief" (technically, chairman of the board of directors) from his father's death in 1970 until 1977. By the latter year dealings with state and federal agencies were demanding ever more formalized and bureaucratic forms of tribal operation rather than the kind of leisurely, personalized, contingency-based local-level mobilization of effort that was Houston's forte. The stress of these changes led to Houston's resignation; he was succeeded briefly by Kent McGhee, then in 1978 by Eddie Tullis. The powwow now is itself a highly structured event with a routinized allocation of specific responsibilities among tribal councilmembers and an elaborate schedule of performances, contests, and presentations.

The powwow has grown from an event attended by a few hundred locals Indians, visiting relatives, and a few others to an award-winning attraction drawing thousands of visitors, being named by the Southeastern Tourism Society in 1985 as one of the "Top Twenty Events in the Southeast." At early powwows the "Indian" activities consisted almost solely of local, self-taught "fancy dancers" and an Indian princess contest, with only an occasional visitor from another tribe. Over the years the tribal council has actively sought and financed the participation of Indians from other tribes. These other Indians have included craftsmen, dancers, and guest speakers from the Florida Seminoles, the Mississippi Choctaw, the North Carolina Cherokee and Lumbee, the Chitimacha of Louisiana, the Oklahoma Creeks, the Wisconsin Chippewa, and even San Juan Pueblo in New Mexico as well as representatives of such intertribal organizations as the National Congress of American Indians. In a sense, the Poarch Creeks have imported much of the local color that bolsters their public image as Indian. All of these events have, in recent years, been avidly reported by local and regional news media. Since the early 1980s Dale Gehman, the Poarch Creek owner of a local radio station, has broadcast continuously from the grounds on powwow day.

The powwow grounds themselves, located behind the former Poarch schoolhouse that is now a tribal administration building, have been expanded and improved since the inception of the annual powwow by fencing, erecting buildings, and constructing a large earthen platform—the newest Indian mound in the South, as it were. All of these additions have been made by the tribal council, initially with volunteer labor but increasingly with resources from a variety of agencies and organizations. Despite the continuing role of the tribal council in organizing and supporting the powwow, over the years the council has relinquished direct control of more and more food concessions. Nowadays, individual tribal members and local Indian churches and other tribal organizations have taken over various powwow food sales, a change that appears to have had beneficial effects on the solidarity of the community and the relationships between the tribal council and its constituents. Similarly, the numbers and types of outside crafts concessionaires, who rent booths from the council, have greatly expanded over the years. Despite changes in fiscal operation, the powwow remained until federal recognition virtually the only source of unrestricted revenues for tribal council activities.

For the very first powwow, in 1970, the Poarch Creeks' honored guest was the county circuit judge, Hugh Rozelle, who as a young attorney had helped them in a suit against the local school board in 1947. The tribal council continues to be very attentive to inviting representatives of city, county, state, and federal government to attend and sit on the dais for public introduction at the powwow. Overall, those on the dais each year have represented ever-widening circles of political interests of tribal leaders. Since 1978, however, the lineup of honored guests and, especially, principal speakers has been increasingly dominated numerically by representatives of other Indian tribes and national organizations, including such notables as Ladonna Harris and Billy Mills. The most noticeable exception in the trend toward Indians as principal speakers for the powwow was in 1983 when Congressman Jack Edwards announced the positive findings of the Bureau of Indian Affairs on the Poarch petition for federal recognition. Balancing this national linkage in 1983 was a previously arranged congratulatory telephone call from Governor George Wallace that was broadcast over the powwow grounds.

The powwow is not the only medium for Poarch public relations. Since about 1976, an annual late winter, tribal council banquet, though more modest in scale and serving primarily as a vehicle for maintaining internal esprit de corps, likewise provides a setting for acknowledging "friends of the Creeks," especially at the local level. Similarly, on an even more private scale, the tribal council has sponsored in recent years a memorial service for Calvin McGhee that, according to some, is primarily for the benefit of "members of the family," though it should be noted that McGhee regarded his people as "all of one family" (Paredes 1980:184–85).

The Poarch leadership has furthered a positive image of their group through a variety of channels. At the local and regional level, especially in the early to mid-1970s, younger Creek leaders were quick to accept invitations for the "dance team" to perform at various functions in nearby cities and to participate in the powwows of Indian descendant organizations in the region as far away as Baton Rouge, Louisiana. In a similar vein, through visits to the Mississippi Choctaws, the Oklahoma Creeks, and the Florida Seminoles; by participation in national Indian organizations, such as the National Congress of American Indians (NCAI); and, in the recent past, hosting meetings and workshops of regional Indian organizations and agencies, a select group of leaders such as Tullis, Rolin, John Arthur McGhee, Frank Flournoy, and Eugene Madison have given high corporate visibility to that peculiar little group of Indians down in Alabama that had for so long been identified so strongly with a single, colorful character: Calvin McGhee.

Beyond these interpersonal channels of public relations the Poarch Creeks have employed a variety of standard advertising devices, including ever more professional-looking folders, brochures, and letterheads. At one point in the late 1970s, with funds from a Comprehensive Employment and Training Act of 1973 (CETA) grant, the band operated a media center complete with television equipment, but the project was discontinued for financial and personnel reasons and the equipment transferred to the Mississippi Band of Choctaws. (The Creeks' media campaign took even me by surprise one day in late 1985 when I was driving home from work in Tallahassee, more than 200 miles away, and my eye was caught by a flashy but very slick roadside billboard advertising the Poarch Creek Indian Bingo Palace, but I am getting ahead of the story.) Not to be overlooked either is the extent to which the present writer's scholarly works and other writings have served to publicize the Poarch Creeks (cf. Paredes 1976b).

## Political

As early as 1960 Calvin McGhee was politically extending his efforts well beyond building merely local organizations of Indian descendants for pressing the land claims and other local causes. He curried the favor of state and national politicians and willingly posed in Plains-style Indian costume for news photographers. Calvin McGhee participated in such intertribal meetings as the 1961 Chicago Indian Conference (cf. Lurie 1976); later, McGhee was part of the subsequent intertribal leaders delegation that called upon John F. Kennedy at the White House in 1962. These activities served McGhee and his Creeks well. Even in the 1980s the band

*Left:* Christy Godwin O'Barr, Poarch Creek Indian Princess 1987, sings at 1987 Thanksgiving powwow (see text); her costume is of a type, partially inspired by traditional Mississippi Choctaw dress, that was adopted by the Creeks during the 1970s and 1980s, replacing the fringed, Hollywood-inspired Poarch creations of the 1960s and early 1970s. Note contrast with the photograph on the opposite page, below, in treatment of shade over the dais. In the foreground above are spectators at edge of powwow mound. (Photo: Elizabeth D. Purdum). *Below:* Poarch Creek Indian domestic scene, summer 1972. Girlie Rolin (left), now deceased, and Florence Tullis shell peas while Girlie's husband Tracey Rolin looks on; Florence, now deceased, is the mother of the tribal chairman, Eddie Tullis, and the Rolins are parents of Buford Rolin. (Photo: J. Anthony Paredes)

*Right:* Council Chamber in Poarch Creek Indian Tribal Center. (Photo: Michael Duncan, courtesy Poarch Band of Creek Indians and Michael Duncan). *Below:* U.S. Congressman Jack Edwards announcing BIA's positive recommendation on Poarch Creeks' petition for federal recognition, Thanksgiving powwow 1983. On the dais in the foreground are, left to right (standing) Buford Rolin, Eddie Tullis, Edwards, Escambia County (Alabama) Probate Judge Martha Kirkland, Mayor of Atmore Patricia McKenzie, and 1983 Poarch Creek Princess Edith Marie Tullis. In the background (to the left of Edwards) is the author. (Photo: Charles J. Stevens)

*Above:* Dedication of the Poarch Creek tribal center, 3 April 1987. Oklahoma Creek Sam Proctor (at rostrum) presides over traditional Creek blessing portion of the ceremony. (Photo: Elizabeth D. Purdum). *Below:* Poarch Creek Indian Bingo Palace, 1984. Note tribal logo to left of word "Creek." (Photo: Sara Paredes Dominguez)

still benefited from the goodwill that McGhee created among non-Indian politicians; such individuals continued to mention respectfully McGhee's name in public addresses to the Creeks. Moreover, it was principally Calvin McGhee who guided the early stages in the development of what was to become the Poarch tribal council, even though oftentimes during the latter years of McGhee's leadership, according to oral history, for all intents and purposes tribal government *was* Calvin McGhee.

Soon after McGhee's death the Poarch Creeks formally organized under the laws of Alabama as a nonprofit corporation, The Creek Nation East of the Mississippi, with a board of directors, popularly referred to as "the council." Regular popular elections of councillors, however, were not instituted until 1976. Since that time the council and the general membership of the band at large have gone through at least two formal reorganizations, the most recent in June 1985, in connection with establishing a constitution acceptable to the Bureau of Indian Affairs. In retrospect, during the post–Calvin McGhee era, though not always fully cognizant of where they were headed, the Poarch Creeks and their council moved inexorably toward establishment of the government that is the present Tribal Council of the Poarch Band of Creeks.

The historical hinge in these developments was an event that, as is so often the case, was seemingly trivial at the time. As a matter of personal tastes, Eddie Tullis became an active member of the Republican party as a young man. By his own account it was his election to office in the local Young Republicans organization that led fortuitously to Tullis meeting, in 1968, a key individual through whom the Poarch Creeks were invited to participate in the formation of the Coalition of Eastern Native Americans (CENA) at a Boston meeting in 1971. Though now defunct, CENA was the umbrella organization for the first CETA program to the Poarch Creeks in 1974.

By 1975 the Poarch council (not yet the "tribal council") was its own "prime sponsor" for CETA programs that continue to the present, though now known as JTPA (Job Training Partnerhsip Act). With CETA funds, the Poarch Creeks for the first time had the money and incentive to employ paid administrators. One of the first hired, Glenda Rackard Carlton (a band member), is still a tribal employee, now in the position of credit and finance director. Participation in these and later federally funded programs was an important part of the process by which Poarch Creek leaders were spiraled upward through ever-widening circles of state and federal bureaucracy. Also, participation in such programs had a feedback effect on the local Poarch organization in that the council began fine tuning tribal organization to meet governmental guidelines for administering programs; regular, secret-ballot elections of council members by tribal voters was one of these adjustments. Following federal recognition in 1984 and with the adoption of a new constitution, elections are now held in June rather than at the Thanksgiving powwow as previously done.

Of equal importance with the internal organizational effects of participation in federally sponsored programs was the network connections to the larger world of "Indian politics" provided the Poarch Creeks by their participation in these programs and in such organizations as CENA. In short, it was through such connections that the Poarch Creeks initiated an aborted bid for federal recognition in 1975 (cf. Anderson 1978); became, in 1979, members of the National Congress of American Indians, of which Tullis has served as southeastern vice-president and first vice-president and Rolin has served as treasurer; and, with the assistance of the Native American Rights Fund, petitioned for and ultimately achieved in 1984 federal recognition as an Indian tribe under the provisions of 1978 federal regulations (25 CFR 54, now designated 25 CFR 83). As the Poarch Creeks have become well established in the national arena of Indian affairs, they have not neglected their longer-standing ties to local and state politics and involvement in regional Indian activities.

From the outset of their quest for legitimization as a federal Indian tribe the Poarch Creeks have relied upon the cooperation of local and state officials. Through the local school superintendent, the Poarch leadership began as early as 1973 to have the old schoolhouse site and its building, now extensively remodeled, transferred to federal trust should recognition come. Such linkages remain an important part of Poarch successes. For example, the tribal chairman has been careful to maintain good relations with local law enforcement (the county sheriff, an amateur vocalist, sang the national anthem in the opening ceremonies of some recent powwows). The Creeks still host political rallies for candidates for city, county, and state offices, as in Calvin McGhee's day; the city council of Atmore joined with the band to host a training workshop for southeastern Indian CETA workers in 1982. The band was successful in obtaining the signatures of the entire Alabama congressional delegation on a letter of support for the Poarch petition for federal recognition. Strong support for the Poarch Creeks was engendered among the Florida Seminoles and Miccosukees through Buford Rolin's several years of service, while living in Pensacola, Florida, as a member of the Florida Governor's Council on Indian Affairs.

In light of their eventual federal recognition, the Poarch leaders appear in retrospect to have been unnecessarily preoccupied with the machinations of various Indian descendant organizations in Alabama, Georgia, and Florida, especially those claiming a Creek identity. These organizations typically consist of assimiliated, geographically dispersed "Indian descendants" (the Mowa Choctaw, however, whatever question there might be about their specific tribal claims, are in contrast a distinct and territorially concentrated ethnic group). Although in some cases not even Indian ancestry, much less continuous community existence, can be verified, a number of these organizations have petitioned for and been denied federal recognition as an Indian tribe (cf. Roth, Chap. 9 this volume; Quinn 1987, 1990; Walker 1977). These organizations were initially stimulated in large part by Calvin McGhee's popularization of Indianness and encouraged by McGhee to a certain extent. In the 1970s and 1980s, however, these groups were seen by Poarch leaders as potential threats to their own Indian movement if not appeased and incorporated into Poarch activities. This aspect of Poarch political process has emerged in its most contentious form in the events surrounding the formation, dissolution, and reformation of various Alabama Indian affairs commissions since 1975.

The first Alabama commission was appointed through state government at the instigation of self-proclaimed Indian descendants from other parts of the state, and elsewhere, without the participation of the Poarch people. But through their political allies at the state level the Poarch Creeks reformed and gained control of the commission and used it to their advantage in their efforts at federal recognition (including funding for contracting with me to prepare a supplement to their petition). Then, the Poarch Creeks lost control and ultimately the commission itself in 1983. A new commission was established by the state legislature in 1984. In this new commission the Poarch Band had no superior status, despite its impending federal recognition, among the other five (and then six) Indian organizations specified as representatives on the commission. The Poarch Creeks still participate in the commission to keep abreast of activities but are reluctant to lend their credibility as a federal Indian tribe to activities of the various state-recognized Creek, Cherokee, and Choctaw groups now intensively involved in the commission. More important now for the Poarch Creeks is their membership in the United South and Eastern Tribes (USET). Besides, the Creeks must focus their attention on the much greater political and economic stakes that have mushroomed since having become federally acknowledged.

## Economic

In my 1973 paper on the Poarch Creeks (Paredes 1974:77) I suggested that "blunt economic motivations for asserting Indian identity should be given more serious consideration. Given the special governmental status of reservation Indians and romantic thirst of the American public for things Indian, an identity as Indian ultimately may be the most important economic asset held by poorer, smaller Indian communities." Subsequent events at Poarch have further confirmed the correctness of that view.

Since the 1960s the Poarch Creeks have been peripheral beneficiaries of various state and federal agencies and programs to serve the needs of poor people, such as the Head Start program. Even in these kinds of programs, which were not "Indian programs" per se, the Poarch people had some measure of control through membership on the local Community Action Project board, and some of these activities were conducted within the Poarch community. Involvement in these programs, however, was because the Poarch Creeks were poor (some abjectly so) not because they were Indians. Similar state-federal programs have benefited the Poarch community increasingly over the years. Such programs have included dental services, various state-sponsored health programs, legal aid, agricultural extension, senior citizens communal meals programs, and a federal Title IV Indian education program—paradoxically, one of the smallest such programs in the state even though the Poarch people are the only group in Alabama officially recognized as Indian by the United States (but that— the larger programs—is another story involving what some Indian leaders see as outright fraud). The tribal council has been instrumental in establishing these programs in the community but most of these programs still have income-based eligibility criteria and technically are not exclusively for Indians. Nonetheless, council members take pride in seeing themselves as having provided leadership and inspiration to other Indian groups, including federally recognized tribes, for seizing opportunities offered by various programs outside the usual Indian channels. Indeed, the Poarch Creeks have manifested an entrepreneurial spirit and quickness to respond to new programs, despite languishing for so long in their uncertain legal status as Indians, that evokes the spirit of Indian Agent Benjamin Hawkins's 1816 commentary on some of the Poarch Creeks' mixed-blood ancestors living along the lower Alabama River: "They embraced the plan of civilization first and by their conduct merited the attention of the Agent for Indian Affairs" (Grant 1980:768).

The first big break on the economic front for the Poarch Creeks came with their CETA programs and, soon afterward, grants from the U.S. Department of Health and Human Services' Administration for Native Americans. These programs and others, along with material support from private organizations, enabled the Poarch Creeks to develop a paid support staff, from executive directors to custodians; experiment with potential economic development ventures, such as a quilting and sewing enterprise (including distinctive patchwork and ribbon-appliqué items); and build an infrastructure of personnel, physical facilities, record-keeping systems, and management procedures that prepared them for what was to come. Likewise, the tribal council was gaining more and more experience in the complexities of tribal administration. And, through their dealings with the Bureau of Indian Affairs in monitoring the progress of their petition for recognition and in their dealings with other tribal leaders through participation in various organizations (e.g. the National Congress of American Indians and federal task forces),[2] the Poarch leaders were gaining valuable knowledge of events in "Indian country." When federal recognition came they were ready.

## The Poarch Band as Federal Indians

Following the required waiting period after the 1983 positive recommendation of findings, in August 1984 the Poarch Band of Creeks was officially recognized as an Indian tribe with a "government-to-government" relationship to the United States of America. By April of the following year the several parcels of land totaling 229.51 acres acquired by the Creeks through purchase and donation were taken into trust and declared a reservation. In the meantime the Poarch Creeks had already negotiated a very favorable contract with a private firm in Texas (later the Texas firm sold the contract to a company based in England) for financing, building, and managing a Creek bingo hall. Within days after the site officially became a reservation, the 1,700-seat Poarch Creek Bingo Palace was opened for business and busloads of avid players from near and far were literally banging on the doors during the dedication ceremony to get inside and try for the big money in the newest high-stakes Indian bingo parlor. The bingo operation proved to be quite lucrative and became the cornerstone for other economic ventures of the tribe. (As of June 1990 the Poarch Band of Creeks had become full owners of the Creek Bingo Palace.)

While waiting for the declaration of reservation status and, thus, the manifestation of sovereignty that empowers tribes to run high-stakes bingo operations, the tribal council was busily gearing up. Through training workshops, needs assessments, constitutional revisions, and a variety of other activities, the band leaders were preparing to assume their full responsibilities as a government. Formerly established programs such as CETA and the senior citizens programs continued, but in addition now there was a sudden influx of "start-up funds" from the Bureau of Indian Affairs and Indian Health Service to get tribal operations fully underway (but, it should be added, with the tribal chairman still at his old job at a nearby chemical plant to put in the last few years he needs for retirement). That process is still continuing. It is worth noting that by the grand opening of the Poarch Creek Bingo Palace in April 1985 two members of the band already had been selected and trained as police officers, and on the very day of the bingo palace dedication the men were sworn in as deputies in the local county sheriff's department. Since then the band has established its own six-person police department plus a tribal court system and fire department.

By March 1986 the Poarch Creeks were well on their way to a firm base of operation. Federal funding included approximately $550,000 from the Bureau of Indian Affairs for adult education, social services, credit and finance, fire protection, law enforcement, and community services; $250,000 from Housing and Urban Development to begin family and senior citizens housing projects and a new 10,500-square-foot tribal center; and $725,000 from the Indian Health Service to operate a clinic, including on its staff a nurse-practitioner, and to contract physicians' services; plus continuing previously established "non-Indian money" federal- and state-supported programs, along with a couple of new ones, for a total budget—including powwow proceeds and even some corporately held funds from the original land claim judgment—of nearly $2,000,000. But this amount did not include proceeds from tribal enterprises. By 1989 the Poarch Creeks had a tribal budget including receipts from tribal enterprises totaling nearly $8,000,000.

In November 1985 the tribe secured a federally guaranteed loan from a local bank and purchased a Best Western motel on the nearby interstate highway. The motel is an independent enterprise not on federal trust lands that the tribe undertook in part to demonstrate their entrepreneurial capabilities and to expand bases for economic independence away from federal sources of support. With a payroll of approximately 260 people, not all of them Indians, by 1986 the Poarch Band of Creeks had become the fifth largest employer in Escambia County, Alabama. By 1989 the band had 350 employees; only fourteen years earlier the band had hired, with CETA funds, its very first employee, Linda Gail Rolin. The band's membership plaque from the Atmore Chamber of Commerce is prominently displayed in the tribal office.

By 1986 ground had been broken for the housing projects and the new tribal center, and modernization of office equipment was proceeding apace. (The sight of a computer terminal on every desk and the man from Wang scurrying about training the tribal staff observed on a field visit in 1986 were almost just too much reverse culture shock for me to handle.) The tribal center was completed at a cost of $1 million and was dedicated in April 1987. In 1988 the band added a kitchen-equipped senior citizens' center at the outer edge of the powwow grounds opposite the rear of the "old schoolhouse." Eighty housing units—family houses and duplex apartments—had been completed by 1989. And by fall 1989 the band had completed a modern fire station housing a spiffy new fire truck painted in the "official" green and white colors of the band. Finally, in late 1989 many tribal services were being moved to a new 14,000-square-foot tribal annex built immediately behind the new tribal center; financing of the annex was in significant part derived from a lease to the Indian Health Service of office space for some of its personnel with region-wide duties. At the same time the band's computer system was greatly expanded and upgraded, completely replacing the modest system first installed just three years earlier. (As if all this high-tech sophistication were not jarring enough, the band's stationery letterhead was amended in 1989 to include their FAX number!)

Happily, there are a few touches of the "old ways" that are still around to warm the romanticist anthropologist's heart. Impromptu Saturday afternoon cookouts, quiet socializing with a beer and plaintive country music on a portable radio deep in the woods, and "just riding around" continue for some, even though some formerly important livelihoods such as "paperwooding" are virtually gone. And there is still "that old-time religion": in 1986 there were some indications of declining church attendance in some denominations, but others seemed to be enjoying a new vigor. Poarch Creek Gail Thrower, employed by the band as librarian-archivist-genealogist, has received summer grants from the Alabama Arts Council to teach other tribespeople some of the local folk crafts, such as pine-straw baskets. To further the development of native arts and crafts and a museum, in 1988 the Poarch Band established by tribal ordinance a Creek Indian Arts Council (I serve on the advisory board of the council) with its own endowment fund.

Some of the youths of the community seem to have a new seriousness of purpose in making authentic war dance costumes and learning powwow dancing. In 1986 their mentors were a young Comanche Indian recently (and, it turns out, only briefly) employed by the tribe and a member of the Brotherton Band of Wisconsin who has resided in the area for many years and had worked closely with former Poarch councilman Billy Smith and the local fancy dance team in the past. In 1986 a detribalized version of the sweat bath was even added to the dance team's Saturday practice sessions, under the direction of the Comanche instructor. (Following the 1985 powwow a Native American Church service was conducted by a visiting Nebraska Winnebago in a tipi on the powwow grounds.) In 1987 a traditionalist Creek from Oklahoma, Sam Proctor, was hired by the Alabama Creeks for a few weeks initially to teach native heritage and Muskogee language classes, then he worked for several months at Poarch as project coordinator for the band's housing authority. (Even more recently a few people from Poarch have begun to participate in Creek religious ceremonies in Oklahoma, and some of them reportedly are working toward reestablishing in Alabama a traditional "square ground" with a properly sanctified "fire." Principal among the mentors of this movement are the Brotherton Indian mentioned earlier, Gordon Fay, and a married-in Oklahoma Creek, Larry Haikey, who first came to Poarch as a graduate student under my direction in 1977. This group has come into open, though not too volatile, conflict with tribal government over plans for a museum and tourist attraction at Wetumpka, in Elmore County, Alabama, near Montgomery, on a tract of tribally owned land situated near an important historic Creek Indian site of the late eighteenth and early nineteenth centuries.)

The tribal council continues to support powwow dance team activities, and the chairman looks forward to developing a craft enterprise. But, for the moment, staying on top of developments in governmental operations and medical and social services and firmly establishing business enterprises that promise lucrative returns and permanent jobs dominate the thoughts of tribal leaders and, perhaps, frighten them a little. (By 1989 the band owned or had interests in at least seven other enterprises besides the still-thriving bingo operation.) In a related vein, mention must be made of the strong, continuing interest by tribal leaders and the membership at large in furthering higher education among the band's young people. By 1989, fund raising for the band's scholarship fund was especially prominent, and since the mid-1970s a number of band youngsters have attended area junior colleges and state universities; among these, for instance, was the Poarch Senior Princess of 1987, Christy O'Barr who was also the band's first entrant into the national Miss NCAI contest (offering in the contest's talent competition her solo rendition of "In the Sweet Bye and Bye" sung in both English and Muskogee, the latter having been learned from the Oklahoma Creek teacher in cultural awareness classes a few months earlier).

This has all been rather heady stuff for tribal leaders who strived so long to achieve what they have. But there are a few sour notes: accusations of favoritism in hirings and providing services (some of that has been around since well before federal recognition), concern for a clock-watching mentality among some staff workers, complaints and misunderstanding by tribal members about limitations on social and medical services offered, concern about out-marriage and blood quanta requirements, litigation with the bingo backers (decided in the Creeks' favor), impatience that things are not happening fast enough, and uncertainty about how long new-found opportunities will last. Among some it was rumored in 1986 that a callous cynicism exists among tribal leaders expressed as, for instance, "the Poarch Band of Creeks is just a business" or "if it doesn't make money they're not interested in it—I'm not criticizing, that's just the way it is now." In recent years tribal elections have become more tense and open seats more vigorously contested—including some surprising upsets—as tribal office becomes more important with the new-found successes of the band.

It does appear to be the case that much of the leadership of the band is currently caught up in a spirit of adventuresome entrepreneurship, which is, nonetheless, not without its mental stresses for key tribal leaders. It is equally true, however, that the fact of federal recognition brought with it a broad-based sense of satisfying closure to processes of community transformation and ethnic intensification that began more than forty years earlier. In addition to the political and economic opportunities that federal recognition brought, the action gave official reaffirmation to the Poarch people's long-standing awareness of their Indian identity, a reaffirmation of a very positive sort that stands in stark contrast to the earlier stigma that had been attached locally to being "one of them Indians." At the 1983 ceremonies when Congressman Edwards announced the BIA's positive recommendation on the Poarch petition, all available current and former council members who could be recalled were brought to the powwow mound and presented to the audience. As they were leaving the mound I overheard one elderly former councilman, Kinsey McGhee, say, with a touch of irony, "Now we're really Indians."

# 7

# CHOCTAW SELF-DETERMINATION IN THE 1980s

## *John H. Peterson, Jr.*

T he Mississippi Choctaws entered the twentieth century at perhaps the lowest ebb they had experienced since the removal period some seventy years previously (Peterson 1979).[1] Following the major removal efforts in the 1830s, the remaining Choctaws in Mississippi experienced continued pressure to give up their lands and move west. Southern politicians such as Jefferson Davis continued to press for the removal of the remaining Choctaws, and several small removal efforts were made as late as the 1850s. From this point, the Choctaws slipped into obscurity, living as isolated squatters on the unoccupied marginal land generally owned by out-of-state investors (Peterson 1971).

Following the end of the Civil War, the expansion of the rural white population, and the extension of the sharecropping system, the Choctaws gradually reemerge into the historical record. At this time the Choctaws were living in isolated farming communities, living as sharecroppers on the land they had previously farmed as squatters. Not only was the land they occupied generally marginal in soil type, but also the locations tended to be isolated from major travel by unbridged rivers and swamps. In general, these locations resemble those described for the scattered Indian settlements in the coastal plains of other southern states.

By the 1880s the rural church was emerging as an important institution in the Choctaw communities (Langford 1986; Farr 1948). Rural churches were soon followed by rural schools housed in the churches. By the 1890s schools were established in most Choctaw communities (Halbert 1894).

As rural communities centered around their own churches and schools, the Choctaws resembled white and black rural communities of the time, although remaining distinctively Choctaw in language and social customs such as playing of stickball, retaining Choctaw social dances, wearing distinctive clothing, and cooking special foods, especially homemade hominy.

This pattern was severely disrupted as a by-product of the transformation of Oklahoma from Indian territory into a state during the early 1900s. The Dawes commission, responsible for adjudicating Indian claims, investigated the case of the Mississippi Choctaws. The commission decided that because many of the Choctaws remaining in Mississippi had never received land promised under the Treaty of Dancing Rabbit Creek in 1830, any Mississippi Choctaws who removed to Oklahoma by a stated date could participate in the allocation of land in Oklahoma on the same basis as the Oklahoma Choctaws. White lawyers put forth a massive effort to assist Choctaws in removing to Oklahoma in exchange for a land claim. The result was a complete disruption of the Mississippi Choctaw communities. Entire communities sold their churches and removed west as a group. Many of these Choctaws either did not receive or failed to be able to retain the lands they received and many gradually returned to Mississippi. But the Choctaw school system had been discontinued and many of their churches disbanded. The final blow was the influenza epidemic of 1917 that had particularly disastrous impact on the poorly housed and clothed Choctaws.

In some ways the disasters of the early twentieth century had beneficial results. The publicity surrounding the hearings of the Dawes commission and the death toll of the influenza epidemic brought the condition of the Mississippi Choctaws to the attention of political leaders in Mississippi and in Washington. As a result, congressional hearings were held in Union, Mississippi, that resulted in the establishment of the Choctaw Agency in 1918 (Kidwell 1986).

As important as was federal recognition of the Mississippi Choctaws as Indians, the programs of the Choctaw Agency only slowly improved the condition of the Choctaw people. An Indian hospital was built in Philadelphia, Mississippi, near the agency headquarters in 1926 and the health conditions of the Choctaws began to gradually improve. The agency began a program of school construction in the scattered Choctaw communities, with the school to serve the educational needs of the Choctaw children and also as a basis for outreach programs in farming assistance and home economics. But the agency operated on a small annual appropriation, and it was almost fifteen years after its establishment before elementary schools were established in the six major Choctaw communities of east-central Mississippi.

The agency program did not envision the establishment of a reservation. Rather, efforts were made to concentrate the Choctaw population in the areas surrounding the schools by purchasing small farm plots from white farmers in the areas where the Choctaws were already clustered as share-croppers. In the aftermath of World War I, cotton prices fell below the cost of producing a crop and the boll weevil made the possibility of making a living through cotton farming almost impossible. As a result the agency was gradually forced to acknowledge the failure of the farm credit pro-gram as individual Indian farmers forfeited on their loans. The agency was left with title to these farm lands, which, almost by default, were consoli-dated into a reservation. Many of the Choctaws continued as subsistence farmers on land that now made up the reservation. Larger number of Choctaws continued as sharecroppers on the white-owned farms sur-rounding the reservation lands.

The Indian Reorganization Act of 1934 had little initial impact on the Choctaws. A tribal constitution was not adopted until 1945. Fifteen years later, the Tribal Council of the Mississippi Band of Choctaw Indians still met in the kitchen of the home economics department of the agency, and the superintendent's secretary took the minutes of the meeting. During this time the tribal council only served as an advisory board to the agency superintendent. It had no power or control over reservation affairs.

In 1968, fifty years after the establishment of the Choctaw Agency, no marked changes in the living conditions of the Choctaw people had oc-curred (Peterson 1970). Slightly over half of the population lived on trust land, and the median years of school completed by Choctaw heads of household was three. Over a third of the heads of household were unem-ployed and approximately a third worked only as temporary farm la-borers. The increasing mechanization of agriculture in Mississippi in the 1950s and 1960s had resulted in a sharp decrease in the need for agri-cultural labor, and the Choctaws faced the alternatives of unemployment, welfare, or migration to other areas.

Increasing numbers of Mississippi Choctaws were beginning to leave Mississippi to escape the dual oppressors of a pervasive racism and the absence of any alternative to the vanishing sharecropping system. Because a high school for the Mississippi Choctaws was not established until 1964, most Choctaws were educationally ill equipped to compete for non-agricultural jobs. Further, because Choctaw is spoken in most Choctaw homes, many Choctaws had limited use of English as well as educational deficiencies. While out-migration was increasing, many people returned, defeated in their efforts to succeed. Thus, it was with some justification that the Bureau of Indian Affairs selected the Mississippi Choctaws for a massive training program in urban relocation in the late 1960s. In 1968, almost 10 percent of the total Choctaw population below the age of forty-four was enrolled in this program. This relocation program was in addition to the ongoing governmentally unprompted heavy out-migration of young males. It seemed as if a third Choctaw removal was underway, this time by individual choice and economic necessity. The long-term prospects for the continued existence of the Choctaws in Mississippi was again in doubt (Peterson 1972).

Fortunately, 1964 marked the beginning of two decades the tribal government later called "An Era of Change." The establishment of the Choctaw Central High School, with the first graduating class in 1964, was an educational turning point. This development was in response to determined efforts by Choctaw parents to persuade a reluctant government to implement a long overdue program. Previously Choctaw students were denied admission to the white segregated schools in the Choctaw area and refused to attend the academically substandard schools for black children. The only Choctaws who received high school educations prior to 1964 had to attend Indian schools in North Carolina or Oklahoma or go to public schools outside the Choctaw area (Peterson and Richburg 1971).

The year 1964 also marked the enactment of the Civil Rights Act, which opened some positions in local factories to the Choctaws for the first time. These were primarily jobs for women in local garment factories. Finally, in 1964, as part of the civil rights era and its poverty programs, the Economic Opportunity Act was initiated and OEO funds became available in Mississippi.

By the 1960s, the Choctaw tribal council began to become more actively involved in reservation affairs, as individuals who had attended school and worked out of state returned and were elected to office. In addition to having higher levels of education, many of these returning Choctaws also had military experience through which they had become acquainted with bureaucratic governmental processes. Representative of this group of emerging new Choctaw leaders were Phillip Martin and Robert Benn. Martin had received his high school education in Cherokee, North Carolina, and had over ten years of experience with the U.S. Air Force. Benn had received a college degree from Mississippi College and had four years of experience as an officer in the navy. Martin was to provide the major leadership for the tribal government for more than two decades, while Benn became the agency housing officer, holding the first professional non-teaching job in the Choctaw Agency held by a Mississippi Choctaw. Benn later became the first Mississippi Choctaw to become superintendent of the Choctaw Agency.

In 1964 the tribal government, under Tribal Chairman Phillip Martin, established a Community Action Agency and applied for a $15,000 planning grant. From this beginning, in less than twenty years the Choctaw Tribe was directly administering over $10 million in federal grants and contracts. When the initial grant was received, Martin resigned as tribal chairman to become the director of the Choctaw Community Action Program. An older tribal leader, Emmette York returned to office as tribal chairman. Over the next six years these two men initiated a massive change on the Choctaw Reservation, working in concert from their respective positions as director of the Choctaw Community Action Program and as chairman of the tribal council. Utilizing the "poverty program" resources available to the tribe, the Choctaw Community Action Program developed an aggressive program of assistance to the Choctaw people across the entire range of social programs. Such programs included early childhood education (Head Start and related programs), community health aides, emergency food distribution, and other social services. Several of these programs included provision for advisory councils through which an increasing number of the Choctaw people were able to have an active voice in the operation of programs on the reservation. To operate these programs effectively, the Choctaw Community Action Program began to develop fiscal and administrative procedures to serve the diverse programs.

By 1970, Martin and others were realizing that further self-government and self-development on the Choctaw Reservation required entering a new stage with efforts directed less at the immediate circumstances of Choctaw poverty and more on long-range objectives. The individual program-specific efforts could not address these longer objectives. The new emphasis required a restructured and more assertive tribal government operating all programs in terms of the long-range goals of tribal self-government and self-development (Mississippi Band of Choctaw Indians 1972a).

This was a direct challenge to the authority of the agency superintendent as the power on the reservation, and the threat of tribal control also was upsetting to many agency employees, both white and Choctaw. Martin and his supporters dominated the tribal council after the election of 1971, and he was elected chairman by his supporters on the council. There followed a major restructuring of programs. The diverse programs that had operated under the Choctaw Community Action Program were consolidated under the tribal council. Thus, rather than a separate Choctaw Community Action Program and tribal council, a single entity now existed that could represent the Choctaw people in relationship with the Choctaw Agency and other state and federal agencies. Further, a single consolidated tribal administration and a planning department now served as tribal programs and entities. Unified personnel, fiscal, and procurement procedures were established and administrative personnel, both Choctaw and non-Choctaw, were recruited and trained.

While this effort at governmental development was taking place within the tribal government, a struggle for dominance was also taking place between the tribal chairman and the superintendent of the Choctaw Agency. Direct confrontation was rare. But at one time, a recall petition was being circulated against the tribal chairman while at the same time the tribal council was petitioning the Bureau of Indian Affairs to replace the agency superintendent. The final outcome of this struggle was the appointment of a Mississippi Choctaw, Robert Benn, as agency superintendent with the strong support of the tribal council.

It is important to realize that while the unrecognized Indian groups of the Southeast have at times envied the federally recognized tribes for the level of services available on the reservation, the recognized tribes had a different struggle during the 1970s, that of gaining control of affairs on their reservations without destroying the support services that came from the Bureau of Indian Affairs. Some of the newly recognized tribes did not experience the period of federal paternalistic support, since the fight for the strengthened voice of the Indian people on their reservations had begun to be won by the federally recognized tribes during the 1970s.

Because of the basic dissimilarity of their problems, the Choctaws had limited relations with the nonrecognized tribes during the 1970s. Instead, the Choctaws early took the lead in establishing closer linkages between the federally recognized tribes in the Southeast through the United Southeastern Tribes, Inc. As additional groups in the East gained federal recognition, this organization was changed to the United South and Eastern Tribes, Inc., with no change in its initials, USET. Throughout recent decades, a great deal of intertribal sharing of experiences has occurred between federally recognized tribes. The quarterly meetings of USET resulted in tribal chairmen or chiefs and members of their tribal councils sharing ideas and exchanging views. While quite different problems existed on the major southeastern reservations, there was a general sense of movement toward greater tribal self-government among all the tribes. Furthermore, the existence of USET promoted exchange between the growing technical staffs working for the tribal governments on each of the reservations.

With a Mississippi Choctaw in charge of the Choctaw Agency and the consolidation of various community action programs under the tribal government, the tribal government began negotiations to contract for certain service elements of the Choctaw Agency. This process was initially aimed at positions that were small and distinct, such as adult education, and for which the tribal government has a comparable component through other governmental funding. Adult education was an early contracted program and resulted in a massive coordinated effort to have out-of-school Choctaws complete high school through competency examinations. This form of consolidation under the tribal government proceeded by functional areas. In all cases, this consolidation made possible an improved program because programs were no longer competing in a similar area and because the source of funds was now more diversified. However, it must also be noted that this process of contracting did not meet with universal approval. Employees of the Choctaw Agency generally recognized that long-term salary levels and retirement benefits would be greater for employees of the federal government. Where small programs were concerned, this was a minor problem, but the tribal government moved more slowly on contracting for major programs that would antagonize more Choctaw voters. Additionally, the tribal government was very sensitive to the need to demonstrate an ability to successfully manage each individual program taken under its control. As a result, the tribal government delayed contracting major programs such as the school system (Mississippi Band of Choctaw Indians 1972b, 1981).

The development of a consolidated tribal government that operated most governmental services on the Choctaw Reservation seems now to have been an inevitable process. But this view ignores the alternatives that were considered as one set of goals was achieved and was replaced by another. At each stage alternatives were considered. Beginning with the development of the Choctaw Community Action Program, Choctaws faced two alternatives for new program development. One of these alternatives was to allow program development to keep pace with the slow increase in numbers of young Choctaw men and women who could qualify for professional and supervisory positions. The other alternative was to develop new programs as rapidly as possible where needed and to rely on hiring non-Choctaws for managerial and supervisory positions until Choctaws were able to fill these positions. The latter of these alternatives risked blocking the upward development of Choctaws by filling positions with non-Indians. The other alternative risked either delaying needed programs unnecessarily or alternatively risking program success by the premature promotion of Choctaws to positions of authority before they were fully trained.

Paralleling these major alternatives were what might be called two views of what an ideal Choctaw reservation might be. One view was toward fuller employment and emphasized the desirability of providing for the Choctaw communities the range of alternatives available in all communities in Mississippi. The other alternative stressed more the need to preserve the Choctawness of the reservation community even if it meant limiting alternatives. The tourism development at Cherokee, North Carolina, served as a reminder for Choctaws that economic development could be dominated by non-Indians not under the control of the tribal government.

Phillip Martin and his followers saw the problem not as postponing development until Choctaws were trained but rather as keeping control under the tribal government. Some of Martin's opponents saw employment of whites in supervisory positions as a threat to Choctaw control over their own affairs and to the preservation of Choctaw values in the operation of the reservation affairs. Some saw little advantage in having Choctaw leadership in control of reservation affairs if such leadership did not appreciate and promote community-based Choctaw culture (Thompson and Peterson 1975).

The reality of the need for Choctaws to move elsewhere if economic opportunity was not expanded locally was a major deciding factor for Martin's approach. Both the more traditional opposition and the employees, white and Indian, of the Bureau of Indian Affairs were threatened by Martin and his supporters' program of development. But clearly the programs of the Choctaw Community Action Program had provided expanded employment for Choctaws and better service to Choctaw people.

Once the Choctaw tribal government had established uniform personnel and fiscal policies and consolidated all programs under central administration, the next major objective was a revision of the tribal constitution to permit the direct election of a tribal chief and the clear separation of administrative responsibilities for the chief and the legislative and policy powers in the tribal council (Brescia 1982:x–xiii). The Choctaw voters rejected the first proposed constitutional revision, at least partially because it provided for a four-year term for the tribal chief while retaining two-year terms for tribal council members. This arrangement would clearly make the chief too powerful and too knowledgeable as compared with the council members. A revision providing four-year staggered terms for both chief and council was passed and set the stage in 1975 for the first election of a Choctaw chief since the nineteenth century. In this election, Phillip Martin lost a close election to an experienced Choctaw educator and principal of Choctaw schools, Calvin Isaac. Isaac had campaigned on the policy of slowing down the pace of change and consolidating the achievements of the past decade. The four-year term of Chief Isaac saw few new developments. On the other hand, the developments of the previous decade were not dismantled.

There seemed to be two major aspects of the ensuing four-year pause in Choctaw development. In the first place, the Choctaw people demonstrated that no one individual, even an innovative leader like Phillip Martin, was essential for the operation of the Choctaw government and its program. There was a maturing aspect of this pause for consolidation. At the same time, it also became clear that a leader with innovative vision such as Phillip Martin was required if progress in Choctaw self-determination was to continue.

One major development of Isaac's four-year term as chief was the working out of a new relationship between the tribal council and the chief as established by the 1975 constitution. Previously, the chairman of the tribal council had been a member of the council, indirectly elected by the other council members. But with the first reservation-wide direct election of a chief, the responsibilities and demarcation of powers between the chief and the council were subject to testing. The 1975 constitution had increased the terms of the tribal council members from two to four years as well as allowing for a four-year term of office for the chief. The growth and increasing complexity of the tribal government and its related enterprises required more knowledgeable leadership among all elected tribal officials. As a full-time tribal administrator, the tribal chairman before 1975 and the directly elected chief after 1975 had the apparatus of the growing tribal administrative structure to provide expert assistance and technical planning. On the other hand, tribal council members were facing an increasing volume of technical reports and proposals they needed to understand to participate in tribal council meetings.

Even prior to the institution of the 1975 constitution, efforts had been made to establish some sort of committee system within the sixteen-member council, recognizing that all council members could not become completely familiar with all aspects of tribal affairs. But even with a committee system, the tribal council, as the legislative branch, did not have resources available to support its efforts to participate as an equal partner in policy formation and to monitor the operations of the tribal administration. The response by the tribal council in 1977 was the creation of seven standing committees with the chairman of each compensated full-time for his or her legislative work. This development made it possible for the council to be more truly coequal with the chief in knowledge and responsibility for tribal programs and has resulted in an unusual stability in the Choctaw government. Phillip Martin had the opportunity to participate in these developments as a council member for two years before he was returned to office as chief in 1979.

The tribal council also established a roughly parallel structure for the executive branch, with five departments under which the various tribal programs are grouped. This program structure in the executive branch of tribal government thus complements the committee structure of the tribal council for purposes of monitoring and reporting program activities. The directors of each department are appointed only with the concurrence of the tribal council, and quarterly and annual reports are submitted by the programs to the tribal council.

While the tribal council and tribal executive structures were being clarified and strengthened, conditions remained more uncertain in terms of the judicial responsibilities and authorities on the Choctaw Reservation.

In the early 1970s, the growing Choctaw housing program being carried out by the Choctaws' own construction company was resented by some local whites who previously had no Indian competition for construction contracts on the reservation. Complaints of this situation reached the Mississippi State Tax Commission, which proceeded to assess state sales tax against the materials purchased by the tribally owned construction company, which as an Indian enterprise doing business exclusively on tribal lands was exempt from state jurisdiction. At the same time, a police jurisdiction case was brought by tribal attorneys who were attempting to establish that the Choctaw Reservation constituted Indian country and thus came under federal jurisdiction for major crimes rather than state jurisdiction. While the technical aspects of the two cases were quite different, the basic point was fundamental.

Were the Mississippi Choctaws a federally recognized Indian group and was the Choctaw Reservation Indian country within the meaning of federal law and jurisdiction? Both state courts and the U.S. Court of Appeals ruled against the Choctaws, thus threatening all the progress of the previous decades (U.S. Fifth Circuit Court of Appeals, Case C.A. 5, no. 76–1518, 1976). If this ruling was not successfully overturned, the Choctaw schools, government, and all social, educational, and economic progress had no legal basis. Indeed, in the time in which this case was pending, the rulings of the lower courts effectively blocked all attempts at economic development because the legal basis for the tribal lands was in question. The Choctaw tribal government was forced to take primary responsibility for its own defense in pursuing this case over several years to the U.S. Supreme Court. A full-time tribal attorney argued the case before the Court, resulting in a decision in 1977 that upheld the legal existence of the Choctaw Tribe (Supreme Court of the United States, Case no. 77–836, 1977). This decision marked the clearing of a major barrier to Choctaw economic development.

The term of Chief Isaac from 1975 to 1979 offered Phillip Martin a chance to expand his knowledge of tribal affairs and Indian economic development. No longer involved in daily tribal administration, Martin faced the necessity of earning a livelihood. This he accomplished by forming a private Indian management and consulting firm and entering into contracts with Indian governments throughout the eastern and southwestern United States to help them develop the fiscal and personnel administrative structures that he had implemented in the Choctaw government. His firm also provided technical assistance in all types of program development that he had carried out on the Choctaws' reservation. This was Martin's first experience as an individual businessman, head of his own firm. This experience and his work as a management consultant with other tribes con-

*Above:* After Phillip Martin (right) won a third consecutive landslide election to the office of tribal chief in 1987, more than 2,000 attended inauguration ceremonies. He and Tribal Council Secretary-Treasurer Beasley Denson are shown during the administration of the oath of office. *Below:* A line worker at Chahta Enterprise. (Photos: Julie Kelsey, Courtesy *Choctaw Community News*)

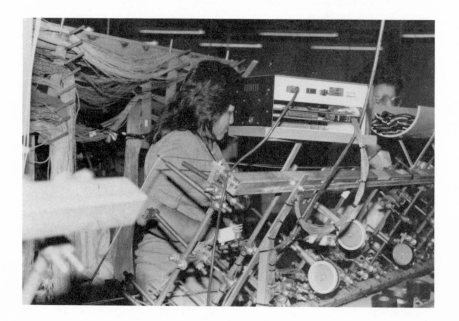

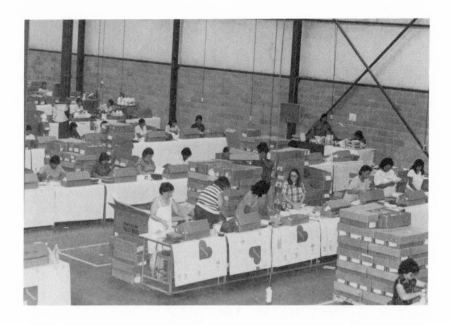

*Above:* At Choctaw Greetings, seasonal greeting cards are hand finished, as shown in this section of the plant interior. (Photo: Julie Kelsey, Courtesy *Choctaw Community News*).
*Below:* Groundbreaking ceremonies for the Chahta Enterprise Plant II expansion project were held in 1982. (Photo: Edward John, Courtesy *Choctaw Community News*)

*Left:* Choctaw stickball, "the oldest field sport in America," is a traditional game of the Choctaws. (Photo: Ami Regier, Courtesy *Choctaw Community News*). *Below:* The Choctaw Early Education Center, opened in 1986, is the administration center for Head Start and other early childhood education programs. At the ribbon-cutting ceremonies for the center, children performed traditional dances for those in attendance. (Photo: Julie Kelsey, Courtesy *Choctaw Community News*)

vinced Martin that Indian tribes must place a greater emphasis on economic development involving the private sector rather than the government as a source of jobs. Martin was not the only Choctaw with such a viewpoint. But he had promoted Choctaw self-development since returning to the chairman's position in 1971.

Many efforts at economic development had been tried in the 1960s and 1970s. Under Emmette York, Martin's predecessor as chairman in the late 1960s, the Choctaw Tribe tried to produce jobs through forestry or agriculture on tribal lands. An effort was made to begin growing soybeans on tribal lands along the Pearl River and later to establish a tribal feeder pig operation. The tribe lacked the capital necessary to establish a successful farming program, and the younger tribal members were rarely interested in working in agriculture, which they associated with economic bondage and grinding poverty.

In the early 1970s, the Choctaws initiated a reservation housing program to meet the acute housing needs of the Choctaw people. The first group of houses was built by outside contractors, but the Choctaws formed a tribal construction company that first provided the interior finishing of the houses and later undertook bidding on total construction projects. Although Choctaws had been receiving construction skill training for some years, and in spite of the civil rights legislation, Choctaws were not noticeably successful in getting construction jobs on projects on the reservation until the formation of Chata Development Company. By 1976 Chata had completed over six million dollars of construction on the reservation and was a model for further industrial development on the reservation (Chata Development Company 1976). It was the success of Chata that prompted the state challenge to tribal existence.

With the success of Chata, the Choctaws investigated the possibility of bringing small manufacturing plants to the reservation. Most of the prospects the Choctaws could interest at this time were marginal operations that expected major financial assistance the tribe could not produce. Really good prospects found the Choctaws unprepared for industrial development. To further improve the possibilities for industrial development, in 1971 the Choctaws broke ground for an industrial park complete with utilities and sewage treatment. This park was to remain vacant for eight years until other conditions changed on the reservation to make industrial development possible.

In addition to an interest in industrial development, the Choctaws continued to look at tourism development. The examples of both the Cherokees and the Seminoles were attractive to the Choctaws, not so much because they liked the appearance of the commercial "Indian" shops but because they saw the jobs generated by the tourism traffic and the higher prices for good traditional craftwork, especially baskets. But Choctaw Reservation is an hour's drive away for the main north-south interstate highway connecting the Midwest with the Gulf Coast at New Orleans. There seemed to be no way to attract an economically viable portion of this tourist traffic to the Choctaw's reservation, which unlike the Cherokee's reservation did not have any other nearby point of interest such as Great Smoky Mountains National Park. Some non-Choctaw economic developers tried to promote plans to develop a Choctaw tourist complex in non-Indian communities closer to the main flow of tourist traffic. But such plans had the fatal flaw of providing most of the jobs and economic benefits to non-Choctaws. Such plans also required that older traditional craftspeople and Choctaw students be willing to live and commute to work from some distance from the reservation communities.

In the 1980s the Seminoles and later the Cherokees (and still later the Creeks) developed reservation bingo as a major source of reservation funds and the Choctaws again looked at this possibility. It proved unrealistic for the same geographic reasons that tourism proved unrealistic. Perhaps the best that can be said of the Choctaws' efforts in economic development in the 1960s and 1970s was that they looked at a large range of possibilities and rejected them without losing tribal resources in the process. The failure of the land operation and farming operation in the late 1960s served its purpose in demonstrating that the most attractive plans may not succeed. In the decade that followed, the Choctaws learned to say "no" to a host of superficially attractive opportunities while developing and learning to operate successfully their tribal entities such as the construction company, housing authority, and utility commission.

Not until 1979 did economic development become the top priority of the Choctaw tribal government (Mississippi Band of Choctaw Indians 1981:19). But also by 1979 the Choctaw Tribe had spent a full fifteen years preparing for economic development. Initially, from 1964 until 1971, a major effort had been made to address social issues and needs. From 1972 until 1979 a major effort had been to strengthen tribal government. During these years, the Choctaws had proven that they could accomplish program development, meet their own social needs, and administer and direct their own programs and tribal enterprises. The Office of Economic Opportunity Indian Desk, the Office of Native American Programs, and the Administration for Native Americans had provided critical funds for planning and implementing these major policy directions.

In the election of 1979, Phillip Martin ran and was elected chief on a platform of continued self-determination and aggressive efforts at economic development. The stage was set for what appeared to be a Choctaw economic miracle (McKee and Murray 1986; Michelmore 1984; Krebs

1986). The first plant to locate in the Choctaw industrial park was the Packard Electric Division of the General Motors Corporation, which was establishing dedicated supplier plants at about five locations in Mississippi. In 1979, the tribal council utilized an Economic Development Administration grant and a Bureau of Indian Affairs loan guarantee to establish Chahta Enterprises, which located in a 42,000-square-foot plant. Now known as Chahta Enterprise Plant I, this operation employed 200 people to assemble electronic wiring and components into the "wiring harnesses," the electronic assembly for trucks and automobiles.

Later in 1979, officials from American Greeting Corporation of Cleveland, Ohio, visited the reservation. Officials of this corporation had first visited the Choctaws in the late 1960s, but they failed to see much possibility to encourage a plant location. But, ten years later, there had been tremendous growth in educational and training programs, housing, tribal-owned enterprises, and a strong and stable tribal government. Most of all, Chahta Enterprises was standing as an example of tribal initiative with an efficient Choctaw labor force and the highest quality index of any of Packard's dedicated suppliers. Negotiations were begun for a 120,000-square-foot building in which to hand finish greetings cards. Financing proved to be a major problem with the withdrawal of the Economic Development Administration as a source of funds. Overlapping jurisdictions and regulations among several different bureaucracies created further difficulties. But the Choctaws became the first Indian tribe to construct an industrial building on a reservation using state industrial development revenue bonds. This enterprise, established by the tribal council as the Choctaw Greeting Enterprise, now employs 200 people and has the capacity to expand to around 400 if the market will permit such expansion.

Meanwhile, production in Chahta Enterprise Plant I was reaching the capacity of the plant and the needs of Packard Electric. This success led the tribal administration to plan an expansion that would permit the Choctaws to enter the competition for business in the open wiring and cable market. The Choctaw Tribe was successful in becoming the first industrial enterprise of an Indian tribe to receive an Urban Development Action grant from the U.S. Department of Housing and Urban Development. This $600,000 grant was important, but perhaps more important was that with a Bureau of Indian Affairs loan guarantee, the tribe itself was able to finance the remaining $2.3 million for the construction of an additional 42,000-square-foot plant and for the necessary raw materials and equipment to begin production. Unlike Plant I, where parts and the assembly line were provided, in Plant II the Choctaws had to produce electronic components to the specifications of a potential contractor, being provided only with blueprints from which to work. The Choctaws were successful in securing a contract from Ford, and between November 1983 and November 1985 the number of employees in Plant II grew from 10 to 300 and the total contract for the second year of operations was $7 million.

By 1985, the Choctaw success was attracting wider interests. Oxford Speaker Company of Chicago had been considering resorting to foreign sources for the high quality radio speakers they were producing for Chrysler. Upon investigation they decided that the Choctaw industrial park offered a suitable alternative closer to the market and with top quality standards. They entered into still a different form of financing for developing the fourth industrial plant on the Choctaw Reservation. This was a joint capital venture in which the tribe maintained a 51 percent interest with Oxford Speaker having the balance.

These first plants were all located in the Choctaw industrial park in the Pearl River community. Pearl River is the largest and most centrally located of the Choctaw communities and in it are also located the tribal administration and Choctaw Central High School. By 1984, it was becoming apparent that further industrial development would require dispersing plants to other Choctaw communities in neighboring counties. The continued expansion of the wire harness business now made it possible to develop Chahta Enterprise Plant III and to locate this plant near DeKalb in neighboring Kemper County east of the Pearl River community. The location of this plant in the Tennessee Valley Authority service area opened up still another source of financing, was closer to the Choctaw community of Bogue Chitto, and made possible the support of a new group of locally elected non-Choctaw officials. U.S. Senator John Stennis, who had been interested in and helpful to Choctaw progress for several years, was especially helpful in securing funding for this development in his home county. Senator Stennis participated in the plant opening in August 1986.

Only two months later, in October 1986, still another plant was opened west of Pearl River on the boundary between the Choctaw community of Red Water in Leake County and the industrial park owned by the city of Carthage. This was the second joint capital venture for the tribe, this time in association with Richmond Industries of Richmond, Michigan. This company designs and produces electrical components, circuitry, and electronic testing equipment for General Motors. As in the previous joint venture, Richmond provided the technology, expertise, and sales of the project, while the Choctaw Tribe provided the building, equipment, and operating capital. For all these plants major construction was carried out by the tribal construction company.

To summarize, in 1979 the Choctaw industrial development began with a small $.5 million contract and 25 people assembling parts furnished by Packard Electric. By 1987 the Choctaw industrial effort involved over

1,200 employees and a total budget of $35 million. Of the total of six plants opened between 1979 and 1986, two plants opened late in 1986. The total budget of the Choctaw industrial enterprises was expected to reach $50 million in 1987. In employees alone, the Choctaw industrial effort is already the fifteenth largest industrial enterprise in the state of Mississippi.

In seven short years the Choctaws moved from a contractual relationship as a dedicated supplier, with the parts and equipment being furnished by a parent firm, to complete production on the open competitive market and to joint ventures financed cooperatively between established firms and the Choctaw Tribe. In all cases, the Choctaws offered an alternative to automotive and related electronic fabrication and assembly plants to foreign sourcing by U.S. corporations. In the process the Choctaws have built an industrial enterprise based on centralized financial strength of a tribal government and related tribally owned enterprises.

In the process of accomplishing all this, the Choctaws have turned from a population seeking employment in the few industries in the surrounding area to an industrial enterprise that is employing approximately 25 percent non-Choctaws. The overall increase in the local economy is greatly appreciated by the non-Choctaw workers and public officials throughout east-central Mississippi. As a result, the base of public support for the Choctaws has grown enormously. Only ten years ago local citizens and officials and the Mississippi state government were attempting through the federal courts to challenge the legal existence of the Choctaw Tribe. Local and state officials are now thankful that this effort failed, inasmuch as the existence of a tribal government and reservation has been essential for the economic development the Choctaws have brought to east-central Mississippi.

This growing relationship between the tribal leaders and non-Choctaw elected officials has been carefully cultivated over twenty years. When the tribal government first became assertive in defense of Indian rights and began to promote Choctaw economic opportunity, many Mississippians were still resentful of the federal government civil rights efforts. It was difficult if not impossible for non-Choctaw officials of a federal agency to generate any appreciation or concern for the Mississippi Choctaws. Initially, the growing strength and authority of the Choctaw tribal government was viewed by many local white officials as personally threatening, much as they viewed black militancy of the 1960s and early 1970s. Not only was the tribal jurisdiction case viewed as a financial threat to white-owned concerns that hoped to dominate construction on the reservation, but the idea of a Choctaw reservation with its own police jurisdiction raised irrational fears of many local whites. There was a time of confusion before state and federal officials began to recognize that a tribal government existed that could represent the Indian people. As late as the early 1970s, plans could be made for construction of a major reservoir on the Pearl River that would flood tribal lands without formal consultation with the tribal council (Peterson 1975).

As the tribal government grew in strength, many local whites found to their surprise that the Mississippi Choctaws were not unlike the Mississippi whites and blacks in their aspirations. As late as 1980 on the 150th anniversary of the Treaty of Dancing Rabbit Creek, a local committee planning to commemorate the event was unsure about inviting the Choctaws. But Chief Martin won their respect by talking about moving together in the future to seek better opportunities for the people of the area. In much the same fashion, state and national political leaders found that they could communicate better with an elected Choctaw tribal leader than they could with non-Choctaw, non-Mississippi employees of the Bureau of Indian Affairs. Indeed, by the 1980s, a visit to the annual Choctaw fair became an important event for the governor of Mississippi and candidates for major state office. Both the Republican senator, Thad Cochran, and the Democratic senator, John Stennis, have supported Choctaw economic development, as has Representative Sonny Montgomery. But perhaps equally important is the increasingly close working relationship between local political leaders and tribal leaders. Choctaw industrial development does not compete with other local economic activity, rather it retains in the United States jobs that otherwise might be lost to other countries. Thus Choctaw economic development is a cause that non-Choctaws can support regardless of political position.

But while the development of the Choctaw industrial effort has resulted in a closer and more cooperative relationship between Choctaw and non-Choctaw elected officials, the rapid industrial expansion has also brought an increased consciousness of the dependence the tribe has on non-Indian technical personnel to run industrial enterprises and, to a lesser extent, tribal social and educational programs. The increased technical level of the jobs being created on the reservation has forced a recognition of the limited skills of the mass of the Choctaw labor force. The initial industrial development first attracted the most highly skilled tribal members, but the growth of industrial jobs has required recruiting and training the two-thirds of the Choctaw work force that is basically unskilled. Because the majority of these individuals have attended the Choctaw schools since the opening of the Choctaw high school in 1964, it is no longer sufficient to identify the lack of opportunity as the educational problem of the Choctaws. Instead, there is the difficult problem of improving the quality of education in the Choctaw schools and preparing Choctaw youth to be able to respond to the technical jobs that are now available locally.

There is also a problem with Choctaw youth who have graduated from the local high school but who are unable to complete college. Only seventy-two tribal members have completed a college degree, and the tribal government estimated that fewer than 20 percent of Choctaw students enrolling in college actually graduate. Thus while opportunities have rapidly expanded on the reservation, there is a lag in the ability of the Choctaw people to respond to these opportunities. Although the academic and motivational problems in the Choctaw school system are obvious (Spencer, Windham, and Peterson 1975), changing the direction of an entire system is difficult and the detailed reasons for continued failure remain difficult to identify.

The Choctaw school system remained, until the fall of 1989, the only major component of the Bureau of Indian Affairs not being operated under contract by the Choctaw Tribe. During the 1980s, perhaps the outstanding unresolved problem on the Choctaw Reservation was how best to achieve change in the Choctaw schools. Early in the process of contracting for the operation of the programs of the Choctaw Agency, the tribal government proposed contracting for community schools. A community referendum indicated the majority of individuals were opposed to this idea. By 1982, however, 81 percent of those surveyed believed that the tribe should contract to run the school in their community. But the overriding need for jobs made economic development a higher priority for most of the decade. The size and complexity of the school system also required careful examination of alternatives. By the latter part of the decade, it was apparent that Choctaw economic development was being limited by the quality of education being received in the Choctaw schools. Continued economic development required significant changes in Choctaw education. Thus the Choctaw schools opened for the fall of 1989 under tribal control for the first time. It is much too early to anticipate the results of this latest step in Choctaw self-determination. But the willingness of the Choctaw people to undertake the most difficult problem on the reservation reveals the widespread acceptance of the philosophy of Choctaw self-determination.

Choctaw self-determination began with the development of social programs under the federal poverty programs of the 1960s. By the 1970s this social effort was expanded to include a restructuring and strengthening of tribal government. By the 1980s, the Choctaws began a massive and successful effort to provide economic development and jobs in east-central Mississippi. With twenty years of growing experience, there is little doubt that eventually all educational programs will be operated by the tribe. This last may be the most difficult step of all.

Yet as one visits the new industrial operations, it is impossible not to be impressed by the pride in Choctaw accomplishment. Everywhere one finds an emphasis on quality. While the top management may be largely non-Choctaw, the supervisory level is increasingly filled by young Choctaws. Ten years ago, many of these young people would have had to go to Chicago or Detroit to look for jobs.

Have the Choctaws become less Choctaw as a result of these changes? Certainly the work on a production line requires a different attitude toward work than hoeing cotton, which was the "traditional" Choctaw subsistence activity from the 1880s through the 1950s. "Do you believe the Choctaws will respond to work on a production line? Sometimes it can be tiresome and boring." This was the question, with commentary, an early industrial prospect put to a group of Choctaw tribal council members. "Have you ever tried chopping cotton?" was the honest answer he received. The Choctaws who practiced a broadly based agricultural and hunting subsistence in the eighteenth century became increasingly agricultural as the deer trade reduced game. Subsistence agriculture merged into sharecropping to produce a market crop for the landowner as the Choctaws lost control of their land. Sharecropping was vanishing to be replaced by welfare. Dissolution of the Choctaw communities through out-migration was predicted by the end of the century. The current tribal industrial development is only the latest transformation the Choctaws and other southeastern Indian people have experienced across the past four centuries.

Today, the Choctaw communities look like any small town or subdivision, with nice brick homes centered around schools and churches. Increasingly these towns contain industrial plants that make it possible for the community to continue to exist. As a result, the vast majority of Choctaw youth continue to live in Choctaw communities and to marry other Choctaws. As of 1990, approximately 6,000 of the 8,080 people enrolled in the Mississippi Band of Choctaw Indians lived on or adjacent to reservation lands (personal communication, Robert Ferguson, Choctaw Tribal Office, 1990). Most Choctaw families continue to speak Choctaw at home. The traditional Choctaw identity based on kinship groups, individual Choctaw communities, and the Choctaws as a language group is continuing (Thompson and Peterson 1975). But upon this basis is being developed a new identity in which Choctawness is equally based on pride in traditions and pride in current achievements in the modern world. Choctaw social dances are scheduled regularly but they take place in the well-lighted air-conditioned community building in each community. The Choctaws are still enthusiastic supporters of kin and locality-based sports. But more people play softball than stickball (Blanchard 1981). The economic developments that have transformed the Choctaw communities have also made possible the continued existence of the Choctaws in Mississippi. A recent review of tribal enterprises (Cohen 1989:43) cites the Mississippi Choctaws as a tribe for whom consistent leadership and consensus among the members seems to ensure further consolidation of their economic success.

Yet the Choctaw struggle is not ended. Too many of the Choctaw people remain at the poverty level without the education or skills that will permit them to enter the industrial economy that is emerging on the reservation. The tribal government has developed over the past twenty years as a strengthened stable institution with experience in administering a large number of social, health, and educational programs. But as is true for all reservations, there is no tax base, and there is the continuing dependence on federal funding for basic programs contracted through the Choctaw Agency. Funds are limited or nonexistent for remedial education programs for the young people who have been passed through the Choctaw schools but who have skill levels too low to compete in what is rapidly becoming a high-technology economy. The very mark of pride in Choctaw heritage, the level of retention of the Choctaw language, is declining, but limited skills in written English remain a problem. The Choctaw struggle to continue to exist as an identifiable people and to control their own affairs will continue until these problems are addressed and overcome. No doubt the future will bring new problems. But the Choctaws' capability to meet and overcome the challenges from the dominant society surrounding them seems better than at any time in recent history.

# 8

# THE LOUISIANA TRIBES:
# ENTERING HARD TIMES

*Hiram F. Gregory*

In 1980 the United States census enumerated 12,064 American Indian residents of Louisiana. Recent summaries of tribal populations (Anonymous 1985) published by the Louisiana state Office of Indian Affairs counts 11,925 people on the official rolls of the eight organized tribes or communities in the state.

The state commission on Indian affairs has requested a special census for Louisiana, because it is highly unlikely that there are so few Indians outside the eight organized groups. Certainly the tribal rolls are accurate, but it leaves numbers of nontribal people in the state uncounted. Scattered Indians are known to be in all the state's urban areas, and several rural communities are known to have strong Indian identities as well. Cherokee, Osage, Ute, Apache, Caddo, Winnebago, Sioux, Creek, Powhatan, Texas Choctaw, Seminole, and Chickasaw Indians have been identified in Louisiana in the past few years, and it is likely there are others. This matter is mentioned here only to suggest that Louisiana remains in need of more adequate census data. Relatively large populations of "Redbones" (populations labeled only by that pejorative, which generally implies triracial ancestry) exist in western Louisiana. These communities have had little or no contact with either anthropologists or other Indian identity groups. They remain both geographically and socioculturally isolated. This chapter deals only with the eight organized tribes/communities in the state.[1]

Three tribes are federally recognized: the Chitimacha in St. Mary Parish (county) with 520 people; the Coushatta (Koasati) in Allen Parish with 350 people; and the Tunica-Biloxi in Avoyelles Parish with 250 people (Anonymous 1985).

The Chitimacha have been federally recognized since 1916, and their 238 acres of land have been held in trust since 1919 when it was donated to the U.S. Congress by the late Sarah Avery McIlhenny, a friend of the tribe (Hoover 1975:50–53).

The Coushatta (the Choctaw version of the tribal name often used by non-Koasati) had federal services, essentially education and health services, in the 1940s and 1950s, but those were terminated before 1960. The tribe organized the Coushatta Alliance in 1965 to provide a crafts outlet and by 1973 had regained federal recognition as the Coushatta Tribe of Louisiana. In 1889 a Coushatta tribal member, Sissy Robinson, had her land patent taken in trust by the federal government. That land was released from trusteeship in 1953 (Johnson 1976:60). The newly recognized tribe was able to place 35 acres of land in federal trust. Ten acres were purchased for the group by the Association on American Indian Affairs and another 20 acres were donated to the tribe by the J. A. Bel Estate (Johnson 1976:98). By 1977 the tribe had acquired an additional 100 acres of land.

The Tunica-Biloxi had begun seeking the federal relationship in the 1930s and in the late 1970s petitioned the Department of the Interior for federal recognition according to the *Code of Federal Regulations for the Recognition of an Indian Tribe or Entity* (25 CFR 54, now 25 CFR 83). The tribe was recognized in 1981 (ASIA 1981a). Their 130 + acres, held since Spanish colonial times as a communal land base, provide them with a trust land base.

The other Louisiana Indian groups lack the federal relationship, but four of them, the Clifton Choctaw, the Ebarb (Choctaw-Apache), the Houma, and Jena Choctaw, have petitioned for it (personal communication, George Allen and Kirby Verrett, 1985–86, and George Roth 1990). All these groups currently (1990) await review of their petitions by the federal agency. The five unrecognized groups are: the Houma (some 11,000 strong) dispersed from Terrebonne Parish across Lafourche Parish and into St. Bernard Parish; the Jena Choctaw (150 people) mainly in LaSalle Parish; the Choctaw-Apache (2,500 + people) located primarily in Sabine Parish; the Clifton Choctaw in Rapides Parish (250 people); and the suburban agglomerate of Choctaw, the Louisiana Tribe of Choctaw, in West Baton Rouge Parish (150 people).

All eight tribes, including the federally recognized tribes, hold.Louisiana state legislative recognition as Indian communities. In order to provide the state's Indian groups with a liaison to the various state agencies, an official state Office of Indian Affairs was established in 1970, with a commissioner of Indian affairs who serves by the governor's appointment. Since 1974 that office has been held by Coushatta, Chitimacha, Houma, Jena Choctaw, and, presently, a Chitimacha. The commission is now all

Locations of Modern Louisiana Indian Groups (Map prepared by Jared Jones)

Indian and is composed of the elected tribal leaders of the eight tribes.

In an effort to make this a coherent endeavor, and not to slight various groups in any way, this chapter can only hope to discuss certain trends observed in Louisiana's recent Indian affairs. Some efforts have been made to check these etic ("outsider") notions with tribal leaders and members, and most of the communities have been visited regularly. Nevertheless it is difficult to generalize about a population as large and as diverse as that of the Louisiana Indians. It is hoped that this attempt to stop midstream will not seem too impressionistic and that in the 1990s some systematic efforts to check and correct these observations will be made.

A number of areas stand out when one looks back across twenty years of development. Notable are: economic development (especially entrepreneurship), self-determination, and developments in education and traditional culture.

## Self-Determination

Clearly, there is now a tendency away from dependencies on Indian "help" organizations and toward more cooperation between the tribal/

community groups *within* Louisiana. Even the Indian Angels, a pantribal organization that operated in Louisiana in the 1970s to generate interest and activism among the Louisiana Indians, has virtually disappeared. Formed to lend support to the activists of the American Indian Movement, the organization flourished briefly, and now, subsequent to the death of its urban leader, Sarah Peralta, it has no appreciable impact on state Indian affairs.

The Coalition of Eastern Native Americans (CENA), which encouraged the unrecognized tribes in the state to organize and actively sought to find them financial and economic aid, has also disappeared from the scene. The Institute for the Development of Indian Law, which provided all sorts of aid, especially to the Tunica-Biloxi, has no real impact now. Once the Sioux activist, Vine Deloria, Jr., left that organization in the late 1970s, its activism and help declined in Louisiana. Deloria's friendship with the Tunica-Biloxi traditionalist, Joseph Alcide Pierite, was a strong factor in that tribe's petition for recognition as well as for the gathering of CENA influence across the state.

Even the more conservative Association on American Indian Affairs (AAIA), a group that worked with the Coushatta and Jena Choctaw on various projects, has not had any recent influence among the tribes. Although AAIA helped the Jena Band of Choctaw with an organizational grant and began work on that group's petition for federal recognition, the tribe finished that work with help from the federal Administration for Native Americans (ANA) on its own. In recent years the Coushatta, once actively involved with AAIA, have had no apparent ties to that group.

Volunteers from the Mennonite Central Committee in Akron, Ohio, have been active in Louisiana since the late 1970s. Volunteers have worked on petition research, genealogy, and crafts cooperatives for some of the tribes. Volunteers served two-year terms at the discretion of the tribal organizations. In only one case, at the Tunica-Biloxi community, were volunteers requested to withdraw. All the other tribal groups—Clifton Choctaw, Houma, and Choctaw-Apache—actually requested volunteer extensions. Only the Louisiana Band of Choctaw (also known as the East Baton Rouge Choctaw) did not participate in the Mennonite program.

These volunteers should not be confused with missionaries, inasmuch as they were not allowed to proselytize any Indian people. They tutored, wrote grants, worked with the office of the Inter-Tribal Council of Louisiana, and performed a wide range of community services. The tribal groups helped, to the best of their ability, with volunteer maintenance and guidance in the communities.

Today no Mennonite volunteers are in any Indian community in the state, nor do any work with the Inter-Tribal Council office. Their programs are still working, most notably the Houma crafts cooperative and their recently completed Houma petition for federal recognition; but, in all cases, they are now completely administered by the Indian communities themselves.

The Native American Rights Fund (NARF) has been involved in various Tunica-Biloxi litigations in both federal and state courts. It was with NARF legal aid that the Tunica-Biloxi recently won possession of artifacts looted from one of their eighteenth-century cemeteries (Brain 1979). It was a major legal victory for the tribe, and although they now employ independent counsel they are quick to acknowledge the contribution of NARF.

The federally recognized tribes—Coushatta, Chitimacha, and Tunica-Biloxi—work with the United South and Eastern Tribes. One Coushatta actually worked in that group's Nashville office, where it operates as a clearinghouse for Indian Health Service and other activities for the southeastern tribes. The recognized tribal leaders were also invited to belong to the now-defunct National Tribal Chairmen's Association. Such advantages are not readily available to the unrecognized groups. As unrecognized tribes, most (five of the eight organized groups in Louisiana) of the Louisiana communities depend, at least in part, on input from the recognized tribes and two newly formed Louisiana Indian organizations. The oldest of these is the Inter-Tribal Council (ITC) of Louisiana, which was founded by the Chitimacha, Coushatta, and Jena Choctaw in 1975. Ostensibly, ITC formed to seek grants and to protect tribal grants from overhead paid into the state administrative bureaucracy. The Houma and Tunica-Biloxi eventually became members. In 1983–84 a related organization, the Institute for Indian Development, began. While the initial stimulus for the Inter-Tribal council was grants-in-aid, mostly federal, the newer effort was to extend those possibilities to all eight communities. ITC membership seems to be composed only of groups with, or who have filed petitions for, federal recognition under the regulations of the *Code of Federal Regulations* (25 CFR 83). Moreover, the institute has taken as its major mission the articulation of the Indian communities with the larger society of Louisiana. As part of this extension, it seeks funding from business and the private sectors. A tide of entrepreneurship developed from this lead, stimulated by the successes of the neighboring Mississippi Choctaws. Nevertheless, all eight tribes are members, and the Inter-Tribal Council and the institute have written new needs assessments funded by an ANA grant to the institute (personal communication, John Faine, Western Kentucky University, 1986).

In 1970, in keeping with his campaign promises to the Indians of the state, Governor Edwin Edwards established the state Office of Indian Affairs and the Governor's Commission on Indian Affairs. In 1970 the first commissioner was non-Indian, David Garrison, but soon his assistant, Ernest Sickey, a Coushatta Indian, took his place. Subsequently, M. D. Regions (a nontribal Indian), Helen Gindrat (a Houma), Clyde Jackson (a Jena Choctaw), and now (1990) Diana Stouff Williamson (a Chitimacha) have held that position. Again the directorship and the membership of this group have moved resoundingly into Indian hands. By the administration of Governor David Treen, the commission had shifted to the elected chief executives of the eight tribal groups, and it has remained so, with two additional full-time staff.

There is little doubt that these organizations have effectively removed much of the need for pantribal or non-Indian groups from outside the state to lobby, help, or advise the Louisiana Indian people. Federal and state grants, along with some private sector support, have been more and more channeled into these local all-Indian organizations. Only in the area of legal aid has the "outside connection" remained an advantage for the tribal communities. In spite of some statewide politicking within the Indian groups, only recently a strongly Democratic and pro-labor Indian organization developed. Its chief activity seemed to be active campaigning for the Democratic candidate, Edwin Edwards, for governor; but it did recruit many of the old Houma activists, formerly closely aligned to the Indian Angels organization, and they worked the nonrecognized groups. This organization, Louisiana Indians for Equality (LIFE), lobbied actively against the Republican appointees to the state commissioner's office. The newly elected governor, Edwards, held a meeting with tribal leaders and, with the wisdom of a Louisiana politician, reappointed Jena Choctaw Indian, Clyde Jackson, as commissioner; but he designated a person acceptable to the LIFE members, a Chitimacha, Diana Stouff Williamson, his "assistant commissioner." Apparently satisfied, little has emanated from LIFE since those decisions. Jackson eventually resigned and Williamson assumed the office.

Again, the tribes have gained an effective voice in state politics—a remarkable shift for a group of people not large enough to statistically determine election outcomes. The tribal groups and communities see this accomplishment, even with some factional differences due to it, as a net gain. It seems that self-determination has a chance.

Once these basic political alignments were made and the Indian people had enough resources and access to power, the communities much ameliorated their pantribal antagonisms. Tribal identities are still strong and the greatest intertribal conflicts seem now limited to the conflicts among the Choctaw. The Jena Choctaw, with a number of Choctaw-speaking full-bloods in their ranks, are the most conservative. The other three Choctaw-related groups have no language retention and few or no fullbloods, so there are frequently conflicts over the degree of "Choctawness." Still, all these groups cling desperately to quarter-blood enrollment; and among the Jena Choctaw, only one full Choctaw marriage has taken place in recent years. Soon there, too, mixed-bloods will predominate. Only people over age forty have retained Choctaw speech to any appreciable degree, a problem that preoccupies their elders. Still, again, these are essentially playbacks of conservative-liberal developments in these groups and are less and less a problem as the communities work together. Nevertheless, it must be pointed out that none of the four organized Choctaw groups has *ever* suggested a union of Choctaw-related groups. This is clearly due to the nature of the different Choctaw incursions into Spanish Louisiana (post-1763) and the subsequent isolation of those communities. Even the suburban Louisiana Tribe of Choctaw will label others the "discovered" tribes: the Clifton Choctaw and the Choctaw-Apache. None of the groups knew of the others until the 1970s. Only the Jena Choctaw seem to have had any interaction with the other tribes prior to that period. The Jena Choctaw school aid kept them in contact with the Coushatta and with the Mississippi Choctaw. Interestingly again, no intermarriages developed, while the long unrecognized Tunica-Biloxi intermarried with both the Coushatta and Mississippi Choctaw.

## Tribal Development

In the 1980s, tribal development started with new alignments and new pantribal strengths. Arguments between and inside Indian communities now began developing all-Indian outlets inside the state. The year 1980 saw a radically different Indian community than had existed only a decade earlier.

Tribal resource development began as early as 1965 when the Coushatta Alliance opened a store to market tribal craft productions (Sickey 1978). Similarly, the Tunica-Biloxi, with the help of the late part-Choctaw artist/ anthropologist Claude Medford, Jr., began a "trading post" on tribal land for the same purpose. Both these efforts to develop various tribal crafts into an economic base for the communities helped in hard times, but both failed due to lack of resources and skills for promotional and developmental efforts. Even a grant to the Coushatta, after federal recognition, administered by the tribe and managed by Claude Medford, Jr., produced a profitable crafts outlet. Still it did not really outlast the grant period. These early successes and failures for the Tunica-Biloxi and Coushatta did not slow tribal efforts but were only preludes to a series of events that string across the 1970s and 1980s.

The federally recognized Chitimacha and Coushatta certainly led the tribes in the 1970s, but all the tribal groups had had some economic and cultural developments by the beginning of the 1980s. The Coushatta saw an amazing amount of development, as did the Chitimacha and, to a lesser extent, the Jena Choctaw. After 1980, the Tunica-Biloxi saw an amazing surge in development. These groups all had a number of Housing and Urban Development (HUD) grants. Each has completed a tribal administrative center on their trust land bases. The Coushatta, Chitimacha, Jena Choctaw, and Tunica-Biloxi have also implemented recreational complexes—a gymnasium and softball fields for the Coushatta, tennis and softball fields at the Chitimacha, and children's recreational areas at the Tunica-Biloxi. Toward the end of the 1970s these tribes, except for the Chitimacha and Tunica-Biloxi who had already had land bases, began acquiring some tribal land. The Coushatta expanded their land from 30 acres to 130 acres and almost immediately began building on it. They now have and maintain a tribal health center, an administrative center, a tribal hall, and a heavy equipment maintenance plant. In the late 1970s, while their crafts outlet functioned, the tribe was given the abandoned depot in nearby Elton, Louisiana. This outlet was on the main thoroughfare, a state highway, and kept tourism away from the tribal area but put their crafts in a better market position. When the crafts program disappeared in the mid-1970s, the tribe leased out a portion of that building, turning even that early failure into a profit base.

Since 1975 the Coushatta have built administrative buildings and recreational complexes (Johnson 1976). They have also built fifteen to twenty new houses and repaired, or are currently repairing, virtually every other house in the tribal area. Improved sewerage (septic tanks were virtually unheard of until the 1970s) and an improved water system have greatly benefited tribal health, likely contributing nearly as much as their contracted medical services, which began in the early 1970s when Indian Health Service connections became available.

Today, work is complete on a new tribal store with a gasoline station, and the tribal officials are pushing to complete home repairs and the new water system on what they fear may be the last of their rehabilitation grants from HUD. The store is managed by a Coushatta staff.

The Chitimacha had hoped for a crafts outlet, but that effort fell short and the cooperative never developed. They did build a tribal store, a meat/fish preparation center, and a fast food outlet. The fast food outlet was built in expectation of the state of Louisiana's short-lived push to develop the nearby portions of the Atchafalaya Basin (Hoover 1975) as an outdoor recreation area. It stands empty, mute testimony to the hopes of the tribe for economic autonomy through fusion of state and federal developments.

The Chitimachas, too, have had housing rehabilitation moneys, and the Office of Indian Education has expanded their day school, opened in the 1940s, into a full elementary school with a beautiful brick facility located in the center of the Chitimacha land base. In 1989 the tribe, as a cooperative venture with Jean Lafitte National Park, opened its own museum.

The Jena Choctaw used their HUD grant to purchase a tribal land base, albeit just a few acres, their first land ownership since 1900. After they migrated to Oklahoma in the 1890s (Gregory 1979) they returned to Louisiana and to full-time sharecropping. Local planters and bankers systematically refused Indians loans or mortgages, so the purchase of the land base was an especially important event for all the tribal people. By the 1980s one of the heirs to the farmland where the Jena Choctaw had labored so long as sharecroppers returned to the tribe some five acres of land on which the Indians had traditionally maintained their isolated all-Choctaw burial area, White Rock Cemetery. The Jena Choctaw lacked nonrent housing, so housing improvement grants were not available, though the tribal members were able to get some succor from a fuel supplement program that applied to renters as well as home owners.

The Tunica-Biloxi were able to repair three older houses on their land and, with the Coushatta tribal workers and the Summer Youth Corps, attempted to renovate their old "trading post" and use it as a tribal office. It was only totally abandoned after the tribe received a large HUD grant for their new administrative center. Since federal recognition they have had their land surveyed, established a long-term development plan, and finished ten new housing units. Tribal families are returning to the land base. A museum, built under a HUD grant, has opened. It houses the now famous "Tunica Treasure." A new tribal police station has just opened, and the tribe has begun operation of its newest venture, Sikania, a pecan processing plant at Mansura, Louisiana. Moreover, the state of Louisiana had also leased to the Tunica-Biloxi the Marksville Prehistoric Mounds Park and museum on a hundred-year lease. All these developments are part of a long-range plan developed by the tribe (Coco and the Tunica-Biloxi Tribe 1985) that will facilitate economic development and tribal independence. In 1989 the tribe contributed $1.2 million to the local economy and employed some seventy-one people, the bulk of whom are non-Indian (Barbry 1989). Their woodlands and cemeteries are now considered important resources, and traditional sacred areas have been mapped for preservation. An archaeological survey and developmental plan have been completed (Gregory and Pine 1988).

These material changes will not likely sound as impressive as they really are. The substandard housing, without plumbing, sometimes without electricity, will soon be a thing of the past at Coushatta; it is already at

Chitimacha and Tunica-Biloxi. For those who remember the Tunica-Biloxi tribal meetings in the top room of the local cattle auction barn in the early 1970s, or the long evenings crowded into one of the four rooms of the late Chief Pierite's shotgun house, the changes are amazing. Similarly, they are astounding to those who remember the late 1960s when the Coushatta met at St. Peter's Congregational Church or in the back of the shotgun store built by the Coushatta Alliance, with a single pay phone on the outside wall.

From the front two rooms of an abandoned auto repair shop in 1975 to their own tribal center is an equal leap for the Jena Choctaw. It is almost unbelievable how much material change the tribes have been able to generate since 1970.

The other groups have had less physical development, but where it was possible it has taken place. In 1975 the Clifton Choctaw community was strung along a dirt road that wound between the barbed-wire fences of a large private landholding. Today the road is paved, some housing rehabilitation has taken place, a softball field/recreational complex has been built, and, for awhile at least, a tribal office was maintained in a trailer purchased with an ANA grant. In 1989 the tribe maintained an official building on their land. The tribe, like everyone except the Jena Choctaw, also tried a crafts cooperative but never opened a shop. It again was abortive, and only the cane syrup sold by the Clifton Choctaw was close to profitable. The lack of tribal land (all the Clifton families live on individual holdings) seems to slow their development, likely the by-product of federal and state grant guidelines applicable throughout the 1970s and early 1980s.

The Ebarb and Converse communities (Faine and Gregory 1986) of the Choctaw-Apache did manage to receive housing rehabilitation and fuel supplement moneys and for the first time were able to influence the parish police jury (county board) with their presence, potential, and needs. A push to obtain a land base near the public school at Ebarb, on land set aside for the Toledo Bend Reservoir Authority in the 1960s, remains a goal that may yet materialize. Tribal meetings are held today, as in the past, in the community hall of the Catholic church or at private homes. In the last twenty years, all the roads in the communities have been hard surfaced, and today virtually no home is without electric power. In 1961 many had no running water and no electric power and even butane stoves were new. This group, with its roots in the mixture of Lipan Apache slaves and Choctaw bands of the Spanish colonial period, rivals the Houma in size. While it has had access to public education, the communities have suffered from poverty and social isolation. The fact that Spanish surnames and language were common has led to double discrimination because the people are

*Left:* Clyde Jackson (right), Jena Choctaw, past Louisiana Commissioner of Indian Affairs and past tribal chairman, discussing federal recognition with Congressman Jerry Huckaby (Dem.) of Louisiana, ca. 1979. (Courtesy Division of Informational Services, Northwestern State University of Louisiana). *Below:* Coushatta Tribal Center, ca. 1985. (Photo: Don Sepulvado, Courtesy Don Sepulvado)

*Above:* A Choctaw-Apache elder, Sabine Parish, Louisiana, ca. 1979. (Photo: Hiram F. Gregory). *Below:* Ana Juneau and Norma Kwahajo, Tunica-Biloxi basket makers and apprenticeship workshop of Tunica-Biloxi tribal center, 1988. (Photo: Don Sepulvado, Courtesy Don Sepulvado)

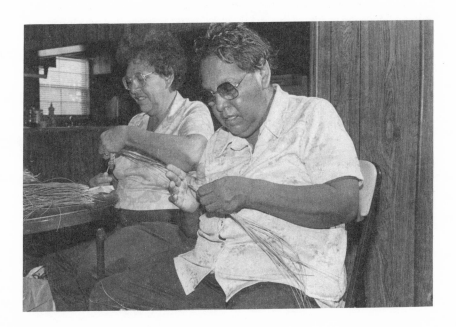

frequently treated as recent Mexican immigrants. Lack of a land base hampers development, but efforts continue for recognition.

The Houma, too, have profited from the various programs available to them as poverty-level people. Like their counterparts at Jena, Clifton, and Ebarb, they have not shared in the Department of Housing and Urban Development nor the Economic Development Administration grants available to tribes with land bases and/or federal recognition. Still, needs assessments led to housing rehabilitation and fuel and food supplements; and gradually the tribe, through ANA grants, was able to establish a tribal office in Houma. The Methodist church has maintained a Houma Indian Center at Dulac, Louisiana, since at least the early 1940s but has not fostered independent tribal control of the facility, maintaining a full-time, non-Indian director.

Spiller Milton (1976:16) has summarized the impact of this Methodist involvement among the Houma for the Dulac area by pointing out that a school built by the Methodist mission board was the only facility available to the Houma in that area until 1953 and that as late as the 1970s the western Houma high school dropout rate was 96 percent. By 1989 the tribe had students enrolled in college and at least one Dartmouth graduate to its credit.

In the 1960s the Houma had successfully mounted a campaign to end legal segregation of their children into all-Indian schools. In 1963, thirty Houma students entered a formerly all-white school, and by 1964 nearly all the Houmas were attending public schools (Fischer 1968:212–235). Still, no Houma land base was established and, so, no center developed. As late as 1979 it was still possible to discuss the Houma as at least two distinct population clusters, those on lower Bayou Lafourche and those in Terrebonne Parish to the west. By 1980 they had united their efforts and some material benefits accrued.

Efforts to mount Houma economic autonomy continued well into the 1980s with the Dulac leadership fighting for a fishing cooperative to break the hold of "company stores" who outfit fishermen and trappers. That is still, as of 1991, one of the strongest pushes of Houma leaders. It has yet to happen.

With the help of Mennonite volunteers the Houma have, however, made a somewhat better effort with a crafts cooperative. Now under the direction of a Houma craftsman, it at least manages some tribal marketing. It still lacks a successful profit margin and relies on various grant funding from time to time.

The Louisiana Tribe of Choctaw, most often termed the East Baton Rouge Choctaw, have likely benefited least from program development. Their employment figures have generally been higher, as have their educational levels. Housing rehabilitation, fuel supplements, and other sources have not been as pertinent to this group.

They have managed to develop some educational programs with some classes in crafts and the Choctaw language and, as might be suspected for an urban group, managed the earliest pantribal powwow held in Louisiana. The powwow seems to have replaced the Indian Angels organization and, in fact, has the same format and many of the same participants. It has been held in Baton Rouge and at the Poverty Point State Commemorative Area. Pantribalism is stronger among this group than any others, and Plains Indian headdresses and Pueblo- and Plains-style jewelry are plainly Indian identity markers. Their interest in cultural and retention programs clearly reflects these urban Indian hallmarks. Whatever direction development takes, it will have to happen in an urban setting, without a land base, and likely will be more programmatic than material in nature. In 1986 the Louisiana Board of Choctaw was in the throes of planning a tribal lottery patterned after one declared legal for the Louisiana State University Alumni Association (personal communication, Ralph Murphy, 1986).

By 1988 a new pantribal organization, the Twin Eagles, had appeared in Shreveport. It is similar in its pantribal organization to the old Baton Rouge urban groups, but it is not politically active, rather preferring to stress powwows and "traditional" Indian religion. It is attracting a number of "New Wave" religionists to its gatherings.

Other tribal developments have been extended through the state Office of Indian Affairs, the most important being the Indian Manpower program of the federally funded Comprehensive Employment and Training Act (CETA)—subsequently, the Job Training Partnership Act (JTPA). Moneys and job training components have been implemented for the Houma, Jena Choctaw, Coushatta, Chitimacha, and Tunica-Biloxi. Administration by the Inter-Tribal Council has meant that some overhead moneys have been made available to that Indian organization to facilitate other grant developments as well. Out of both HUD and CETA, the tribes have developed staff positions, mainly for carpenters, equipment operators, secretaries, administrators, and other tribally related service personnel. At the Jena Choctaw, Clifton Choctaw, and Choctaw-Apache at Ebarb community, ANA grants have allowed the operation of tribal offices by Indian personnel. Both Clifton Choctaw and the Choctaw-Apache of Ebarb are using recently acquired grants to fund federal recognition petition research.

## Education

The Coushatta Tribe actively involved its youth in the federally funded Summer Youth programs and eventually became the regional supervisors for that program in their planning district. The Houma and Chitimacha, and to a lesser extent Jena Choctaw and East Baton Rouge Choctaw, have also been involved in those programs. The loss of CETA funding brought the tribes back to the harsh realities of federal budget cuts. The loss of HUD and CETA jobs, lapses in ANA contracts, and the diminution of health service funding had left tribal leaders and members alike with a new awareness of the fragility of much of their apparent success. Employment problems and educational problems (recently the state Office of Indian Affairs could count only thirty-five college graduates known from the eight organized tribes) seem to be the major concerns of the tribes; and as Clyde Jackson, former state commissioner of Indian affairs, pointed out at Title IV grants meetings in Alexandria, Louisiana, in 1987, these things are seen to be related. The bulk of these programs are for elementary school, and most involve tutorial programs of one kind or another. Arts and crafts programs have been implemented but are burdened with the difficulties of convincing school boards and superintendents about the need for traditional crafts and teachers as pertain to individual tribes.

According to Marilyn Watt of the Tulsa office of CETA, the Louisiana Indian communities are especially notable in that they all have deep involvement between tribal parents' committees and Title IV and parish school officials. In the main, this involvement has had a strengthening effect on program development. The lack of involvement with pan-tribalism had led to conflict between the Tunica-Biloxi committee and their local school officials, so much so that they withdrew in protest over non-Indian art teachers and the Plains-Pueblo arts format implemented in the schools. The board rapidly changed its position and the next arts programs were taught by traditional Tunica-Biloxi craftspeople. No other problems have been noted, and all the tribes now seem to see the need for these programs. Unfortunately, Indian populations (with the exceptions of the Houma, though even they are spread over several school districts) are small and rather dispersed across school administrative areas. The low amounts of money available, the tribal connection to the parents' committees, the program guidelines, and reporting have slowed school participation, but that seems much ameliorated and virtually every school board with Indian children has some involvement at this time.

New job training programs implemented by the state and federal governments seem to be replacing the old CETA-funded programs. The tribes used those funds well, not only to buffer unemployment but also to provide incentive for their high school and upper elementary students to stay in school and to maintain a C grade-point average. The temporary lull in those programs was short enough that most see some improvements at hand.

Education, now heralded for opening jobs to Indians, in a state with serious employment problems due to the decline in the petrochemical industries is both a blessing and a curse to the tribes. In few of the tribal areas—99 percent rural—do adequately developed job markets exist for any educated population. Completion of degrees often means loss of population. The lower socioeconomic and educational levels of Indian communities, even when oil prices were high and developmental funding more plentiful, led to demand for drastic changes in health, housing, education, and welfare. The tribes opened as many jobs requiring advanced education as they possibly could—in office administration, health, construction, and other areas related to their grant capabilities. Now unemployment is rising and the tribal authorities are seeking new ways to maintain and improve on the progress they made in the 1970s and the first half of the 1980s. Education will not likely be the panacea, but it is certainly not a placebo either. The fact remains that in 1989 every tribal group had students in college.

Tribal involvement in development has led to more interaction with the other southeastern tribes, especially among the federally recognized tribes involved in the United South and Eastern Tribes. Stimulated by Seminole and Cherokee successes to the east, the Coushatta began a tribal bingo game on their trust land base. The local sheriff refused to acknowledge federal trust status of the tribal center, seized their equipment, and arrested tribal leaders and workers. After court confrontation the officials were released, but the tribe was much distraught and polarized over the issue. It was the last straw in an old internal political factionalism and led to the complete overhaul of the tribal administration. After the first election in fifteen years, not a single tribal official remained in office.

Chitimacha tribal developments have had severe setbacks in administrative scandal and the loss of a major land claim case. Distraught and with poor public relations, the tribe has managed to spring back. Its regular bingo programs are now funding tribal education funds used to augment Indian education moneys.

Times were worse for the Chitimacha than other tribes because that tribe is so dependent on the oil industry. Even tribal oil income from their land base has dwindled due to drops in prices, and unemployment has increased. Some, always the lowest income Chitimacha, have continued to fish commercially and work in the Atchafalaya Basin, but since the 1940s the tribe has looked to the developing coastal oil industry for jobs.

## Cultural Change and Maintenance

All the tribes have maintained their full complements of traditional arts. The Jena Choctaw, Coushatta, Chitimacha, and Houma were all represented by traditional craftspeople at the 1985 Smithsonian Folklife Festival. The Jena Choctaw remain one of the few groups in the South to continue the traditional tanning of deerskins. Cane basketry, chinaberry necklaces, blowguns, beadwork, and appliqué shirts tie their crafts to those of Choctaw in Mississippi and Oklahoma. Still, these crafts are the products of individuals, and some even refuse to sell their production! There is no tribal outlet, nor is there any overt effort to organize one.

Coushatta maintain their elegant pine-straw basketry tradition, and two women and two men still manufacture their more traditional split-cane basketry. Blowguns, toys, and other woodworks are commonly made. Beadwork, popular in the 1960s, has declined, as has moss weaving (a common activity in the 1930s, it is seldom practiced today). Again, each craftsperson brokers for him/herself and only two or three people seem to have attempted any entrepreneurial skills at marketing or promoting their crafts.

The Houma have done moderately well, but woodcarving, palmetto weaving (basketry and hats), a few blowguns, and other crafts have a limited distribution, even through their cooperative. No Houmas manage to make a living at their crafts.

Mennonite efforts to organize crafts for the Clifton Choctaw and the Choctaw-Apache have failed. Both groups produce white-oak and some local variety of pine-straw basketry, beautiful quilts, and a number of small crafts: yucca whips (toys), gourd birdhouses and dippers, cow-horn carvings and spoons, goose-feather whistles, and other things. These crafts are considered old-fashioned and are not viable as full-time economic endeavors. Isolation and the lack of promotion limit their development.

At Tunica-Biloxi pine-straw basketry, beadwork, doll making, horn spoons, woodwork, and some silverwork all flourished in the 1960s and 1970s. Unfortunately, tribal elders have not been able to maintain production, and the arts have not been passed on to many younger people. Presently, only four or five craftspeople approach any level of income, on even a supplemental basis, from their traditional crafts. Tunica-Biloxi leaders still constantly urge the traditional artists to teach. A series of recent grants have funded apprenticeships between older and younger tribal basket makers.

It is unfortunate that the few efforts at a crafts cooperative have failed. These efforts were frustrated by tribal demands for profits, by the individualistic nature of the craftspeople, and by the fact that these are the most conservative of items and people. Some, like the Jena Choctaw, resist seeing their artistry alienated from tribal tradition. Moreover, the production of crafts, even among the Chitimacha whose basketry tradition supports at least one full-time artisan, has a relatively low status attachment. As late as the 1930s and 1940s, selling basketry and other crafts was something people did in hard times, sometimes only in lieu of begging, and the social situation of having to peddle door to door or having to sit on street corners has been only slightly modified by long days outdoors at various festivals and fairs. The Louisiana tribal traditionalists understand, if no others do, the beauty and quality of their arts. More and more they seem unhappy with the ways and means available to them for marketing their products.

The other traditions, religion, folklore, music, and medicine have long been considered private, almost family traditions. The Corn Feast is held as part festival and part religious celebration. Nontribal people are banned from the traditional religious activities but are invited to a Catholic Mass.

The Coushatta have, with the help of Wycliffe Bible Translators, published two readers for the tribal people, the first time they have seen Coushatta written. Still, because the native language is preferred, they do not fear its loss. Elders note, frequently now, though, that young people only speak "baby talk" and some younger people have to admit that they cannot count in their native language. So in even the most conservative of all the southeastern Indian speech communities, the impact of public schooling and outside contact is taking a toll on the language.

The only other native speech community left in Louisiana, at the Jena Choctaw, is in a much more threatened situation. Most of the Choctaw speakers have married non-Choctaws and the children are virtually monolingual in English. A series of language workshops in 1974, sponsored by a grant that provided a linguist and attempted to train native speakers to teach more or less formal classes to the children, had little effect except that it created wider tribal awareness of the problem. Because less than a third of the population now is fluent in Choctaw, the language does seem in jeopardy.

The impact of federal and state program development on the tribes has only begun to be studied. Coushatta cultural change was the topic of a paper by Dan Jacobson at a national ethnohistory meeting in 1985. He observed more factionalism than he had observed in the 1950s. He also lamented the changes in material culture, pointing out that one of his friends now made his blowguns out of plastic pipe (PVC) instead of cane! One craftsman said herbicides sprayed on local fields had taken their toll on the canebrakes.

Jacobson further stated that there was a decline in attendance at the

Congregationalist church in the Coushatta community. Where that church once dominated the Coushatta, it now competes with three other churches. The expulsion of the non-Coushatta Congregationalist minister in the 1970s was pointed out by tribal leaders as part of the wider move toward Indian autonomy and self-determination. Since that time a native Koasati-speaking minister has served that congregation. The other religions, all sects of one Pentecostal church or another, clearly reflect the increasing contact with Coushattas living near the Alabama-Coushatta in east Texas, where Pentecostalism has actively competed with the Presbyterians and Congregationalists for tribal membership. Rather than ascribe these changes to factionalism due to program development and reorganization, it seems equally viable to relate them to trends toward autonomy and to the effects of increased mobility. Native ministers serve in all these churches and Coushatta language sermons are heard weekly, something never heard in the 1950s.

Marilyn Watt (personal communication, 1985) is currently engaged in a detailed study of program development among the Jena Choctaw, likely the first detailed study of its kind among the Louisiana tribes. It should be added here that certainly at the Jena Choctaw and Tunica-Biloxi the roots of tribal factionalism are older and more deeply rooted in tribal tradition than federal or state program development. Factions exist in all the Louisiana communities; some, doubtless, are traceable to very ancient tribal divisions. However, one recent development in tribal factionalism does seem widespread and certainly seems new. At the Coushatta, Tunica-Biloxi, Choctaw-Apache, Clifton Choctaw, and, to a lesser extent, Jena Choctaw communities a certain amount of tension has developed as urbanized members return and become politically active. At the Coushatta, Clifton Choctaw, and Choctaw-Apache tribal areas, these people have either become tribal leaders or, as was the case at the Coushatta, backed eligible candidates who assumed that role. Less traditional, more assertive, and more interested in development and economic success, these individuals have had powerful impacts on the Indian communities in the state. Their presence and influences are far too recent—none existed before 1980—to evaluate, but it is not likely they will disappear from the scene. They are this generation's equivalents of the World War II veterans who returned from their travels with new ideas and hopes for the future. These people returning from urban experiences in Houston, Los Angeles, and other cities have had some experience in pantribal activism and Indian affairs, most are literate, and many have some business school definitions of development. The older conflicts between traditional chiefs (the last of the traditional chiefs of both the Chitimacha and the Tunica-Biloxi have died within the past two decades) and the new, more bureaucratic, reorganization demands have ameliorated. Programs now demand and often provide more services to the people. Yet the feeling that older ways were somewhat better, less meddlesome, more generous, and in some ways more "Indian" persists. Factionalism, based on conservative versus more progressive conflicts and on kin-based and religious disputes, is a latent foundation for intense tribal politics, and the returning politicians often seem to find fertile places to sow new seeds between the factions.

## Hard Times

One tribal chairman, commenting on the overview of tribal development, expressed more recent tribal developments rather well: "They had fun in the 1970s, but hard times are here with us now."

Part of the problem was, as has been mentioned, the federal budget cuts, but the greater impact has been the declining economic base of the state of Louisiana. The decline of the petrochemical industry hit the tribes of Louisiana as hard or harder than other citizens of the state. Everyone felt the loss. The reform administration of Governor Buddy Roemer has gradually had some impact on the situation, but unsolved problems remain in employment, education, and literacy. As late as 1986 the state led the nation in unemployment and in 1989 the situation had changed only slightly. The tribes, partially as an attempt to survive federal cuts and partially to correct for growing economic woes in their regions, have responded with a new spirit of entrepreneurship. The Tunica-Biloxi have invested heavily in their pecan processing plant, the Coushatta Tribe has an industrial park near DeRidder, Louisiana, and has opened a tribal store on its trust land base. The Tunica-Biloxi and the Chitimacha are also planning on tourist development; both tribes have opened new museum complexes. The Tunica-Biloxi, using a HUD grant, have opened a new facility to exhibit their Tunica Treasure, artifacts regained from a treasure hunter only by several years of litigation. They also have entered into a hundred-year lease with the state of Louisiana to operate and develop the Marksville Prehistoric Mounds Park and museum, a former state commemorative area that was allowed to decline during the state's recent economic decline. Both tribes have entered into a letter of cooperation with Jean Lafitte National Park, providing the tribes with some jobs, training, and technical assistance. These actions in the minds of some tribal leaders at least, have been seen as one more step toward self-determination. Now the tribes have some say as to how Louisiana Indian culture will be depicted and some direct input into the state educational system. That, of course, is a new voice for the tribes.

After the round of bingo fiascoes, conflicts with local authorities have been resolved, and the tribes with trust land bases are operating bingo parlors with some success. The Chitimacha are planning to invest a portion of their profit in education programs for their college students.

Land claims appeared sporadically among the Louisiana tribal groups throughout the 1980s. The Chitimacha filed and lost a large claim for 3,000 acres of their beloved Atchafalaya Basin. The Tunica-Biloxi, with a tentative claim to some 17,000 acres of land, have not yet filed the claim but have not relinquished their opportunity to do so either. The Coushatta Tribe quietly, with little local publicity, won a $1.3 million land claim, and 20 percent of that amount has been set aside for tribal development. So land claims have had a mixed impact. Local public relations have not been easy inasmuch as Louisiana citizens do not understand the nature of claims nor why the tribes are entitled to them. Tribal governments, now in competition with local business interests, have found local competitors quick to stir emotional anti-Indian controversies by warning people of "land claims." Tribal leaders can, as the Tunica-Biloxi chairman recently did, respond that they are now providing jobs and increasing local incomes (Barbry 1989). They can also explain that their bingo operations must have federal clearances and that the nature of their land claims is such that their neighbors will not be adversely affected by them. Still, the narrow economic base of Louisiana leaves the tribal governments constantly vulnerable to pressures from the non-Indian community. Entrepreneurial skills and competition with non-Indian endeavors still seem to evoke some of the same responses they did in the days of the nineteenth-century Indian removals. Today the tribes have some skill at combating these pressures, though members of most tribal groups state they feel the negative pressure and it hurts their feelings. Still most tribal groups are pursuing their rights to success, and they take heart in that they can compete and make contributions to the whole region, no matter how narrow their critics.

So the hard times persist. The tribes have had them before and they have always fallen back on their own resources to save themselves. They have maintained their identity and polity to cope with the negative pressures of the society around them. Perhaps this negative pressure has always been a functional component of tribal life. The tribes and communities face the future with new tools and a lot of fortitude. As one Choctaw leader has stated (Gregory 1977:9), "We draw strength from our culture."

It is that strength that has saved them before and likely will again.

# 9

# OVERVIEW OF SOUTHEASTERN INDIAN TRIBES TODAY

*George Roth*

The tribes discussed in the chapters in this volume are extremely diverse in size and character.[1] Some are among the larger tribes in the country—for example, the Lumbee of North Carolina, with approximately 40,000 members, and the Houma of Louisiana with approximately 11,000. Membership size ranges down to the Eastern Chickahominy of Virginia, with a formal membership of 42 adults, while a significant number of the tribes are intermediate in size, with between 1,000 and 5,000 members.

Only a few of the tribes have maintained any significant degree of traditional culture, most notably the Seminole, Miccosukee, and Mississippi Choctaw. The Eastern Cherokee, Coushatta, and Jena Choctaw have maintained some culture, including the traditional language, among at least part of their membership. A few others, like the Chitimacha, Tunica-Biloxi, and Catawba, are close in time to an era when traditional culture still functioned. The rest are described by the authors as more or less culturally similar to, while socially distinct from, their non-Indian neighbors.

An important distinction for this review is between tribes with clear-cut and accepted tribal origins and identities and ones whose Indianness or specific tribal origins presently or in the past have been the subject of debate and disagreement with non-Indians and sometimes with other tribes. Examples of the former are the Poarch Creek and Tunica-Biloxi. Examples of the latter are the Lumbee and various South Carolina tribes. In some instances, the authors note tribes that have only just recently begun to define themselves and claim specific tribal origins.

An important dimension for understanding the recent history and present character of the southeastern tribes is the status of their recognition as tribes by the various states and by the federal government. Federally recognized status means that the federal government recognizes a "government-to-government" relationship with the United States and the existence of a trust responsibility for the tribe. This recognition gives such tribes a unique legal status within the United States as partially sovereign entities. State recognition varies in significance from state reservations established by treaty to a simple designation by the state government that carries no appreciably different legal status from non-Indians in the state. Three tribes have state recognition and reservations that derive from the colonial era and give them distinct legal statuses within their states. These are the Pamunkey, Mattaponi, and Catawba. In the modern era, many federally unrecognized tribes have gained a limited form of state recognition.

Five tribes had federally recognized status before 1970: the Chitimacha, Mississippi Choctaw, Eastern Cherokee, Miccosukee, and Seminole. The Coushatta were recognized from at least the 1930s until 1953, when services were administratively withdrawn. No congressional action, however, was taken to terminate them. They were re-recognized in 1973. The Catawba were federally recognized in 1943 and terminated in 1962. The Catawba are the only terminated tribe in the South and one of the few remaining in the country. Two tribes, the Poarch Band of Creeks and the Tunica-Biloxi, have become federally recognized in the past decade through the administrative process established in 1978.[2]

The regulations governing the federal recognition process establish a particular definition of tribe for purposes of establishing a government-to-government relationship with the United States. This definition is derived from the case law that forms the basis of the unique legal status of federally recognized tribes in the United States. As such, it reflects non-Indian concepts about the nature of "tribes," although it is influenced by ethnological considerations as well.

To be federally recognized, a group must demonstrate that it has existed as a distinct community, within which tribal political processes have existed, since first sustained contact with non-Indians. The group must have been identified as an Indian group throughout history by entities outside itself, such as the federal government, local governments, other Indian tribes, or scholars. In addition, the membership must be able to demonstrate ancestry from the historic tribe (or tribes that have combined, for example, the Tunica-Biloxi) from which the present tribe is derived. The definition of tribe in the regulations may, and in all likelihood does, differ from the meaning or meanings of tribe implied in the chapters by the various authors in this volume. As an alternative to the administrative process, a number of unrecognized groups have in the past several years sought federal recognition through legislation. These include the Houma, Mowa Choctaw, Jena Choctaw, Florida Tribe of Eastern Creeks, and Lumbee.

Research by federally unrecognized tribes in preparation for petitioning for federal recognition has greatly expanded knowledge of the history and character of these peoples. The authors have undoubtedly been cautious in their characterizations, based on research that is not yet complete, because of the perception that these could subsequently influence the process of consideration for recognition. For the same reason, this author, as part of the staff that conducts the federal government's rather detailed study and evaluation of petitioning tribes, has avoided stating (or reaching) any independent conclusions about the character of the tribes described in this volume.

## Changes in the Past Twenty-Five Years

The southeastern tribes, particularly the unrecognized ones, have undergone a significant series of changes in the past twenty-five years. Though these changes vary in degree from tribe to tribe, they have many common features as a result of changes in the larger society and through interaction between the tribes. Part of the variation between tribes today appears to reflect the appearance of changes among some tribes earlier than among others who are nonetheless following somewhat the same path.

Changes have occurred in the organization, character, and identity of the tribes and in their relationship to local, state, and federal governments. The tribes have developed more formal and more complex governmental and other organizational characteristics. They have become service providers and have developed new institutions such as tribal offices (sometimes with permanent staff), tribal meeting centers, and annual powwows. To a degree they are becoming corporate organizations, with a defined membership and common resources used for the benefit of the group. Tribal identities have evolved, strengthening and changing in character.

The tribes' relationships to local, state, and national governments and to each other are responsible for much of the change in tribal character. These relationships have become more intense and widespread as the tribes have become less isolated and more sophisticated in drawing on the resources of the larger society. The tribes have increasingly used these relationships to advance their goals.

The tribes have changed along with the changes occurring in southern society beginning in the 1960s. The chapters in this volume describe groups whose members before the 1960s were largely poor, rural, and with limited education. Even the federally recognized tribes had few resources and few formal political institutions. In the segregated southern past the position of the Indian (with the possible exception of the Seminoles, who may have been outside the system altogether) was a third category in a system that had established a strong color line based on only two categories, white and black. Indians, as nonwhites, had maintained a distinct racial and social position, but a low status one. Different tribes had varying degrees of success in gaining complete acceptance as Indian depending on their particular character and history. Federally recognized tribes had relatively less difficulty than recognized ones because of their legal recognition as distinct Indian entities; even the Mississippi Choctaw, however, were forced to maintain a complete separation from both whites and blacks in order to achieve a separate identity (Thompson and Peterson 1975:180). Indians sought to avoid identification with the black population of these eras and to avoid thereby the social disabilities associated with that status.

The post–Civil War era had seen a sharpening of the racial divisions in comparison with the earlier part of the nineteenth century. As a result, the populations identifying as Indian drew into themselves, more strongly asserting identification as Indian and becoming more endogamous. Indian status in some areas declined beginning in the late nineteenth century, as rural areas became less isolated. Land status was threatened, economic relationships with whites changed, and formal education became more important. The Indians' independent farming and hunting existence tended to be replaced with sharecropping or wage-work in the lumber industry, as farm laborers, or in other unskilled jobs.

The early 1960s brought changes on several fronts. The 1964 Civil Rights Act had the effect of providing access to better-paying jobs (e.g., at factories), which had previously been denied to Indians as well as blacks. Rural populations, including the Indians, became better educated and more knowledgeable about the outside world and had more personal economic resources.

The Civil Rights Act also brought desegregation of schools—which was seen as a mixed blessing by various tribes. Many, if not most, of the tribes had managed between the 1880s and the 1920s to establish separate Indian schools (refusing for the most part to attend black schools and being denied entrance to white ones). These schools were often the result of Indian community labor and financial support and thus were a focus of community institutions. Better education was a primary community goal. The tribes had managed through various efforts and political activities to influence local and state authorities either to establish or eventually to assume responsibility and support for these schools after the Indians had established them. The schools were thus symbols of recognition of identity as Indian as well as major focuses of the community.

In the decade beginning in the early 1960s, most of these schools were closed and the children sent to now-integrated schools. A trade-off for the loss of separate schools was access to better quality education. In the era of separate Indian schools the education was generally of a low quality and access to high school and college was limited. Although some Indians managed higher education, it was usually necessary to leave the state (e.g., to go to mission-run schools or the like).

The various authors see the development of tribal center buildings (frequently with federal funding from non-Indian programs) as a replacement for the schools as social centers and symbols of the tribe. In some cases the tribes have managed to retain the former school building for use as a tribal center. The tribal center buildings serve as meeting places as well as a kind of visible, territorial symbol of the existence of tribes.

Annual powwows have also flourished in the modern era as tribal symbols and assertions of Indian identity. The Chickahominy Fall Festival was initiated in 1951, that of the Haliwa-Saponi in 1965, the Poarch Band's in 1970, and a variety of others in the 1970s and 1980s. The celebrations typically draw dancers and visitors from a variety of southeastern tribes as well as sometimes from farther away. Besides being events for the tribe itself, they sometimes play a role in enhancing local non-Indian acceptance of the group as Indian (see especially Paredes's discussion of this strategy in Chap. 6). These celebrations draw to varying degrees on the Plains Indian–oriented pan-Indian tradition as well as developing local traditions and reviving tribally specific traditions. An example of the latter is Oklahoma Creek tutelage of members of the Poarch Creek Band. Lerch (Chap. 3) describes the Waccamaw powwow as adopting symbols that may be pan-Indian but that celebrate a local Indian identity.

Beginning in the late 1960s and continuing throughout the 1970s and into the early 1980s, new forms of organization and relationships between the tribes and non-Indian society emerged and spread from tribe to tribe and state to state.

An important force in the early era was the Coalition of Eastern Native Americans, commonly known as CENA. Formed in 1971, this organization of unrecognized tribes east of the Mississippi worked to strengthen Indian tribes. It promoted greater use of federal moneys from programs outside the BIA as well as the establishment of relationships with states and use of state programs. It also worked to strengthen the organization of the tribes. For example, CENA advised the Tunica-Biloxi and others concerning the development of written governmental charters. At least four of the (then) unrecognized southeastern tribes were among the earliest members: Poarch Creek, Chickahominy, Catawba, and Four Holes Edisto.

Although a few of the unrecognized tribes already had formalized governing structures (e.g., defined councils, election of members, etc.), these became widespread in the fifteen years between 1968 and 1983. These structures were created because of the advice of groups like CENA, as a result of acquaintance with them in other tribes, or in response to the demands of administering various state and federal social programs of the era. More generally, the tribes were apparently influenced by the idea that such formalized governing structures were necessary to deal more effectively with non-Indians and to mobilize the efforts of the membership. Early examples are the Lumbees' Lumbee Regional Development Association in 1968 and a nonprofit organization formed by the Waccamaw in 1972 that eventually became the Waccamaw Siouan Development Association. These are characterized as having evolved subsequently into governing bodies. The Tunica-Biloxi adopted their first written governing document in 1974. In Virginia, beginning with the Rappahannocks in 1974, nonreservation tribes formed corporations under state law, in some cases reestablishing formal organizations begun fifty or more years earlier and subsequently abandoned (see Rountree, Chap. 1).

Relationships to state governments have been and continue to be a major focus of the efforts of Indian tribes in the different states to improve their conditions. State relationships took on a new shape with the establishment of state Indian commissions that gave the Indians a formalized position within state governments to advocate for their needs. The commissions often serve as vehicles for administering grants and programs and providing technical advice benefiting multiple tribes. The earliest appear to have been the Louisiana Governor's Commission on Indian Affairs, established in 1970, and the North Carolina Commission of Indian Affairs, established in 1971. Equivalent offices followed in Florida in 1974, Alabama in 1975 (subsequently dissolved in 1983 and reformed in 1984), South Carolina in 1979, and Virginia in 1983.

A major driving and facilitating force for change was federal social programs, which not only improved social conditions but provided resources to assist in the development of tribal organizations. Many began with the passage of the Economic Opportunities Act in 1964, the same year as the Civil Rights Act. Strengthening tribal organizations was not necessarily a deliberate aim initially, but it had become so with the transfer in 1973 of many programs to the Office of Native American Programs (ONAP) of the Department of Health, Education, and Welfare that in turn became the Administration for Native Americans (ANA) in 1977. The CETA jobs program between 1973 and 1981 was of particular importance, helping provide staff positions for infant tribal offices in many of the tribes. HUD and Economic Development Administration grants contributed to the ability to create physical facilities for tribal centers. Tribal members also benefited from a variety of federal and state social and educational programs, such as Job Corps, VISTA, Head Start, and legal services, either directly or through state Indian organizations.

Though particularly pertaining to the unrecognized tribes, some of these trends applied to the federally recognized tribes as well. The recognized tribes also began to deal directly with states more frequently, to participate in national organizations, and to participate in government social programs. The Seminoles, Miccosukees, and Mississippi Choctaws modified and greatly expanded their formal governmental structures in response to the requirements of new programs and functions and the desire to control these programs themselves. For the recognized tribes, the self-determination policies and laws instituted in the 1970s provided new opportunities by providing for the tribes to take over programs formerly run by the BIA and the Indian Health Service.

The organization of both the recognized and the unrecognized tribes was affected by the opportunities and requirements of federally funded social and poverty programs. These programs provided both experience and awareness of new possibilities for tribal governments. Peterson and Kersey (Chaps. 7 and 5) describe Mississippi Band of Choctaw and Seminole Tribe participation in and control of these programs as key processes in gaining experience and sophistication in learning how to organize and run programs, experience transferred from social programs into tribal government and tribally sponsored economic and business projects. Paredes (Chap. 6) describes a similar effect, though on a lesser scale, for the Poarch Band of Creeks before they became federally recognized.

## Expanded Relationships with Indians and Non-Indians _____

In the past, many of the southeastern tribes were quite isolated from contact with, or even awareness of, other Indian tribes. Federally recognized and unrecognized tribes and their individual members have become much less isolated in the past three decades. Contact between tribes occurs within the framework of state Indian councils and the like and to some degree through organizations such as the United South and Eastern Tribes (USET). Powwows and similar events bring visitors from other tribes in the South as well as from elsewhere in the country. Reducing isolation is a deliberate part of efforts, particularly on the part of certain of the tribes, to enhance tribal development by building wider relationships with other Indians and with non-Indians.

An aggressive style of interaction with the local non-Indian populations as a way of promoting the tribe's interests is described for only some of the tribes. Differences in dealing with local non-Indians appear to reflect variances in the character and aggressiveness of the tribes' leadership and quite possibly different individual possibilities for success, for example, because of local prejudice. Powwows are one of the most common arenas of interaction with local non-Indians. As well as being assertions of Indian identity to the non-Indian community, powwows in part have become tourist attractions, stimulating interaction with local non-Indians.

A deliberate strategy of enlisting local support is not totally new, especially for the unrecognized tribes, but its character and aggressiveness have changed from earlier eras. In the past, racial prejudice and the Indians' depressed economic status limited the possibility of local relationships with non-Indians that were supportive of Indian identity and more than limited availability to Indians of education, good jobs, and services. Lerch provides a good indication of the character of Indian relationships with local communities in past eras in her description of Waccamaw efforts to obtain separate schools and avoid black schools.

The best descriptions in this volume of tribes' increasing interaction with local populations and local governments (i.e., below even the state level) are those of the Poarch Creeks and the Mississippi Choctaws. Both tribes have made long-term intensive efforts to enlist local support. Poarch's Chief Calvin McGhee perhaps started earliest, in the 1950s, building local organizations of Indian descendants and currying favor with local politicians. The Mississippi Choctaw have been developing relationships with state and local politicians for twenty years, overcoming suspicion of the tribal government with cooperative working relationships. Rountree (Chap. 1) describes the Virginia tribes as "carefully managing" relations with non-Indians. The Eastern Cherokee have recently shifted from few local relationships to greater cooperation with local (e.g., county) agencies as well as more participation in local social programs.

All of the southeastern states reviewed in this volume except Mississippi have some form of state recognition of Indian tribes. Recognition of Indian tribes by the states is largely, though not entirely, a recent development. It dates mostly from the 1970s and is an aspect of the push by southeastern tribes, especially the unrecognized ones, for a state as well as a federal relationship.

Important exceptions to state recognition as a recent phenomenon are three surviving colonially derived state reservations, those of the Pamunkey and Mattaponi tribes in Virginia and the Catawba in South

Carolina. Like federally recognized tribes, and unlike the other state-recognized tribes that are not also federally recognized, these state-recognized tribes have a distinct legal status from that of non-Indians.

North Carolina legislation in 1885 established in law a distinct status as Indian for the Lumbee (designating them as Croatan Indians) and provided for a school system separate from blacks. Though not colonially derived nor involving the distinct legal status of the colonially derived reservations, this North Carolina action was perhaps the earliest and strongest postcolonial state-Indian relationship before the modern era.

The Lumbees were granted modern state recognition by North Carolina in 1953, followed by the Haliwa in 1965, the Waccamaw in 1970, and a number of others in the state in 1971. Virginia legislation in 1983 gave state recognition of the limited kind common to other states to four tribes in Virginia. Louisiana recognized several tribes in the 1970s, and Alabama recognized six in 1984 (*Code of Alabama* sec. 41-9-700–707). In several of the states—Louisiana, Alabama, North Carolina, Florida, and South Carolina—additional groups are seeking state recognition or are expected to in the future. In North Carolina and Louisiana, urban Indian associations as well as historical communities have been accorded state recognition. Following somewhat deliberately on the federal model for administrative recognition, some states have now adopted or are considering adopting formal guidelines and criteria for recognition of additional groups.

State recognition in the modern form is a step beyond the state forming a commission or having a specific state official to deal with Indian needs. However, it generally constitutes little more than the state taking official notice of the existence of the tribe as a tribe, usually together with defining access to state programs for Indians. State recognition is of greatest significance to the tribes that are not federally recognized because, although much less significant, it provides a degree of ratification of distinct status. In addition, it has become, and may be increasingly becoming, the partial equivalent on a state level of federal recognition. That is, it usually denominates the groups that get special state funding and attention to which other groups in the state claiming Indian tribal status do not have access. In South Carolina, the state has provided programs to a number of the tribes besides the Catawba, even while avoiding recognizing them because of concerns regarding possible land claims litigation. In addition, a number of federal programs outside the Interior Department include Indian tribes that are state—but not federally—recognized within their eligibility criteria. This eligibility adds to the significance of state recognition, taking it beyond state assistance in getting federal programs not limited to Indians. State recognition of recently designated tribes is unlikely to evolve

further, however, into something like the legal status of the colonially derived state reservation tribes of Virginia and South Carolina.

Contributing to the tribes' ability in recent decades to work with local
and state governments is the fact that conflicts with non-Indians over Indian rights have been relatively limited in comparison with other parts of
the country. Conflicts, or at least resistance to cooperation, have been as
common between different tribes within states as between tribes and non-
Indians. The tribes have been fairly skillful in managing relationships
where conflicts with whites have occurred. The Mississippi Choctaw have
managed to turn their relationship with local non-Indians from one where
special Indian rights on the reservation were seen as competition to one
where the tribal enterprises based partly on those rights were viewed as a
benefit to the non-Indian community. In Louisiana, however, some conflicts between the federally recognized tribes and local governments have
occurred over Indian bingo and other enterprises as well as land claims
suits. In South Carolina the Catawba land claims suit has made the state
government reluctant to provide for Indian programs and recognition of
additional tribes. A Pamunkey land claims case, now settled, does not appear to have generated sufficiently negative non-Indian opinion to affect
Indian-white relationships in Virginia. Kersey describes not only significant conflict with state and local governments concerning Seminole Tribe
bingo operations and "smoke shops" but also the ability to operate politically to successfully influence state legislation concerning the Indians.

State recognition and other relationships with the states have produced
some degree of rivalry between tribes. This rivalry is noted by the authors
here as deriving from varying degrees of reluctance on the part of the
federally recognized tribes and the colonially derived tribes in Virginia and
South Carolina to share their legitimacy with the unrecognized ones. This
reluctance is in part derived from attitudes of older periods where Indian
status was viewed as shaky and subject to question by whites.

Federally recognized tribes at times have been either reluctant or entirely
unwilling to participate in state Indian commissions. Paredes notes that
the Poarch Band unsuccessfully resisted the inclusion of what he terms
"descendant organizations" on the Alabama State Indian Commission.
According to Neely, the Eastern Cherokees had been involved in the formation of the North Carolina Commission of Indian Affairs but then did
not participate in it until very recently. Louisiana produced a more complex division, with the then two federally recognized tribes initially siding
with two of the federally unrecognized tribes against the other federally
unrecognized tribes. Rivalries have extended at times to some state-recognized tribes questioning the legitimacy of others already state recognized
or seeking state recognition.

Regional Indian organizations do not appear to have had a major role after the early 1970s, when CENA was disbanded. USET, formed in the 1970s, has become an important vehicle for dealing with the federal government, obtaining funding, and exchanging information. It has been limited, however, to the federally recognized tribes. The Indian Information Project of United Indians of America, a Lumbee-affiliated organization in Washington, D.C., played a role in helping several tribes in North and South Carolina organize and obtain funding.

National organizations such as the National Congress of American Indians (NCAI) and the Association on American Indian Affairs did not, with several exceptions in the 1970s, play a major role in the changes of the past several decades. However, some of the unrecognized tribes have been members of NCAI and through this sought legitimacy. Similarly, although it has some board members from the southern tribes, the efforts of the Native American Rights Fund have primarily been limited to working on the relatively few land claims cases and to helping some of the tribes seek federal recognition.

Federal recognition has been a goal by some groups since the 1930s (and earlier in some cases, such as the Lumbee). Attempts by a variety of unrecognized tribes to gain federal services and/or tribal recognition between the 1930s and the 1950s were generally not successful or the services and assistance were limited and short-lived. With the increased activism and the advent of more favorable federal Indian policies beginning in the 1960s, federal recognition again became prominent as a goal because of the advantages it conferred in terms of improving conditions and asserting Indian identity and tribal status. Federal services to the Coushatta, withdrawn in 1953, were restored in 1973. Several other tribes were rejected in the 1970s before the present acknowledgment process was established or their requests were deferred.

Federal consideration of a revised, more highly structured process for deciding on requests for recognition as tribes began in 1975, in part as a result of an increasing number of requests from tribes and groups in the Southeast and elsewhere in the country. As a result the present administrative process for federal recognition was established in 1978. As of May 1990, a total of thirty-eight groups from the southeastern states (these include many not discussed in this volume) had petitioned for federal recognition. Only a small portion had completed preparation of the documentation necessary for their petitions to be reviewed under the acknowledgment regulations. Two tribes, the Poarch Band of Creeks and the Tunica-Biloxi, have been acknowledged under the regulations. The final section of this chapter briefly discusses the character of some of the groups that were found not to meet the requirements for federal recognition.

## Changing Character of Tribal Identification

A major element in the evolving character of unrecognized southeastern Indian tribes and their relationship to non-Indians continues to be, as was the case in the past, the establishment, reinforcement, and elaboration of the Indian identity of the tribe. This process appears to have had two elements: gaining recognition of the claim to be Indian and the definition of origins in a specific early historical tribe or tribes.

Taukchiray and Kasakoff (Chap. 4) describe the establishment of origins in a specific tribe as important because of its significance to non-Indians in accepting the legitimacy of a group as Indian. This is not peculiar to Indian-white relationships but reflects the general importance to any group's definition of its ethnic status, and that definition's acceptance by others, of a declaration of specific cultural origins, whether factually correct or not (Despres 1975). Definition of specific tribal origins and associated history is an important part of the processes described here for groups that have been able to maintain some degree of acceptance in the past as Indian as opposed to black but have not been able to retain a clear sense of their specific tribal origins, or whose origins have been the subject of debate and disagreement with non-Indians and sometimes with other tribes. Recency of claiming a specific tribal background is not necessarily an indication that the claim is inaccurate, because it may reflect new research.

Several of the chapters (e.g., those by Lerch and Taukchiray and Kasakoff) provide some indication of the degree to which claimed origins of specific tribes (where these are not clear-cut) are not or cannot yet be clearly established by research. The authors are less clear on the degree to which recent claims of tribal origin reflect past oral tradition or differ from past self-identification.

Taukchiray and Kasakoff note South Carolina communities that have only just recently begun to define themselves and claim specific tribal origins. The tribal designation of Monacan for the Indians of Amherst County, Virginia, is a new one. Rountree notes they have a long if somewhat inexact tradition of Indian ancestry, perhaps largely from the Monacan. In the past this group has to a degree claimed Cherokee ancestry (Beeler 1977).

In some cases, research efforts by anthropologists and other scholars have become part of the process of providing better information about or stronger foundations for Indian status in general or for specific tribal identities. Frank Speck's work in Virginia and other states is one important example. Gregory's research helped document the historical links of the Ebarb community with Apachean groups that oral tradition had suggested (Gregory 1982:82). In recent years, anthropological and historical research for the groups' petitions for federal recognition (e.g., as reflected in Chap. 3) have been a major element in this process.

Attribution of specific tribal origins to groups with status as Indian but without a clearly known origin has not been confined to the modern era.[3] Rountree (1972b) has noted the role earlier in the century of anthropologist Frank Speck in defining the origins of some of the Virginia tribes, for example, the tribe now known as the Upper Mattaponi (see Speck 1928:265). The Lumbees, although their Indian status in North Carolina has been well established for over 100 years, have long struggled with the question of specific tribal origins, asserting first Croatan and subsequently Cherokee and Tuscarora origins (the latter two still asserted by part of the Indians of Robeson County) but then taking the designation as Lumbee in the 1950s (Blu 1980). The latter name is derived from the nearby Lumber River rather than being based on origins in a specific historic tribe. Based on their most recent research, the Lumbee have described their origins as primarily derived from the historic Cheraw Tribe (Lumber River Legal Services 1987).

A different approach to defining tribal identity is adoption of a name relating to the local geography, for example, the Lumbee, as noted above. The Haliwa designation is likewise a geographical one, derived from the names of Halifax and Warren counties where major portions of the membership reside (American Indian Policy Review Commission 1976:152). The tribe presently designates itself the Haliwa-Saponi, the specific tribal origin of Saponi being added as a result of additional research. Another example of a geographically based name is that of the Pee Dee Indians of South Carolina, based on the river name rather than the historical tribe (see Chap. 4).

Paredes has characterized the evolution of the Poarch Band as one in which "more fundamental sentiments of affiliation based on kinship and descent" were part of the vehicle for the subsequent intensification of the existing Creek "ethnic" identity among the band (Paredes 1980:167). It is likely that a similar phenomenon of shifting emphasis from kin and local community ties and identification to tribal-wide identification has occurred in many of the southeastern tribes described here, those with clearly accepted tribal origins and traditional culture as well as those without. The past twenty to thirty years of greater interaction between Indian tribes as well as the growth of federal and state programs in which specific tribal status is the vehicle for participation would tend to promote such a result.

For many of the southeastern tribes, of course, the establishment of a specific tribal background has not been an issue. The federally recognized groups all have clearly accepted tribal origins, although, as Kersey notes, the claimed Seminole-Miccosukee distinction projects a historical division on a more complicated modern situation. Similarly, the formerly federally recognized Catawba have a clearly accepted identification as such, even though their actual historical composition reflects the amalgamation of parts of several tribes in the eighteenth century. The tribal origins of some of the unrecognized (or recently recognized) tribes, such as Poarch Creek, Jena Choctaw, Pamunkey, and Tunica-Biloxi, were clearly recognized in the past as well as present.

The symbols of the tribes with some remaining traditional culture appear to be culturally specific. In the past, some of those with little or no remaining traditional culture but whose specific tribal origins have been well known and unquestioned have adopted some of the Plains-oriented pantribal symbolism in public representations of Indian identity. Examples are the two reservation tribes in Virginia, the Tunica-Biloxi, and the Poarch Creek. Rountree notes, however, the appearance in Virginia of Algonquian-specific rather than Plains-style pan-Indian headdresses recently, while the Poarch Creeks have sought, through connections with Oklahoma Creeks, to relearn and reestablish elements of Creek culture. Use of pantribal symbolism appears to have been an older and somewhat superficial symbolism in comparison with establishing and reinforcing tribally specific traditions.

In analyzing the effects of the modern era of decreased discrimination and increased economic opportunity on the evolution of southeastern Indian tribes, the authors in this volume have avoided simply repeating the usual anthropological commentary that Indians continue to survive despite non-Indian expectations that, through one historical cause or another, they will amalgamate with non-Indian society. It is not surprising that Indian identity and organization are strengthening and increasing rather than decreasing in the Southeast. With the decrease in racial discrimination, the external world is now much more receptive to Indians, as being Indian has acquired a much higher status than in the past. In part through the efforts of the tribes themselves, state and federal government programs (both Indian-related and general) have increasingly provided resources for support of tribal organizations and programs since the 1970s. Furthermore, the members have acquired a higher economic status and thus have greater personal resources to build and maintain the tribes and their institutions and programs.

## Divisions

The authors describe divisions of different kinds within some of the tribes. At least part of the population of each of the tribes with divisions has retained a significant degree of traditional culture. Internal distinctions between more and less acculturated, or more progressive versus conservative populations (not necessarily the same thing), are noted within the Mississippi Choctaw, the Eastern Cherokee, and various Louisiana tribes, and as distinguishing among the several elements of the Florida Seminole population. These internal divisions are of a somewhat different character in the different tribes.

The modern distinction between the Seminole and Miccosukee tribes is described by Kersey (Chap. 5) as the result of formally organizing legally recognized separate tribal governments along progressive-conservative divisions within the Florida Seminole population. These divisions reflect differences in degree of acculturation and degree of conservatism of attitudes toward cultural change. Despite the modern tribal names, the present tribes only partially correspond with historical community distinctions between Miccosukee- and Seminole-speaking populations. A third, even more conservative population, the Traditional Seminole, is left over after the organization of the other two.

The Mississippi Choctaws have had somewhat different, and less sharp, distinctions between more or less "progressive" populations, sometimes corresponding to local community differences (Thompson and Peterson 1975). These distinctions are apparently reflected in the internal debate described by Peterson (Chap. 7) over how fast to develop the tribe, utilization of non-Indians in technical positions, and how to maintain Choctawness in the process.

In the Eastern Cherokee case, the division is between groups with some retained culture and those without. The continuance of nontraditional populations in the Eastern Cherokee case is attributed by Neely (Chap. 2) to the permanent legal status as Indian afforded to such individuals by the recognized federal reservation status of the tribe. Neely indicates that the "white" Cherokees find an economic advantage to maintaining tribal membership if not necessarily a strong Indian identity. Taukchiray and Kasakoff indicate that the absence of such a mechanism of formal, legally defined membership in the unrecognized South Carolina lowland groups has meant that populations losing social ties with the tribe have lost Indian identity or affiliation with the tribe. Conversely, they state that the formal definition of membership among the Catawba has meant that it is not necessary for a Catawba to marry an Indian to maintain ethnic identity. Because there are no longer any fullbloods and no endogamous marriages within the younger generation, it is not clear whether there remain significant divisions among the Catawba along "traditional" versus "conservative" lines.

The apparent lack of this particular kind of social division among the other tribes may reflect the absence of a culture significantly distinct from surrounding non-Indian populations or simply a lack of reporting in some of the chapters. A probable additional factor is that for unrecognized tribes, formally defined membership and significant community resources are recent, with the result that, at least in the past, populations that became more socially oriented to non-Indian society lost contact rather than remaining within the community as a subdivision. Effects of formal definitions of membership, generally a recent phenomenon in both recognized and unrecognized tribes, are not reported for all of the tribes discussed in this volume, however.

## Economic Development and Economic Status

Before the 1960s, improved education and better jobs were major focuses of effort for the unrecognized tribes. With the civil rights era and better access to general education, along with the poverty programs and increased activism, emphasis shifted to obtaining social programs such as health education and services, job training, housing improvement, and the like. As tribes' sophistication and organizational structures have improved, some attention has begun to be paid to economic development, not only to improve the economic condition of members but also as a source of funds for the tribal organization itself.

Successful economic development has been limited to the federally recognized tribes, and only some of these. Gregory (Chap. 8) notes the failure of attempts at tribal crafts cooperatives in the 1970s among both federal and nonfederal tribes in Louisiana. Successful economic development has rested to an important degree on the advantages of federal status, that is, tax-exempt trust land, enhanced tribal government powers, and access to federal Indian programs. Two of the tribes, the Seminole and the Mississippi Choctaw, are more successful economically than all but a few tribes in the country. Both have reached the level of providing a significant job base for their membership. They are able to provide some funding of tribal government programs independent of federal funds, with consequent greater flexibility of tribal government. Seminole success rested initially on Indian bingo, while the Mississippi Band of Choctaw Indians succeeded in making manufacturing plants viable with an integrated program of education and tribal government funding and initiatives. In the process, both have developed their tribal governments to a complexity and sophistication far beyond anything dreamed of a few years ago.

The Eastern Cherokees have also been fairly successful economically. Their success, based largely on tourism, began earlier than that of the

Choctaw and Seminole tribes. However, the Cherokees are now taking advantage of Indian bingo and developing a light industrial base while expanding the older tourism-based portions of their economy.

The Poarch Band of Creeks quickly put the advantages of federal status to work. This is consistent with a tribal governmental structure that even before federal recognition in 1984 was already one of the most dynamic and forceful in the Southeast. Besides a bingo parlor, opened simultaneously with the establishment of a reservation, they have acquired several business enterprises and are expanding rapidly. The other recently recognized tribe, the Tunica-Biloxi, has also gained economically by federal recognition but has moved considerably slower in economic development than has the Poarch Band.

Lerch's description of the Waccamaw indicates they have been something of an exception to the generalizations made here. The Waccamaw initiated economic development as early as 1950, with some evident success, apparently well before other unrecognized tribes in the region.

## Other Populations

Several other populations of Indians in the Southeast are not discussed in this volume or are only described briefly in some of the chapters. These are urban Indian populations, a variety of groups in various states that are not state recognized and usually are less well defined than those that are, and organizations that are not tribes at all but claim such status.

Relatively little is said in the chapters concerning urban Indians in the southeastern states. Urban Indian associations in Louisiana and North Carolina are described as participating strongly in the Indian affairs of their respective states. The members of those associations appear to be almost exclusively drawn from Indians within each state. In South Carolina, the membership of the urban Indian organizations is predominately drawn from out of state, while urban Indians from South Carolina tribes maintain ties with their home communities instead.

From a different perspective, some glimpses of the position of urban Indians in the various tribes are provided. Rountree reports increased urbanization of Virginia Indians as a result of improved education and economic status. She reports that two Virginia tribes, the Upper Mattaponi and the Nansemond, have mostly urban members while the Chickahominy have made efforts to retain the younger generation in the home community. Peterson reports Mississippi Choctaw success in providing a sufficient economic base at home to keep the younger, better educated population from moving to the cities.

The Catawba population on or near the reservation has increased sharply in the past decade, apparently as a result of the revived political activity there and a residency requirement for voting. The Mississippi Choctaw and some of the Louisiana tribes have been influenced by the return of former urban residents to the home area or reservation. These individuals have a different perspective and experience and either add to existing factions or result in new internal divisions. Gregory describes existing factionalism based on kin and religious disputes, as well as progressive-conservative differences, as fertile ground for tribal politicians returning from urban centers. Rountree notes no such distinctions among the Virginia tribes, however, despite the increasing urban portion of their membership.

Beyond the tribes discussed in this volume are a number of other groups of various kinds that are presently state recognized or are claiming tribal status and seeking state and federal recognition or that may come forward and seek recognition in the future. The chapters mention such groups in Alabama, Louisiana, South Carolina, and North Carolina. Besides the states covered in this volume, Georgia presently has three petitioners for federal recognition, and Tennessee has large populations sometimes identified or identifying as Indian though none has petitioned for federal recognition. In the past these carried the pejorative designation by outsiders as "Melungeon" (Cavender 1981). Several of these groups are presently identifying themselves as Cherokee (Tennessee Commission on Indian Affairs 1987).

Somewhat perversely illustrative of the changes in Indian status in the South in the past twenty-five years has been the appearance of nontribal groups claiming to be Indian tribes. These are groups that have formal organizations and claim tribal identities and histories but have in fact no past history at all and little or no present social structure beyond the organization itself. The membership of these groups appears to a large degree to be drawn from populations not historically classified as nonwhite. The membership has typically been lower-middle- and lower-class whites, usually, though not exclusively, from rural areas or small towns.

Three such groups that petitioned for federal recognition and were rejected are the Lower Muskogee Creek Nation East of the Mississippi—actually two linked organizations—and the Principal Creek Nation. These groups claimed Creek Nation origins. Although about a quarter of the Lower Muskogee Creek Nation group's membership and most of that of the Principal Creek Nation could demonstrate Creek ancestry, the groups had no tribal history or present tribal social structure. These groups were stimulated by the earlier outreach efforts of Poarch Creek Chief Calvin McGhee (ASIA 1981b, 1981c, 1984). Formed in the early 1970s, they have their origins in part in McGhee's umbrella organization of Eastern Creeks. Part of McGhee's efforts was to encourage the application to the BIA of individuals of Eastern Creek ancestry to share in claims money awarded to descendants of the Creek Nation of 1814. The claims process and McGhee's efforts stimulated interest in Indian identity among the many nontribal Eastern Creek descendants in the South.

Another group claiming Creek tribal status, also rejected for federal recognition and hence studied in detail, is the MaChis Creeks of Alabama (ASIA 1987, 1988). This group was found to have neither the claimed Creek ancestry or any Indian ancestry at all except for a small portion of the membership. It also had no historical existence before the early 1980s. No connection was found between it and the Creek descendant organizations described above, except perhaps by example. The MaChis Creeks are recognized as a tribe by the state of Alabama.

Somewhat different in character is the Southeastern Cherokee Confederacy (SECC), which was denied federal recognition (ASIA 1985). The organization, although terming itself Cherokee, admits to membership anyone claiming Indian ancestry of any kind or degree. Formed in 1976, the organization holds "Indian" dances and powwows, and members wear Indian regalia and adopt stereotyped Indian names. The SECC has developed subgroups, termed "clans," in many southern states and both clans and splinter groups outside the South. There was little evidence that the claimed Indian descent of its membership was verifiable for more than a few of its members.

The appearance of these groups seems to illustrate the sharp change in the valuation of Indian status in the Southeast in the past three decades. Whereas before the 1960s Indian status was problematical because it was often equated with or suggested "colored" ancestry and therefore social stigma, the success of these organizations in attracting members and local and even state support indicates that individuals with Indian ancestry now find it not only allowable but beneficial to claim Indian identity. Furthermore, many individuals without known Indian ancestry have claimed Indian ancestry. In at least two cases, MaChis Creek and the Lower Muskogee Creek Nation, the organizations have achieved some form of state recognition. Some of the state and federal social programs that the unrecognized tribes utilized have been used by these groups as well, although access to these programs was not necessarily the major motivation for forming these groups.

# Conclusions

The past twenty-five years have been an era of extensive change for the tribes of the southeastern states, particularly the unrecognized tribes. Despite these changes, however, the numerous tribes remain quite diverse in character. Many if not most of the recognized and unrecognized tribes have changed greatly in ways barely anticipated twenty-five years ago. They have become formally organized, with written governing documents, and they maintain a variety of programs for their members. Tribal identities are more strongly asserted and have evolved somewhat in character. State relationships and programs and state recognition of tribes have become major factors, especially for the large number of tribes that are not federally recognized. One of the primary forces of change has been the federal social and economic programs, for the most part outside the BIA and not directed specifically at Indians, which began in the 1960s. The economic growth of the New South has provided expanded opportunities. A major cause of change has been the reduction in racial discrimination that had previously relegated many Indians to an uncertain middle category between white and black. Indian status has risen substantially, to the point of evoking Indian identity and tribal claims from groups with no history or Indian ancestry.

# NOTES

1. In January 1958 armed Lumbee Indians broke up a Ku Klux Klan meeting called to intimidate them; the event received national news coverage, including photographs in *Life* (see Blu 1980:88–89).

## Chapter 1 _____

1. Most of the information in this chapter was collected in interviews with the Indian people concerned, particularly the tribal leaders. I sent out a preliminary draft of the chapter in 1986, and accordingly I am greatly indebted to the following Indian people for reading, commenting upon, and correcting my text: Chief William H. Miles and Warren Cook (Pamunkey); former Chief Curtis L. Custalow, Sr., and Gertrude Custalow (Mattaponi); former Chief Linwood Custalow, Treasurer Eunice Adams, Councilman Malcolm Tupponce, and Shirley Custalow McGowan (Upper Mattaponi; Custalow and McGowan also read the draft with their Mattaponi Reservation upbringing in mind); the late Chief O. Oliver Adkins, Council on Indians member Stephen R. Adkins, and Ronald Jefferson (Chickahominy); Chief Marvin D. Bradby (Eastern Chickahominy); Council on Indians member Nokomis Fortune Lemons, Judith Fortune, and former Assistant Chief Oliver W. Fortune (United Rappahannock); Chief Emeritus Oliver L. Perry, Sr. (Nansemond); and Lloyd E. Johns (Monacan). Phyllis Hicks, Monacan tribal secretary, helped me with the update on her group.

2. As this book went to press, two Virginia groups, the Pamunkey and the Nansemond, were consulting the Native American Rights Fund about applying for federal recognition, before changing their minds and shelving the matter.

3. A United Rappahannock informant adds here, "Some women [in my tribe] have M.A.'s in childrearing, dishwashing, and housecleaning." Though none of them currently holds a chiefly office, Virginia Indian women are becoming more vocal all the time.

4. The Chickahominy had W. H. Adkins and then O. W. Adkins (father and son), the Eastern Chickahominy E. P. Bradby, the Rappahannock George Nelson and then Otho Nelson, the Upper Mattaponi Jasper Adams. These men were the first chiefs of their newly organized tribes. Jesse Bass, father of Earl Bass, was considered the chief by his group, but the group was not formally incorporated during his lifetime.

5. The former Upper Mattaponi chief, the late Andrew Adams (son of Jasper), normally "dressed down" at powwows in his later years when he suffered from emphysema. At the 1986 Nansemond Spring Festival, the temperature was about 90° F. and everyone had to sit in the sun. The Pamunkey chief, William H. Miles, who owns full regalia, "played it sensibly" (his words to me), wearing "civvies" all day and donning his feather bonnet only when he took his place among the guests of honor. As the chief of the premier Indian tribe in Virginia, he could do that; the others wore their regalia and sweltered. At the same time, chiefs are not expected to wear regalia if they have just come from another, more ordinary appointment, which is sometimes the case with these busy men.

6. Fissioning in the Virginia tribes has taken place for various reasons. The Chickahominy split of 1925 occurred because of disagreements about seeking a reservation and also about retaining a tribal church's minister (Rountree 1990: chap. 8). More recent splits, such as the Rappahannock one, are due to differences of opinion over tribal chiefs and their policies; these are sensitive matters about which people are reticent with outsiders. The Rappahannock dissidents of 1982 took a name but have not followed through on incorporation or state recognition. The latter course is no longer open to them: late in 1989 the Virginia Council on Indians formulated rules for recognition that forbid newly fissioned-off groups from even applying (personal communication, Oliver Perry, 1990).

7. Chief Earl Bass, a much respected elder and long-time informal representative of his people, was contacted by United Native Americans but did not respond. He is at heart a country farmer and bear hunter, and knowing he lacked the necessary sophistication, he did not feel up to the task of organizing his people and then collecting documents about them. He tells me he is relieved and utterly delighted that his cousin has now come forward and done all of that for the group.

8. In 1985 I was approached myself about filling a 1986 vacancy on the council, which would have made me a second female member. However, I have declined to get involved until after my Powhatan history book was published, fearing conflict of interest.

# Chapter 2

1. I wish to acknowledge the Eastern Band of Cherokee Indians, especially the residents of the Snowbird community, for their help and kindness in my ongoing

research on the historical and contemporary Cherokees. I would also like to acknowledge tribal attorney Ben Bridgers for his assistance. The descendants of the late Susie and Gaffney Long have been my key informants. I am grateful to Ned and Shirley Long and their children and to Ella Jackson and the late Ed Jackson and their children. These families and everyone associated with the EBCI have always treated me with generosity.

I also wish to express my gratitude to various scholars of Native American cultures who have either trained or advised me, especially the late John J. Honigmann and John Gulick and other anthropologists at the University of North Carolina, Harriet J. Kupferer, Duane H. King, and my colleagues who have contributed to this volume on southeastern Indians, especially J. Anthony Paredes, who kept after us to do our jobs.

## Chapter 3

1. *Proceedings of the Thirty-First Annual Session of the Burnt Swamp Baptist Association*, 1910, p. 6. Archives of the Lumber River Legal Services, Pembroke, North Carolina.

2. James Mooney (1894:65, 76) was the first anthropologist to classify the southeastern tribes as "Eastern Siouans." Mooney based this classification on assumed linguistic and cultural similarities among the tribes of the region. John R. Swanton (1934, 1946) and Alfred Lewis Kroeber (1932:92–95) accepted Mooney's typology and offered only slight modifications to it. Milling (1969:203) placed the "Carolina River Tribes" in the Siouan language family, too. Hudson (1970:7–8) raised some objections to the category of Eastern Siouan, claiming that for many of the tribes (Cape Fear, Waccamaw, Winya, Pee Dee, Sewee, Santee, Congaree, and Waxhaw) little or no actual linguistic evidence exists on which to base this judgment. Hudson prefers a typology based on political organization rather than language (1970:11, 28).

3. Abraham Freeman and Shadrack Jacobs are among the first household heads to appear in the 1790 federal census. They were involved with land transactions with many of the earliest ancestors of contemporary Waccamaw. However, although they are often cited as lineal ancestors by older residents of the tribe, direct genealogical ties are less conclusive. Thus I have preferred to call them "stipulated" ancestors, similar to mythological clan ancestors common to tribal groups (Lerch 1988). Their activities, however, do cast light on the earliest members of the Waccamaw community, and thus tracing their history has proven to be useful to understanding the early history of the Waccamaw Indian community. A neighbor, John Jacobs (ca. 1800), proves to be a more conclusive ancestor of the Waccamaw.

4. Gordillo captured 140 Indians from the land called Chicora (Quattlebaum 1956:11–12; cited by South 1972:32). If the Guacaya were indeed the Waccamaw, this early encounter is the only one documented until 1701.

5. The Lord Proprietors and Puritans from Massachusetts Bay were simultaneously interested in settling the Cape Fear area in 1662 and 1663. William Hilton's second voyage in 1664 reported more extensively about the Cape Fear

Indians (Salley 1911:33–61). Settlement by the proprietors was initiated in 1664 and by 1666 the settlement stretched for some sixty miles along the "Charles River," as the Cape Fear River was then known. The colony, centered at Charles Town on Town Creek, soon established a lucrative trade with the local Indians; but, despite a promising start, the colony was abandoned in 1667 (Lee 1965:17, 19).

6. Rights (1947:39) and Lee (1965:67) both believe that the Waccamaw and the Woccon are the same people. Hudson (1970:8) identified the Woccon as Siouan speakers, thereby strengthening the case for the Siouan classification of the Waccamaw/Woccon. In 1705 the Woccon lived south of the Neuse River along the frontier of the North Carolina settlements (Lee 1965:67); Lawson placed them within ten leagues of the Tuscarora in the Woccon towns of "Warepere and Yupauremau" (1714:255, 251). Evidence that the Woccon/Waccamaw were involved in the Tuscarora War is indirect. Colonel John Barnwell's letter describing his campaign against the Tuscarora made note of the various tribes that accompanied him. In one Captain Bull's company were Waterees, Pee Dees, Weneaws, Cape Fears, Hoopengs, and Warepeles (Barnwell 1908:31). The Warepeles may have been the Woccon (Rights 1947:39), a connection apparently based on a similarity in pronunciation of Warepere and Yupauremau, the two Woccon towns listed above by Lawson (1714). I would like to point out another tenuous link between the Warepere/Woccon/Waccamaw. In April 1716, an old Waccamaw warrior came to Charles Town (South Carolina) to speak to the Commissioners of the Indian Trade, but no one present when he arrived could understand his language. Incredibly, as it turns out, only a certain Captain Bull, who was in town recovering from an illness, knew the Waccamaw language (McDowell 1955:69, 71). If this Captain Bull is the same one who went with Barnwell in 1712, then we may have another connection between the Warepere/Woccon/Waccamaw. Hostilities between the Tuscarora and the Woccon may have been responsible for their abandoning the area sometime between 1709 and 1712 (Lawson 1714:251).

7. This description is based on the assumption that the Woccon and the Waccamaw are the same people.

8. An account given by an unknown traveler making a trip to the Carolinas in 1734 describes the Lake Waccamaw region: "There is an old Indian field to be seen, which shows it was formerly inhabited by them, but I believe not within these fifty years, for there is scarce one of the Cape Fear Indians, or the Waccamaws, that can give any account of it" (Sprunt 1916:40). It appears that the traveler interviewed the Cape Fear and the Waccamaw at or near this field near Lake Waccamaw. He returned to Colonel Moore's home that same evening. Moore's residence, Orton Plantation, lay southeast toward the former colonial settlement known as Brunswick Town, Brunswick County, North Carolina.

9. Letter from James Glenn to Board, 17 July 1755. Records in the British Public Records Office Relating to South Carolina, vol. 26, pp. 184, 194, 203—11. Microfilm Reel no. 3292.

10. Minute Book I, 3 March 1898, p. 108, Columbus County Board of Education, Whiteville, North Carolina.

11. Minute Book I, 7 July 1885, p. 5; 12 December 1892, p. 67; 5 June 1893, pp. 72–73.

12. Minute Book I, 8 July 1903, p. 220; 4 October 1904, p. 304.

13. Minute Book I, 1 January 1920, p. 561.

14. In 1913 Senator Angus W. McLean of Robeson County, and later governor of North Carolina, put forth a theory that the Indians of Robeson County and possibly other counties were really descendants of Cherokees, who, like those in the mountains, refused to move from the state in 1830 (U.S. House of Representatives 1913:20, cited in Blu 1980:40).

15. Minute Book I, 2 February 1920, p. 565.

16. Letter from Donald McRackan to Dr. E. C. Brooks, 18 April 1921, Department of Public Instruction, General Correspondence of the Superintendent, County Files, Box 2, State Archives, Raleigh, North Carolina.

17. Ibid.

18. Letter from State Superintendent of Public Instruction to Donald McRackan, 27 April 1921, State Archives.

19. Minute Book I, 3 January 1921, p. 594.

20. Minute Book II, 8 August 1923, p. 226.

21. Minute Book II, 12 November 1923, p. 269.

22. Minute Book II, 4 February 1924, p. 289; 8 October 1924, p. 374.

23. Minute Book II, 4 February 1924, p. 294.

24. Minute Book III, 4 April 1927, pp. 68–69.

25. Minute Book III, 6 June 1927, p. 80.

26. Outside the state, "Croatan" was seen merely as a "convenient label" for a group with mixed ancestry (Mooney, in Hodge 1907:365, cited by Blu 1980:77) and it did not guarantee any other rights. Even within North Carolina, the label "Croatan," shortened to "Cro(w)," was being used by some whites to mean "Negro" (Johnson 1939:520; Berry 1963:33, cited by Blu 1980:78).

27. Minute Book III, 4 February 1929, pp. 168–69.

28. Minute Book III, 8 January 1930, p. 214.

29. Minute Book III, 5 May 1930, p. 214.

30. Minute Book III, 3 April 1933, 5 June 1933, 7 August 1933, Bladen County Board of Education, Elizabethtown, North Carolina.

31. Minute Book III, 28 August 1934, p. 343; 1 January 1935, p. 351; 7 October 1935, p. 400, Columbus County Board of Education.

32. Minute Book IV, 16 May 1945, p. 269, Columbus County Board of Education.

33. Joe Jennings, Superintendent, Cherokee Indian Agency, letter to John H. Provinse, Assistant Commissioner, Bureau of Indian Affairs, 16 February 1950, Records of the Bureau of Indian Affairs, Record Group 75, National Archives, Washington, D.C.

34. Ibid.

35. Letter from Wide Awake Indian Council to Whom It May Concern, 3 September 1940, Records of the Bureau of Indian Affairs.

36. Letter from Butler Prescott, Attorney, to Reverend R. T. Freeman, 21 October 1949, Records of the Bureau of Indian Affairs.

37. Letter from the Council of Wide Awake Indians, Waccamaw Tribe of the Siouan Nation, to the Secretary of the Interior, 14 November 1949, Records of the Bureau of Indian Affairs.

38. In the 1930s, the Robeson County "Cherokee" Indians had formed the "Siouan Lodge of the National Council of American Indians" through which they were seeking federal recognition as the "Siouan Indians of the Lumber River" (U.S. Senate Reports 1934, cited by Blu 1980:172). Gilbert (1948:420) noted in his survey of Indians within the state that use of the word Sioux was widespread.

39. Letter from John H. Provinse to Hon. Frank P. Graham, 6 December 1949, Records of the Bureau of Indian Affairs.

40. Letter from Alexander Lesser to James E. Alexander, 21 December 1949, Association on American Indian Affairs Collection, Box 78, Princeton University Library, Princeton, New Jersey.

41. Letter from Oliver LaFarge to Hon. Clyde R. Hoey, 20 January 1950, Association on American Indian Affairs Collection.

42. Letter from Felix Cohen to James E. Alexander, 3 January 1950, Association on American Indian Affairs Collection.

43. Letter from James E. Alexander to Dr. Alexander Lesser, 16 January 1950, Association on American Indian Affairs Collection.

44. Letter from Oliver LaFarge to Hon. Clyde R. Hoey, 20 January 1950, Association on American Indian Affairs Collection.

45. Letter from Dale E. Doty, Assistant Secretary of the Interior, to J. Hardin Peterson, Chairman of Committee on Public Lands, House of Representatives, 7 August 1950, Records of the Bureau of Indian Affairs.

46. Letter from Oliver LaFarge to Dr. Sol Tax, 27 July 1962, Association on American Indian Affairs Collection.

47. The first pan-Indian powwow was held in 1965 in the Haliwa-Saponi Indian community.

48. The word "powwow" probably derived originally from an Algonquian word meaning "shaman, shamanistic ceremony, or a council" (Kurath 1957:179; Lurie 1971:449).

# Chapter 4

1. We would like to acknowledge Leland G. Ferguson, E. W. Creel, Foxx and Sarah Ayers, Roger Trimnal, Chief Gilbert Blue, Samuel Beck, the late Georgia Davidson, Willie and Lillie Mae Broad, David Babson, Grace Lowry, Murphy Woods, Gene Waddell, and David Moltke-Hansen for their help with this research.

2. The historical information can be substantiated in the papers of Wesley Du-Rant Taukchiray; these papers have been deposited at the South Carolina Historical Society, Charleston, as the Wesley D. White Collection. Twenty-one boxes of materials there are currently available to researchers.

3. See Hudson 1970 and Merrell 1984a, 1984b.

4. In 1989 the Marion-Dillon Indian Association was represented on the council by the Pee Dee Indian Association. In December 1989 the Pee Dee tribal roll, listing members of both communities, had some 3,000 names (personal communication, Murphy Woods, Council of Native Americans of South Carolina, December 1989).

5. The published report lists 117, but 126 were in the manuscript census.

6. The Catawba have assumed something of a leadership role, serving as a conduit for funds coming to the other groups in the state under the Job Training Partnership Act.

7. See the Sale of John Dangerfield included in the appendix of Wikramanayake (1973). Dangerfield was of Indian descent. Judging from other records, this rich and powerful man was never actually enslaved.

8. Five affidavits pertain to current Indians; the names are Clark, Martin, and Dangerfield.

9. Miscellaneous Records, vol. 6G, p. 296, South Carolina Archives, Columbia.

10. This course of events is implied by the fact that about half the names of "free persons of color" in Wikramanayake's book are surnames that later became known as Indian. But not one of the surnames indexed in Williamson's book on Reconstruction is an Indian name. The Indian names are strikingly absent from the rolls of prominent blacks at that time.

11. See Berry 1963 and Steiner 1928.

12. The Low Country groups probably joined the Church of God sometime after 1928 when Steiner (1928) says White Oak was Methodist. Berry (1963:184) mentions a Church of God in a South Carolina Indian community in 1930.

13. We know that the school at White Oak existed as early as 1923 (see Steiner 1928). With the exception of the Sardis Indian School, we first hear of these schools in the 1920s.

14. Before the Civil War free persons of color were concentrated in cities (see Wikramanayake 1973) and in rural areas with many slaves. They were absent in the pine barrens.

15. Despite the dramatic increases, there is probably still quite a bit of undercounting, especially of the Pee Dee.

16. See n. 13, above.

17. The office is in Columbia, South Carolina, at the College Place Methodist Church.

18. Under the new bill the Piedmont Indian Association would be represented on the commission. It is not represented on the current commission.

19. On 23 January 1989 the Fourth Circuit Court of Appeals in Richmond ruled 4 to 2 that "the Catawbas still have the right to sue because the statute of limitations did not bar the tribe from filing a claim to the land. The ruling also exempted some landowners from the suit, saying the Catawbas could not sue those who could prove their property was owned continuously by the same person for 10 years between July 1, 1963 and October 20, 1980" (from the *Charleston Observer*, 20 June 1989, "Justices Keep Catawba Suit Alive," by Kim Gazella). Termination took on effect 1 July 1962; the date of the suit was 20 October 1980. By its action the court exempted anyone who held land for any ten continuous years during this eighteen-year period from the suit.

20. As of 1989, the Catawba had four demands in their negotiations for settlement: per capita payments, a larger federal reservation, an economic development fund, and federal recognition. Virtually all of the other tribes terminated in the 1950s have had their federal status restored by acts of Congress. The council is working with the Catawba to achieve this goal apart from the pending suit.

21. The Kussoo or Kusso Indians had lived in St. Paul's parish as late as 1750. There were sixty-five men, women, and children in 1743. The group "had no fixed place of abode" and lived in various places in St. Paul's parish.

22. The two affidavits of Indian descent we described above were filed on behalf of Hosea Martin's father, John Hozendorff Martin.

23. See the *First Baptist Beacon*, First Baptist Church, Walterboro, South Carolina, 4 August 1972, and the Walterboro, South Carolina, *Press and Standard*, 24 July 1969, p. 6-A.

24. The figure comes from Georgia Mucklevaney who visited this community, from Creeltown, in 1925 at age fifteen. She remembered the five heads of household: Ervin Muckenfuss, Fred Pratt (called Fed), Johnny Mucklevaney, Henry Wilder, and Stover Davidson. The same names were listed by Hudson Crummie without prompting.

25. This information comes from John Muckenfuss, Jr., an Indian born at Four Holes but separated from his parents and the community when three weeks old but who returned there in 1959 at age eighteen.

26. There may be a connection with some settlement Indians, part of the Pee Dee Tribe who settled on Four Hole Swamp by 1742 and were still there in 1753. These people may have lived near the present Lake Pee Dee on Four Hole Swamp 4.4 miles south-southwest of Holly Hill.

27. See Berry 1963.

28. The photographs show Geneva (Neva) Varner Clark, granddaughter of William and Mary Varner, and some children, identifying them as Indian; the photographs are located in the Library of Congress.

29. An affidavit of Indian descent about the four Dangerfield brothers was filed in 1849 by a William Beamer (himself an Indian of Johns Island) and is preserved in the South Carolina Archives in the Miscellaneous Records, vol. 6D, p. 301. Also in the Miscellaneous Records, in vol. 3Y, pp. 118 and 125, is an affidavit of Indian descent concerning one William Clark of the parish of St. James Goose Creek, dated 1807.

30. In 1989 the Mecklenberg County School District in Charlotte was receiving funds from the federal Department of Education (Title IV, Part A) to create an alphabet for the Catawba language (personal communication, Murphy Woods, December 1989).

# Chapter 5 _____

1. I wish to express my appreciation for the cooperation extended in support of this research by Chairman James Billie of the Seminole Tribe of Florida; Jim Shore, the Seminole general counsel; and Chairman Billy Cypress of the Miccosukee Tribe of Indians.

## Chapter 6

1. I am deeply grateful to the many friends and acquaintances I have made among the Poarch Creeks over the past twenty years for their kindness and forbearance and to the formal organization of the Poarch Band of Creek Indians and its governing body for their collaborative assistance that have made my research and, hence, this essay possible. Likewise, I acknowledge my indebtedness to the Southeastern Oral Indian History Project of the Florida Museum of Natural History, the Florida State University Council on Faculty Research and Support, the Rockefeller-FSU Center for the Study of Southern Culture and Religion, the Alabama Indian Affairs Commission, the Administration for Native Americans, and the Diocese of the Central Gulf Coast of the Episcopal Church for financial and material support of various phases of the research. Finally, I am especially indebted to those patient Poarch Creek friends who read an earlier version of this chapter and identified some factual errors that would have greatly embarrassed me if they had not caught them before publication.

2. Since federal recognition, the involvement of Poarch leaders in Indian affairs at the national level has proceeded apace, especially in the case of Chairman Tullis who, for example, serves (as of this writing) as chairman of the Native American task force for the 1990 census.

## Chapter 7

1. I am indebted to Chief Phillip Martin and to the Choctaw Tribe for the opportunity to have participated in a minor degree in some of the events of the past two decades (Peterson 1987). (The volume editor extends a special note of acknowledgement to John Peterson's colleague Robert Ferguson, a member of the professional staff of the Choctaw Tribal Office, for his obtaining the photographs and for his assistance in the final preparation of this chapter while Peterson was in Africa.)

## Chapter 8

1. I would like to acknowledge the help and support of all the Louisiana tribal governments and communities in the research upon which this chapter is based.

## Chapter 9

1. The comments, conclusions, and views expressed in this chapter are the author's alone and do not reflect the views of the Branch of Acknowledgment and Research or the Bureau of Indian Affairs.

The author's comments and conclusions are not intended to embody conclusions under a determination concerning federal acknowledgment under the federal acknowledgment regulations (25 CFR 83), nor has the author reached such conclusions. Exceptions to this disclaimer are statements concerning groups researched under the federal acknowledgment process—the Tunica-Biloxi, Poarch Band of Creeks, MaChis Lower Creek Indians, Principal Creek Nation East of the Mississippi, Lower Muskogee Creeks, and the Southeastern Cherokee Confederacy.

In particular, the author has for ease of presentation adopted the terminology used in most of the chapters of this volume in referring to all of the groups as "tribes" without intending this terminology as a conclusion independent of that of the chapter authors or as a conclusion under the particular definition of tribe established in the acknowledgment regulations.

2. The author has used the conventional term "recognition" here for both state and federal relationships. The administrative process for establishing federal recognition uses the term "acknowledgment" (as in Branch of Acknowledgment and Research), rather than recognition, because legally the process is viewed by the federal government as acknowledging a preexisting but unacknowledged trust relationship with the United States.

3. The comments in this chapter concerning tribal origins in general, or about the statements concerning tribal origins appearing elsewhere in this volume, in the literature on southeastern tribes, or in the statements made by the tribes themselves, are necessarily made without the author's having reached an independent conclusion about whether the presently claimed origins of one or another specific southeastern tribe have been demonstrated to be valid or can eventually be demonstrated.

# REFERENCES CITED

Adair, James
   1775   *The History of the American Indians, particularly those nations adjoin-ing to the Mississippi, east and west Florida, Georgia, South and North Car-olina, and Virginia, containing an account of their origin, language, manners* . . . London: Edward and Charles Dilly.
Alexander, James E.
   1950   Waccamaw, the Fallen Star. *American Indian* 3(30):30–39.
American Indian Policy Review Commission
   1976   *Report of Terminated and Nonfederally Recognized Indians.* Wash-ington, D.C.: Government Printing Office.
Ammidown, Margot
   1981   The Seminole Tribe, Inc.: Winning and Losing at the White Man's Game. *Florida Anthropologist* 34:238–42.
Anderson, Kurt
   1984   Indian War Cry: Bingo! *Time* 123(1):58.
Anderson, Terry
   1978   Federal Recognition: The Vicious Myth. *American Indian Journal* 4(5):7–19.
Anonymous
   1985   *The Louisiana Indians.* Baton Rouge: State Office of Indian Affairs.
ASIA. *See* U.S. Department of the Interior, Assistant Secretary—Indian Affairs (ASIA).
Barbry, Earl
   1989   Tunicas' Main Desire Is to Boost Local Economy. *Alexandria Town Talk*, 14 December, p. 9–A.

Barnwell, Joseph W.
   1908   The Tuscarora Expedition Letters of Colonel John Barnwell. *South Carolina Historical and Genealogical Magazine* 9 (January):28–54.
   1909   The Second Tuscarora Expedition. *South Carolina Historical and Genealogical Magazine* 10 (January):33–48.
Bastow, Thelma Wilkerson deShields
   1975   *What Happened to the Rappahannocks?* Indian Neck, Va.: Board of Trustees for the Preservation of Rappahannock Indian History.
Beeler, Samuel
   1977   Cherokees of Virginia. Manuscript. Branch of Acknowledgment and Research, Bureau of Indian Affairs files. Washington, D.C.
Berry, Brewton
   1963   *Almost White.* New York: Macmillan.
   1972   America's Mestizos. In *The Blending of Races: Marginality and Identity in World Perspective,* edited by Noel P. Gist and Anthony Gary Dworkin, pp. 191–212. New York: John Wiley and Sons.
   1978   Marginal Groups. In *Handbook of North American Indians,* vol. 15: Northeast, edited by Bruce G. Trigger, pp. 290–95. Washington, D.C.: Smithsonian Institution.
Bladen County Board of Education
   Minute Book, 1931–1954. Elizabethtown, N.C.
Blanchard, Kendall
   1981   *The Mississippi Choctaws at Play: The Serious Side of Leisure.* Urbana: University of Illinois Press.
Blu, Karen L.
   1980   *The Lumbee Problem: The Making of an American Indian People.* Cambridge: Cambridge University Press.
Blume, G. W. J.
   1950   Present Day Indians of Tidewater Virginia. *Quarterly Bulletin of the Archeological Society of Virginia* 6(2):1–8.
Brain, Jeffrey P.
   1970   *The Tunica Treasure.* Lower Mississippi Survey, Peabody Museum, Harvard University, Bulletin 2, Cambridge, Mass.
   1979   *Tunica Treasure.* Papers of the Peabody Museum, Harvard University, vol. 71, Cambridge, Mass.
Brescia, William, editor
   1982   *Tribal Government: A New Era.* Philadelphia, Miss.: Mississippi Band of Choctaw Indians.
Brewington, Tony
   1976   Indian Religion in North Carolina. In *Paths Toward Freedom: A Biographical History of Blacks and Indians in North Carolina,* edited by the Center for Urban Affairs, pp. 19–23. Raleigh: North Carolina State University.
Bryant, Julie
   1979   South Carolina's Native Americans. Status report prepared for the Governor's Office. Columbia, S.C.: Division of Economic Development and Transportation.

Burnt Swamp Baptist Association
  1910    *Proceedings of the Thirty-First Annual Session of the Burnt Swamp Baptist Association*, 17–19 November. Lumber River Legal Services Archives, Pembroke, N.C. Pamphlet.
Bushnell, David I., Jr.
  1909    *The Choctaw of Bayou Lacomb, St. Tammany Parish, Louisiana.* Bureau of American Ethnology, Bulletin 48. Washington D.C.: Government Printing Office. (Reprinted in John H. Peterson, Jr., *A Choctaw Source Book.* New York: Garland, 1985.)
Campisi, Jack, Julian Pierce, Cynthia Hunt-Locklear, and Wes White
  1987    *Lumbee Petition for Federal Acknowledgement*, microfilm reel Z.1.57, North Carolina State Archives. Raleigh, North Carolina.
Carter, Kent
  1988    Wantabees & Outalucks: Searching for Indian Ancestors in Federal Records. *Chronicles of Oklahoma* 66(1):94–104.
Cavender, Anthony P.
  1981    The Melungeons of Upper East Tennessee: Persisting Social Identity. *Tennessee Anthropologist* 6 (Spring):27–36.
Chata Development Company
  1976    *Choctaw Progress Through Economic and Industrial Development.* Philadelphia, Miss.: Chata Development Company.
*Cherokee One Feather*
  1972    Nostalgia Isn't What It Used To Be. *Cherokee One Feather* 5(39):3.
  1975    200 Additional Homes Approved for Qualla Housing Authority. *Cherokee One Feather* 8(5):1.
Coco, Wayne, and the Tunica-Biloxi Tribe
  1985    *Tunica-Biloxi: A Comprehensive Plan for Tribal Development.* Marksville, La.: Tunica-Biloxi Tribe.
Cohen, Daniel
  1989    Tribal Enterprise. *Atlantic Monthly* 26(4):32–34, 36, 38, 42, 43.
Cohen, Felix
  1982    *Handbook of Federal Indian Law (1982 ed.).* Charlottesville, Va.: Michie/Bobbs-Merrill.
Collier, John
  1935    With Secretary Ickes and the Seminoles. *Indians at Work* 2:3–4. Department of the Interior, Indian Office, Washington, D.C.
Columbus County Board of Education
  Minute Books I (1885–1921), II (1921–1926), III (1926–1935), IV (1936–1964). Whiteville, N.C.
Commission of Indian Affairs
  1983    *North Carolina Indians.* Rev. ed. Raleigh: North Carolina Department of Administration.
Cotterill, Robert S.
  1954    *The Southern Indians: The Story of the Civilized Tribes Before Removal.* Norman: University of Oklahoma Press.

Covington, James W.
  1976  The Brighton Reservation, Florida, 1935–1943. *Tequesta* 36:54–65.
  1979  The Seminoles and Selective Service in World War II. *Florida Anthropologist* 32:46–51.
  1981  The Seminoles and the Civilian Conservation Corps. *Florida Anthropologist* 34:232–37.
  1982  *The Billy Bowlegs War, 1855–1858: The Last Stand of the Seminoles Against the Whites.* Chuluota, Fla.: Mickler House.

Dane, J. K., and B. Eugene Griessman
  1972  The Collective Identity of Marginal Peoples: The North Carolina Experience. *American Anthropologist* 74:694–704.

Debo, Angie
  1934  *The Rise and Fall of the Choctaw Republic.* Norman: University of Oklahoma Press.
  1941  *The Road to Disappearance: A History of the Creek Indians.* Norman: University of Oklahoma Press.

Dial, Adolph L., and David K. Eliades
  1975  *The Only Land I Know: A History of the Lumbee Indians.* San Francisco: Indian Historian Press.

Deloria, Vine, Jr., and Clifford M. Lytle
  1984  *The Nations Within.* New York: Pantheon.

Depres, Leo A.
  1975  Toward a Theory of Ethnic Phenomena. In *Ethnicity and Resource Competition in Plural Societies*, edited by Leo A. Depres, pp. 187–207. The Hague: Mouton.

Dorschner, John
  1979  Bury My Heart on Custer Street. "Tropic," *Miami Herald*, 8 April, pp. 11–15, 44–47.

Eastern Band of Cherokee Indians
  1972  *Cherokee Progress and Challenge.* Cherokee, N.C.: Eastern Band of Cherokee Indians.

Eggan, Frederick R.
  1937  Historical Changes in the Choctaw Kinship System. *American Anthropologist* 39:34–52.

Engle, Carole
  1989  Honoring Their Cherokee Heritage. *Southern Living* 24 (October):90–92.

Evans, William McKee
  1971  *To Die Game: The Story of the Lowry Band, Indian Guerillas of Reconstruction.* Baton Rouge: Louisiana State University Press.

Faine, John, with appendix by Hiram F. Gregory
  1986  *The Choctaw-Apache Community: An Assessment of the Status of a Louisiana Indian Tribe.* Baton Rouge: Institute for Indian Development.

Farr, Eugene
    1948   Religious Assimilation: A Case Study of the Adoption of Christianity by
    the Choctaw Indians of Mississippi. Th.D. diss., New Orleans Baptist Theo-
    logical Seminary, New Orleans.
Feest, Christian F.
    1978   Virginia Algonquians. In *Handbook of North American Indians*, vol. 15:
    Northeast, edited by Bruce G. Trigger, pp. 253–70. Washington, D.C.:
    Smithsonian Institution.
Ferguson, Leland G., and Eugene J. Crediford
    1986   *Contemporary Native Americans in South Carolina*. Columbia: South
    Carolina Committee for the Humanities.
Finger, John R.
    1984   *The Eastern Band of Cherokees 1819–1900*. Knoxville: University of
    Tennessee Press.
Fischer, Ann
    1968   History and Current Status of the Houma Indians. In *The American In-
    dian Today*, edited by Stuart Levine and Nancy O. Lurie, pp. 133–47. Deland,
    Fla.: Everett/Edwards.
Fogelson, Raymond D.
    1961   Change, Persistence, and Accommodation in Cherokee Medico-magical
    beliefs. In *Symposium on Cherokee and Iroquois Culture*, edited by W. N.
    Fenton and J. Gulick, pp. 213–25. Bureau of American Ethnology, Bulletin
    180. Washington, D.C.: Government Printing Office.
Fragin, Sheryl
    1985   Indian Bingo Hall Showdown. *Washington Monthly* 17:34–38.
Frazier, E. Franklin
    1966   *The Negro Family in the United States*. Chicago: University of Chicago
    Press.
Freeman, Ethel Cutler
    1960   Culture Stability and Change among the Seminoles of Florida. In *Men
    and Cultures: Selected Papers of the Fifth International Congress of An-
    thropological and Ethnological Sciences, Philadelphia, September 1–9, 1956*,
    edited by Anthony F. C. Wallace, pp. 249–54. Philadelphia: University of
    Pennsylvania Press.
Garbarino, Merwyn S.
    1966   *Big Cypress: A Changing Seminole Community*. New York: Holt,
    Rinehart, and Winston.
Gilbert, William H., Jr.
    1946   Memorandum Concerning the Characteristics of the Larger Mixed-
    Blood Racial Islands of the Eastern United States. *Social Forces* 24(4):438–47.
    1948   Surviving Indian Groups of the Eastern United States. In *Annual Report
    of the Smithsonian Institution*, pp. 407–38. Washington, D.C.: Government
    Printing Office.
Glenn, James L.
    1982   *My Work Among the Florida Seminoles*. Gainesville: University Presses
    of Florida.

Grant, C. L. ed.
  1980  *Letters, Journals, and Writings of Benjamin Hawkins, Vol. II.* Savannah: Beehive.
Green, Michael
  1982  *The Politics of Indian Removal: Creek Government and Society in Crisis.* Lincoln: University of Nebraska Press.
Greenbaum, Susan
  1985  In Search of Lost Tribes: Applied Anthropology and the Federal Acknowledgment Process. *Human Organization* 44:361–67.
Gregory, Hiram F.
  1977  The Jena Band of Louisiana Choctaw. *American Indian Journal* 3(2):2–16.
  1982  Road to Recognition: A Study of Louisiana Indians, 1880–Present. New Orleans: Jean Lafitte National Park. Manuscript.
Gregory, Hiram F., and Clint Pine
  1988  *An Archaeological Survey of the Tunica-Biloxi Reservation, Avoyelles Parish, Louisiana.* Baton Rouge: Louisiana Division of Archaeology.
Griessman, B. Eugene
  1972  The American Isolates. *American Anthropologist* 74:693–94.
Gulick, John
  1960  *Cherokees at the Crossroads.* Chapel Hill: Institute for Research in Social Science.
Halbert, Henry S.
  1894  Indian Schools in Mississippi. In *Biennial Report to the State Superintendent of Public Education to the Legislature of Mississippi, for the Scholastic Years 1891–1892 and 1892–1893*, pp. 574–76. Jackson: Clarion-Ledger. (Reprinted in John H. Peterson, Jr., *A Choctaw Source Book.* New York: Garland, 1985.)
Halbert, Henry S., and Timothy H. Ball
  1895  *The Creek War of 1813 and 1814.* Chicago: Donohue and Henneberry. Montgomery, Ala.: White, Woodruff and Fowler.
Hawkins, Benjamin
  1848  *A Sketch of the Creek Country in the Years 1798 and 1799. Collections of the Georgia Historical Society, vol. III, pt. 1.* Savannah: Georgia Historical Society.
Hodge, Frederick Webb, ed.
  1907  *Handbook of North American Indians North of Mexico*, part 1. Bureau of American Ethnology, Bulletin 30. Washington, D.C.: Government Printing Office.
Hoover, Herbert T.
  1975  *The Chitimacha People.* Phoenix: Indian Tribal Series.
Houck, Peter W.
  1984  *Indian Island in Amherst County.* Lynchburg, Va.: Lynchburg Historical Research Company.

Hudson, Charles M.
  1970    *The Catawba nation*. Athens: University of Georgia Press.
  1976    *The Southeastern Indians*. Knoxville: University of Tennessee Press.
Johnson, Bobby H.
  1976    *The Coushatta People*. Phoenix: Indian Tribal Series.
Johnson, Guy B.
  1939    Personality in a White-Indian-Negro Community. *American Sociological Review* 4(4):516–23.
Jones, A. Bruce
  1979    *The Report of the North Carolina Commission of Indian Affairs 1978–79*. Raleigh: North Carolina Department of Administration.
Kelly, Lawrence C.
  1983    *The Assault on Assimilation: John Collier and the Origins of Indian Policy Reform*. Albuquerque: University of New Mexico Press.
Kersey, Harry A., Jr.
  1970    Educating the Seminole Indians of Florida, 1879–1970. *Florida Historical Quarterly* 49:16–35.
  1973    A Tale of Two Tribes. *Educational Forum* 38:50.
  1975    *Pelts, Plumes, and Hides: White Traders Among the Seminole Indians, 1870–1930*. Gainesville: University Presses of Florida.
  1989a    *The Florida Seminoles and the New Deal, 1933–1942*. Gainesville: University Presses of Florida.
  1989b    Give Us Twenty-Five Years: Florida Seminoles from Near Termination to Self-Determination, 1953–1957. *Florida Historical Quarterly* 67:290–309.
Kersey, Harry A., Jr., and Donald E. Pullease
  1973    Bishop William Crane Gray's Mission to the Seminole Indians in Florida, 1893–1914. *Historical Magazine of the Protestant Episcopal Church* 42:257–73.
Kidwell, Clara Sue
  1986    Choctaw Struggle for Land and Identity in Mississippi. In *After Removal: The Choctaw in Mississippi*, edited by Samuel J. Wells and Roseanna Tubby, pp. 64–93. Jackson: University Press of Mississippi.
King, Robert T.
  1976    Clan Affiliation and Leadership among the Twentieth Century Florida Indians. *Florida Historical Quarterly* 55:138–52.
Krebs, Michelle
  1986    Choctaw Indians Give Big 3 Onshore Source for Parts. *Automotive News*, December, p. 3.
Kroeber, Alfred Lewis
  1932    *Cultural and Natural Areas of Native North America*. University of California Publications in American Archaeology and Ethnology vol. 38. Berkeley and Los Angeles: University of California Press.

Kupferer, Harriet J.
  1966  The "Principal People," 1960: A Study of Cultural and Social Groups
  of the Eastern Cherokee. Bureau of American Ethnology, Bulletin 196,
  pp. 215–325. Washington, D.C.: Government Printing Office.
Kurath, Gertrude Prokosch
  1957  Pan-Indianism in Great Lakes Tribal Festivals. Journal of American
  Folklore 70:179–82.
Langford, Sister John C.
  1986  Holy Rosary Indian Mission: The Mississippi Choctaw and the Catholic
  Church. In After Removal: The Choctaw in Mississippi, edited by Samuel J.
  Wells and Roseanna Tubby, pp. 112–21. Jackson: University Press of Mis-
  sissippi.
Lawson, John
  1714  Lawson's History of North Carolina. Richmond, Va.: Garrett and Mas-
  sie.
Lee, E. Lawrence
  1965  The Lower Cape Fear in Colonial Days. Chapel Hill: University of North
  Carolina Press.
Lefler, Hugh Talmage, and Albert Ray Newson
  1973  North Carolina, The History of a Southern State. 3d ed. Chapel Hill:
  University of North Carolina Press.
Lefley, Harriet P.
  1976  Acculturation, Child-Rearing, and Self-Esteem in Two North American
  Indian Tribes. Ethos 4:385–401.
Lerch, Patricia B.
  1988  Articulatory Relationships: The Waccamaw Struggle Against Assimila-
  tion. In Sea and Land: Cultural and Biological Adaptations in the Southern
  Coastal Plain, Southern Anthropological Society Proceedings No. 21, edited
  by James L. Peacock and James C. Sabella, pp. 76–91. Athens: University of
  Georgia Press.
Lerch, Patricia B., Stuart Berde, and Diane E. Levy
  1986  Indians in North Carolina in the 1980s. Paper read at the annual meeting
  of the Southern Anthropological Society, 24–27 April 1986, Wrightsville
  Beach, N.C. Mimeographed.
Lumber River Legal Services (LRLS)
  1987  The Lumbee Petition. Petition for Federal Acknowledgment as an Indian
  Tribe. Files of the Branch of Acknowledgment and Research, Bureau of Indian
  Affairs, Department of the Interior. Washington, D.C.
Litton, Gaston
  1940  Enrollment Records of the Eastern Band of Cherokee Indians. North
  Carolina Historical Review 17:199–231.
Lurie, Nancy Ostreich
  1971  The Contemporary American Indian Scene. In North American Indians
  in Historical Perspective, edited by Eleanor Burke Leacock and Nancy Ostreich Lurie, pp. 418–80. New York: Random House.
  1976  Comment. Human Organization 35:320–21.

MacCauley, Clay
   1887   The Seminole Indians of Florida. In *5th Annual Report of the Bureau of American Ethnology, 1883–1884*, pp. 469–531. Washington, D.C.: Government Printing Office.

McDowell, W. L., editor
   1955   *Colonial Records of South Carolina. Journals of the Commissioners of the Indian Trade September 20, 1710–August 29, 1718.* Columbia: South Carolina Archieves Department.

McKee, Jesse O., and Steve Murray
   1986   Economic Progress and Development in the Mississippi Band of Choctaw Indians since 1945. In *After Removal: The Choctaw in Mississippi*, edited by Samuel J. Wells and Roseanna Tubby, pp. 122–36. Jackson: University Press of Mississippi.

McPherson, O. M.
   1915   *Indians of North Carolina: A Report on the Condition and Tribal Rights of the Indians of Robeson and Adjoining Counties.* U.S. Senate Doc. 667, 63d Cong. 3d sess. Washington, D.C.: Government Printing Office.

Macy, Robert C., M.D.
   1930   The Indians of the Alabama Coastal Plain. *Alabama Historical Quarterly* 1:406–14.

Makofsky, Abraham
   1980   Tradition and Change in the Lumbee Community of Baltimore. *Maryland Historical Magazine* 75(1):55–71.
   1982   Struggle to Maintain Identity: Lumbee Indians in Baltimore. *Anthropological Quarterly* 55:74–83.

Maynor, Waltz
   1976   Economic and Personal Growth of Native Americans in North Carolina. In *Paths Toward Freedom: A Biographical History of Blacks and Indians in North Carolina*, edited by the Center for Urban Affairs, pp. 36–37. Raleigh: North Carolina State University.

Mereness, N.D., editor
   1961   *Travels in the American Colonies.* New York: Antiquarian (original 1916).

Merrell, James
   1984a   The Indians' New World: The Catawba Experience. *William and Mary Quarterly* 41:537–65.
   1984b   The Racial Education of the Catawaba Indians. *Journal of Southern History* 50:363–84.
   1989   The Indians' New World: Catawbas and Their Neighbors from European Contact through the Era of Removal. Chapel Hill: University of North Carolina Press, for the Institute of Early American History and Culture, Williamsburg, Va.

Michelmore, Peter
   1984   Uprising in Indian Country. *Readers Digest* (November):69–79.

Milling, Chapman J.
   1969   *Red Carolinians.* Columbia: University of South Carolina Press.

Milton, Spiller
  1976   The Houma Indians Since 1940. *American Indian Journal* 2(4):16–17.
Mississippi Band of Choctaw Indians
  1972a   *Accelerated Progress Through Self-Determination: First Annual Report
    of the Choctaw Self-Determination Project, July 1, 1971–July 31, 1972.* Phila-
    delphia, Miss.: Mississippi Band of Choctaw Indians.
  1972b   *An Era of Change.* Philadelphia, Miss.: Mississippi Band of Choctaw
    Indians.
  1981   *Chahta Hapia Hoke: We are Choctaw.* Philadelphia, Miss. Mississippi
    Band of Choctaw Indians.
Mooney, James
  1890   The Cherokee Ball Play. *American Anthropologist* 3(2):105–32.
  1894   *The Siouan Tribes of the East.* Bureau of American Ethnology, Bulletin
    22. Washington, D.C.: Government Printing Office.
Moore, Alexander
  1986   *Lowcountry South Carolina Ethnohistory: A Guide to Indian and Afro-
    American Sources.* Institute for Southern Studies, University of South Car-
    olina, Columbia.
Nash, Roy
  1931   *Survey of the Seminole Indians of Florida.* U.S. Sen. Doc. 314, 71st
    Cong. 1st sess. Washington, D.C.: Government Printing Office.
Neely, Sharlotte
  1979   Acculturation and Persistence Among North Carolina's Eastern Band of
    Choctaw Indians. In *Southeastern Indians Since the Removal Era,* edited by
    Walter L. Williams, pp. 154–73. Athens: University of Georgia Press.
Owl, Henry M.
  1929   *The Eastern Band of Cherokee Before and After the Removal.* Master's
    thesis, University of North Carolina, Chapel Hill.
Paredes, J. Anthony
  1965   Community Celebrations in Northern Minnesota. Paper read at the
    64th annual meeting of the American Anthropological Association. 18–21
    November, Denver. Mimeographed.
  1974   The Emergence of Contemporary Eastern Creek Indian Identity. In *So-
    cial and Cultural Identity: Problems of Persistence and Change, Southern An-
    thropological Society Proceedings No. 8,* edited by Thomas K. Fitzgerald,
    pp. 63–80. Athens: University of Georgia Press.
  1975   The Folk Culture of the Eastern Creek Indians: Synthesis and Change. In
    *Indians of the Lower South: Past and Present,* edited by John K. Mahon,
    pp. 93–111. Pensacola: Gulf Coast History and Humanities Conference.
  1976a   The Need for Cohesion and American isolates. *American Anthropol-
    ogist* 78:335–37.
  1976b   New Uses for Old Ethnography: A Brief Social History of a Research
    Project with the Eastern Creek Indians *or* How to Be an Applied Anthro-
    pologist without Really Trying. *Human Organization* 35:315–20.

1979  Back from Disappearance: The Alabama Creek Indian Community. In *Southeastern Indians Since the Removal Era*, edited by Walter L. Williams, pp. 123–41. Athens: University of Georgia Press.

1980  Kinship and Descent in the Ethnic Reassertion of the Eastern Creek Indians. In *The Versatility of Kinship*, edited by L. S. Cordell and S. Beckerman, pp. 165–94. New York: Academic.

Paredes, J. Anthony, and Sandra K. Joos
1980  Economics, Optimism, and Community History: A Comparison of Rural Minnesotans and Eastern Creek Indians. *Human Organization* 39:142–52.

Paredes, J. Anthony, and Kenneth J. Plante
1982  A Reexamination of Creek Indian Population Trends: 1738–1832. *American Indian Culture and Research Journal* 6(4):3–28.

Parman, Donald L.
1975  The Indian and the Civilian Conservation Corps. In *The American Indian: Essays from Pacific Historical Review*, edited by Norris Hudley, pp. 127–45. Santa Barbara: Clio.

Perdue, Theda, editor
1983  *Cherokee Editor: The Writings of Elias Boudinot*. Knoxville: University of Tennessee Press.

1985  *Native Carolinians. The Indians of North Carolina*. Raleigh: North Carolina Division of Archives and History.

Peterson, John H., Jr.
1970  *Socio-Economic Characteristics of the Mississippi Choctaw Indians*. Social Science Research Center Report no. 34. Starkville: Mississippi State University.

1971  The Indians of the Old South. In *Red, White and Black: Symposium on Indians in the Old South*, edited by Charles M. Hudson, pp. 116–31. Athens: University of Georgia Press.

1972  Assimiliation, Separation, and Out-Migration in an American Indian Group. *American Anthropologist* 74:1286–95.

1975  *Reservation, Reservoir Self-Determination: A Case Study of Reservoir Planning as It Affects an Indian Reservation*. Starkville: Mississippi State University, Water Resources Research Institute.

1979  Three Efforts at Development among the Choctaws of Mississippi. In *Southeastern Indians Since the Removal Era*, edited by. Walter L. Williams, pp. 142–53. Athens: University of Georgia Press.

1985  *A Choctaw Source Book*. North American Indian Series. New York: Garland.

1987  The Changing Role of an Applied Anthropologist. In *Applied Anthropology in America*. 2d ed., edited by Elizabeth M. Eddy and William L. Partridge. New York: Columbia University Press.

Peterson, John H., Jr., and James R. Richburg
  1971  *The Mississippi Choctaws and Their Educational Program*. Community
  Studies, Series 1, Study 21 of the Final Report of the National Study of
  American Indian Education, edited by Robert Havighurst. Washington, D.C.:
  Educational Resources Information Center, U.S. Department of Health, Edu-
  cation, and Welfare.

Pfaus, Mrs. Fred
  1947  *Our Indian Neighbors*. Richmond, Va.: Dover Baptist Association.
  1949  *Our Debt to Virginia Indians*. Richmond, Va.: Dover Baptist Association.

Philp, Kenneth L.
  1977  *John Collier's Crusade for Indian Reform, 1920–1954*. Phoenix: University of Arizona Press.

Pollitzer, William
  1972  The Physical Anthropology and Genetics of Marginal People of the
  Southeastern United States. *American Anthropologist* 74:719–734.

Presti, Susan M., editor
  1981  *Public Policy and Native Americans in North Carolina: Issues for the
  '80s Conference Proceedings*. Raleigh: North Carolina Center for Public Policy Research.

Price, Edward T.
  1953  A Geographical Analysis of White-Indian-Negro Racial Mixtures in the
  Eastern United States. *Annals of the Association of American Geographers*
  43:138–55.

Quattlebaum, P.
  1956  *The Land Called Chicora*. Gainesville: University of Florida Press.

Quinn, William W., Jr.
  1987  Southeastern Indians: The Quest for Federal Acknowledgment and a
  New Legal Status. Paper presented at the Florida Endowment for the
  Humanities–Sponsored Conference, "From Big Game to Bingo: Native Peoples of the Southeastern United States—A Retrospective Occasioned by the
  Sesquicentennial of the Great Removal," organized by J. Anthony Paredes and
  J. Leitch Wright, Jr., 5–7 March 1987, Florida State University, Tallahassee.
  1990  The Southeast Syndrome: Notes on Indian Descendant Recruitment Organizations and Their Perceptions of Native American Culture. *American Indian Quarterly: Journal of American Indian Studies* 14:147–54.

Revels, Ruth
  1981  Economic Status. In *Public Policy and Native Americans in North Carolina: Issues for the '80s*, edited by Susan M. Presti, pp. 65–69. Raleigh:
  North Carolina Center for Public Policy Research.

Richardson, Arnold
  1976  Migrations of North Carolina Indians. In *Paths Toward Freedom*, edited
  by the Center for Urban Affairs, pp. 31–33. Raleigh: North Carolina State
  University.

Rights, Douglas L.
1947   *The American Indian in North Carolina*. Durham: Duke University Press.

Ross, Thomas E.
1987   Population Growth of a Non-Reservation Indian Tribe. In *A Cultural Geography of North American Indians*, edited by Thomas E. Ross and Tyrel G. More, pp. 297–312. Boulder: Westview.

Rountree, Helen C.
1972a   Being an Indian in Virginia: Four Centuries in Limbo. *Chesopiean* 10(1):1–7.
1972b   Powhatan's Descendants in the Modern World. *Chesopiean* 10(3):62–96.
1979   The Indians of Virginia: A Third Race in a Biracial State. In *Southeastern Indians Since the Removal Era*, edited by Walter L. Williams, pp. 27–48. Athens: University of Georgia Press.
1986   Ethnicity Among the "Citizen" Indians of Tidewater Virginia, 1800–1930. In *Strategies for Survival: American Indians in the Eastern United States*, edited by Frank W. Porter III, pp. 173–209. New York: Greenwood.
1990   *Pocahontas' People: The Powhatan Indians of Virginia Through Four Centuries*. Norman: University of Oklahoma Press.

Salley, Alexander S., Jr.
1911   *Narratives of Early Carolina*. New York: Barnes and Noble (reprint 1959).

Seaman, Catherine H. C., and Bertha Pfister Wailes
n.d.   The Issues of AB County: Elements of Cohesion and Dissolution. Manuscript; copy in possession of Helen C. Rountree.

Seminole Tribe of Florida
1977   *20th Anniversary of Tribal Organization 1957–1977*. Hollywood, Fla.: Seminole Tribe. Mimeographed.

Sickey, Ernest
1978   *The Struggle Has Made Us Stronger*. Elton: Coushatta Tribe of Louisiana.

South, Stanley A.
1972   *Tribes of the Carolina Lowland. Peedee-Sewee-Winyaw-Waccamaw-Cape Fear-Congaree-Wateree-Santee*. Columbia: Institute of Archaeology and Anthropology, University of South Carolina. Manuscript.

Speck, Frank G.
1925   The Rappahannock Indians of Virginia. *Indian Notes and Monographs* 5(3).
1928   Chapters on the Ethnology of the Powhatan Tribes of Virginia. *Indian Notes and Mongraphs* 1(5).
1947   Notes on Social and Economic Conditions Among the Creek Indians of Alabama in 1941. *América Indígena* 7:194–98.

1949    The Road to Disappearance: Creek Indians Surviving in Alabama, A Mixed Culture Community. *American Anthropologist* 51:681–82.

Spencer, Barbara, Gerald O. Windham, and John H. Peterson, Jr.

1975    Occupational Orientations of an American Indian Group. In *Career Behavior of Special Groups*, edited by J. Steven Picou and Robert E. Campbell, pp. 199–223. Columbus, Ohio: Charles E. Merrill.

Sprunt, James

1916    *Chronicles of the Cape Fear River 1660–1916*. 2d ed. Raleigh: Edwards and Broughton.

Steiner, Jesse

1928    *The American Community in Action*. New York: Henry Holt.

Stern, Theodore

1952    Chickahominy: The Changing Culture of a Virginia Indian Community. *Proceedings of the American Philosophical Society* 96:157–225.

Stevens, Charles J.

1983    Demographic Variation and Ethnic Differentiation: A Comparative Demographic Analysis of the Poarch Creek Indians and Their Neighbors in the 1900 United Census of Selected Precincts of Escambia and Monroe Counties, Alabama. Master's thesis, Department of Anthropology, Florida State University, Tallahassee.

Stopp, G. Harry J.

1974    On Mixed-Racial Isolates. *American Anthropologist* 76:343–44.

Sturtevant, William C.

1954    The Medicine Bundles and Busks of the Florida Seminole. *Florida Anthropologist* 7:31–70.

1956    R. H. Pratt's Report on the Seminole in 1879. *Florida Anthropologist* 9:1–24.

1971    Creek into Seminole. In *North American Indians in Historical Perspective*, edited by Eleanor Burke Leacock and Nancy Ostreich Lurie, pp. 92–128. New York: Random House.

Swanton, John R.

1934    Probable Identity of the 'Croatan' Indians. In *U.S. Senate Reports, Siouan Indians of Lumber River*, pp. 3–6. Report no. 204, 73d Cong., 2d sess. Washington, D.C.: Government Printing Office.

1946    *The Indians of the Southeastern United States*. Bureau of American Ethnology, Bulletin 137. Washington, D.C.: Government Printing Office.

1952    *The Indian Tribes of North America*. Bureau of American Ethnology, Bulletin 145. Washington, D.C.: Government Printing Office.

Tamarin, Alfred

1974    *We Have Not Vanished. Eastern Indians of the United States*. Chicago: Follet.

Tennessee Commission on Indian Affairs

1987    Private Indian Organizations in Tennessee. Unpublished list. Tennessee Commission on Indian Affairs, 701 N. Broadway, Nashville 37219-5237.

Thomas, Robert
1965   Pan-Indianism. *Midcontinent American Studies Journal* 6:75–83.

Thompson, Bobby, and John H. Peterson, Jr.
1975   Mississippi Choctaw Identity: Genesis and Change. In *The New Ethnicity*, edited by John W. Bennett, pp. 179–96. St. Paul, Minn.: West.

Thompson, Edgar
1972   The Little Races. *American Anthropologist* 74:1295–1306.

U.S. Bureau of the Census
1908   *The First Census of the U.S.: 1790. Heads of Families at the First Census of the United States: North Carolina.* Washington, D.C.: Government Printing Office.
1982–83   *1980 Census of the Population*, vol. 1, chap. B, pt. 35. Washington, D.C.: Government Printing Office.
1984   *1980 Census of the Population. American Indian Areas and Alaska Native Villages: 1980.* Washington, D.C.: Government Printing Office.

U.S. Census Office
1976   *Return of the Whole Number of Persons within the Several Districts of the United States: Second Census/U.S. Census Office.* New York: Arno.

U.S. Congress
1954   *Termination of federal supervision over certain tribes of Indians.* Joint hearing before the Subcommittees on Interior and Insular Affairs. 83d Cong., 2d sess., on S. 2747 and H.R. 7321. Pt. 8, Seminole Indians of Florida, 1 and 2 March. Washington, D.C.: Government Printing Office.
1955   *Hearings before the Subcommittee on Indian Affairs of the Committee on Interior and Insular Affairs.* House of Representatives, 84th Cong., pursuant to H.R. 30, to authorize the Committee on Interior and Insular Affairs to make investigations into any matter within its jurisdiction, and for other purposes. 6 and 7 April. Washington, D.C.: Government Printing Office.

U.S. Department of the Interior. Assistant Secretary—Indian Affairs (ASIA)
1981a   Final Determination for Federal Acknowledgment of the Tunica-Biloxi Indian Tribe of Louisiana. *Federal Register* 46(143):38411. 27 July.
1981b   Final Determination that the Lower Muskogee Creek Tribe—East of the Mississippi, Inc., Does Not Exist as an Indian Tribe. 21 October. Branch of Acknowledgment and Research, Bureau of Indian Affairs.
1981c   Proposed Finding Against Federal Acknowledgment of the Lower Muskogee Creek Tribe—East of the Mississippi, Inc. With Accompanying Technical Reports. 29 January. Branch of Acknowledgment and Research, Bureau of Indian Affairs.
1984   Proposed Finding Against Acknowledgment of the Principal Creek Nation East of the Mississippi of Alabama. With Accompanying Technical Reports. 8 June. Branch of Acknowledgment and Research, Bureau of Indian Affairs.

1985   Evidence for Proposed Finding Against Federal Acknowledgment of the Southeastern Cherokee Confederacy, Inc., Northwest Cherokee Wolf Band, SECC, Inc., and Red Clay Inter-Tribal Indian Band, SECC, Inc. 26 March. Branch of Acknowledgment and Research, Bureau of Indian Affairs.

1987   Proposed Finding Against Federal Acknowledgment of the MaChis Lower Alabama Creek Indian Tribe, Inc. With Accompanying Technical Reports. 27 August. Branch of Acknowledgment and Research, Bureau of Indian Affairs.

1988   Final Determination Against Federal Acknowledgment of the MaChis Lower Alabama Creek Indian Tribe, Inc. 13 June. Branch of Acknowledgment and Research, Bureau of Indian Affairs.

U.S. Department of Interior. Bureau of Indian Affairs

1957   *Constitution and Bylaws of the Seminole Tribe of Florida, ratified August 21, 1957.* Also, *Corporate Charter of the Seminole Tribe of Florida, ratified August 21, 1957.* Washington, D.C.: Government Printing Office.

1965   *Constitution [and Bylaws] of the Miccosukee Tribe of Indians of Florida, ratified December 17, 1961, with Amendments adopted 1964 and 1965.* Washington, D.C.: Government Printing Office.

U.S. House of Representatives

1913   *Hearings before the Committee on Indian Affairs on S. 3258 to acquire a site and erect a building for a school for the Indians of Robeson County, N.C., and for other purposes.* 14 February. 62d Cong., 2d sess. Washington, D.C.: Government Printing Office.

U.S. Senate Reports

1934   *Siouan Indians of Lumber River.* Report no. 204, vol. 1. 73d Cong., 2d sess. Washington, D.C.: Government Printing Office.

Wailes, Bertha Pfister

1928   Backward Virginians: A Further Study of the WIN Tribe. Master's thesis, University of Virginia, Charlottesville.

Walker, Amelia Bell

1977   Instant Indians: An Analysis of Cultural Identity in the American South. *Southern Anthropologist* 6(2):15–24.

Wallace, Anthony F. C.

1961   *Culture and Personality.* New York: Random House.

West, Patsy

1981   The Miami Indian Tourist Attractions: A History and Analysis of a Transitional Mikasuki Environment. *Florida Anthropologist* 34:200–224.

Wikramanayake, Marina

1973   *A World in Shadow. The Free Black in Antebellum South Carolina.* Columbia: University of South Carolina Press.

Williams, Sharlotte Neely

1971   The Role of Formal Education Among the Eastern Cherokee Indians, 1880–1971. Master's thesis, University of North Carolina, Chapel Hill.

Williams, Walter L., editor
  1979   *Southeastern Indians Since the Removal Era.* Athens: University of
  Georgia Press.
Williams, Walter L., and Thomas R. French
  1979   Bibliographic Essay. In *Southeastern Indians Since the Removal Era*, edited by Walter L. Williams, pp. 211–41. Athens: University of Georgia Press.
Williamson, Joel
  1975   *After Slavery.* New York: Norton.
Willis, William S.
  1963   Divide and Rule: Red, White and Black in the Southeast. *Journal of
  Negro History* 48:157–76.
Wilson, Edmund
  1960   *Apologies to the Iroquois.* New York: Farrar Straus and Cudahy.
Wright, J. Leitch, Jr.
  1981   *The Only Land They Knew: The Tragic Story of the American Indians in
  the Old South.* New York: Free Press.
Wroth, Lawrence C.
  1970   *The Voyages of Giovanni da Verrazzano, 1524–1528.* New Haven: Yale
  University Press.
Young, Mary Elizabeth
  1961   *Redskins, Ruffleshirts, and Rednecks: Indian Allotments in Alabama and
  Mississippi, 1830–1860.* Norman: University of Oklahoma Press.

# CONTRIBUTORS

GENE JOSEPH CREDIFORD is assistant professor of media arts at the University of South Carolina. His photographs are in the permanent collections of the Smithsonian, the Museum of the University of Pennsylvania, the Carnegie Library, the South Carolina State Museum, and numerous other collections. He has received grants from the South Carolina Humanities Council to document the Native Americans living in South Carolina, an ongoing project.

HIRAM F. "PETE" GREGORY is professor of anthropology at Northwestern Louisiana State University, Natchitoches, Louisiana, where he is also curator for the Williamson Museum and director of the Claude Medford, Jr., Southeastern Indian Cultural Center. He has published extensively on the Louisiana Indian groups. He has worked on federal recognition petitions for the Tunica-Biloxi (one of only two tribes so far from the Southeast that have been approved), the Houma, and the Jena Band of Choctaw. With Vine Deloria, Jr., and the Coalition of Eastern Native Americans, Gregory sponsored the first intertribal gathering of Indians with anthropologists in Louisiana.

ALICE BEE KASAKOFF is professor of anthropology at the University of South Carolina. She has published articles on the kinship terms and on the marriage patterns of the Gitksan Indians of British Columbia and has been coauthor of articles on the comparative analysis of group boundaries. Currently she is studying the westward migration patterns of New Englanders, using published genealogies, research begun as an NEH Fellow at the Newberry Library and supported by several grants from the National Science Foundation. She is writing a book on migration and the family in the American North during colonization.

HARRY A. KERSEY JR., is professor of history at Florida Atlantic University. He is author of *Pelts, Plumes, and Hides: White Traders Among the Seminole Indians, 1870–1930* (1975) and *The Florida Seminoles and the New Deal, 1933–1942* (1989). As a Fulbright lecturer at the University of Zimbabwe in 1984 and at the National University of Lesotho in 1988, he taught courses in American Indian/ South African comparative frontier history.

PATRICIA BARKER LERCH is associate professor of anthropology at the University of North Carolina in Wilmington. She has published articles on the Waccamaw Indians of North Carolina, Umbanda spirit possession cults of southern Brazil, and tourism in Barbados.

SHARLOTTE NEELY is an associate professor of anthropology at Northern Kentucky University. She has written numerous publications on North Carolina's Eastern Band of Cherokee Indians, many based on her fieldwork in the Snowbird community. She is currently engaged in research with Ohio's Shawnee Nation United Remnant Band.

J. ANTHONY PAREDES, professor of anthropology at Florida State University, is a graduate of Oglethorpe University and of the University of New Mexico. His previous research includes studies of Ojibwa Indians of Minnesota; he edited *Anishinabe: Six Studies of Modern Chippewa* (1980). In 1987 he served on the federal recognition advisory panel of the Association on American Indian Affairs. He has served as an associate editor of *Human Organization: Journal of the Society for Applied Anthropology* and is on the editorial board of the *American Indian Culture and Research Journal*. He is a past president of the Southern Anthropological Society.

JOHN H. PETERSON, JR., is professor of anthropology at Mississippi State University. His work with the Choctaws is described in *Applied Anthropology in America*, edited by Elizabeth Eddy and William Partridge. More recently, he served as a Congressional Fellow in Washington, D.C., and as a Fulbright lecturer at the University of Zimbabwe. He is a past president of the Southern Anthropological Society.

GEORGE ROTH has been staff anthropologist with the Branch of Acknowledgment and Research of the Bureau of Indian Affairs since the inception of the federal acknowledgment process in 1978. He prepared the anthropological studies for the BIA reviews of the petitions for federal recognition of the Poarch Band of Creeks and the Tunica-Biloxi as well as the Lower Muskogee Creek and Principal Creek Nation East of the Mississippi.

HELEN C. ROUNTREE is an associate professor of anthropology at Old Dominion University in Norfolk, Virginia. She received her Ph.D. in 1973 from the University of Wisconsin-Milwaukee, with a dissertation on Indian land policy in Virginia as compared to that policy elsewhere in the country. She has been doing fieldwork with and historical research on the Virginia Indian tribes since 1969.

WESLEY DURANT TAUKCHIRAY has been a consultant (historian and genealogist) for the Indian Law Unit of Lumber River Legal Services since 1982. Since 1985 he has also worked for four other southeastern Indian groups: the Haliwa-Saponi Tribal Office, Lumbee Tribal Enrollment, the North Carolina Indian Cultural Center, and the United Indians of Virginia. He is coauthor of the Lumbee and of the Haliwa-Saponi petitions for federal acknowledgment. His papers are in the collection of the South Carolina Historical Society.

# INDEX